Advance Praise for *Out of the Sierra*

"Forged in more than a decade of participatory research and accompaniment, *Out of the Sierra* offers readers a rare glimpse of how one Indigenous Rarámuri family has battled sublimation and subjugation at the dizzying edge of a modern borderland metropolis. Encapsulating a broad spectrum of beauty, joy, fury, and loss, Blanco details quotidian acts of injustice and resistance, piercing through old narratives of erasure and cultural disappearance to offer up a proud and vivid antidote."   —Francisco Cantú

"In this compassionate witnessing of the Rarámuris' living history, Blanco has intentionally reframed a long history of colonized literary poaching from Indigenous people. By centering their origin story and portraying their daily lives as resistance against cultural subjugation, Blanco's eloquent prose reminds us of the wisdom of the Rarámuris' teaching of *korima,* that gifts from the land are meant to be shared with loving generosity."   —Diane Wilson

"In *Out of the Sierra,* Victoria Blanco writes with delicacy and clarity about the Rarámuris' refusal to assimilate even as they struggle with forced relocation, extortion, and poverty. It is a story that demands recognition of the climate crisis in progress and the human rights abuses it causes and exacerbates."   —Claire Boyles

"Lyric, wise, and urgent, *Out of the Sierra* keeps company with Valeria Luiselli, Elizabeth Rush, and Robin Wall Kimmerer. Blanco's investigative journalism deserves more than a flattering comparison: she is a powerful new voice in ecological nonfiction and her book is not to be missed."   —Kathryn Savage

Out of the Sierra

OUT OF THE SIERRA: A STORY OF RARÁMURI RESISTANCE

Victoria Blanco

COFFEE HOUSE PRESS
Minneapolis
2024

Coffee House Press books are available to the trade through our primary distributor, Consortium Book Sales & Distribution, cbsd.com or (800) 283-3572. For personal orders, catalogs, or other information, write to info@coffeehousepress.org.

Coffee House Press is a nonprofit literary publishing house. Support from private foundations, corporate giving programs, government programs, and generous individuals helps make the publication of our books possible. We gratefully acknowledge their support in detail in the back of this book.

LIBRARY OF CONGRESS CATALOGING-IN-PUBLICATION DATA

Names: Blanco, Victoria, author.
Title: Out of the Sierra : a story of Raramuri resistance / Victoria Blanco.
Description: Minneapolis : Coffee House Press, 2024.
Identifiers: LCCN 2023053226 (print) | LCCN 2023053227 (ebook) | ISBN 9781566896542 (epub) | ISBN 9781566896535 (paperback)
Subjects: LCSH: Gutierrez family. | Tarahumara Indians—Mexico—Social conditions. | Tarahumara Indians—Mexico—Social life and customs. | Tarahumara Indians—Mexico—Chihuahua (Chihuahua)—Social conditions. | Tarahumara Indians—Mexico—Sierra Madre Occidental—Social conditions. | Indians of Mexico—Employment—Mexico—Chihuahua (State) | City and town life—Mexico—Chihuahua (Chihuahua) | Migration, Internal—Mexico—Chihuahua (State)
Classification: LCC F1221.T25 (ebook) | LCC F1221.T25 B57 2024 (print) | DDC 972.16004/974546 23/eng/20240—dc30
LC record available at https://lccn.loc.gov/2023053226

PRINTED IN THE UNITED STATES OF AMERICA

31 30 29 28 27 26 25 24   1 2 3 4 5 6 7 8

For my mom

This land was Mexican once,
was Indian always
and is.
And   will be again.

GLORIA ANZALDÚA

In the late 1500s, Spanish missionaries began drawing the first
Westernized maps of the Rarámuri peoples' homeland, a mountain
range that hid them in its deep gorges and canyons. These maps became
blueprints for the colonizers who followed, then for the Mexican
government that sought to develop this land. I am not including any
Western map of the Sierra and am thereby leaving my readers unsure of
where, exactly, the stories in this book take place. Rarámuri people know
the land in a more intimate way precisely because they do not divide
the land into territories. Even today, they avoid paved roads and walk
on their own paths that take them through the forest. So, instead of a
Westernized map, I offer the Rarámuri women's depiction of communion
with the Sierra, a story that is sewn onto the skirts they wear every day.

The triangles on the skirt are the mountains the Rarámuri people have
been forced to leave behind. The piping, always in a contrasting color,
shows the path their people follow out of the Sierra. The mountains
and the path complete around the circle of the skirt, reminding the
Rarámuris, and everyone else, that their peoples' story is never-ending,
no matter what lines are etched, or by whom, onto their land.

Out of the Sierra

PART 1

Fire wind, brittle soil, angry sun
[Summer and Fall of 2005]

In the beginning, the Sun and the Moon lived together in a cave. The Moon, content in the dark, wanted for nothing. The Sun, who loved spreading light across the earth, desired more beauty. Blending corn and clay, the Sun created a Rarámuri man. The Sun made the man's skin the color of earth, to remind him he would always be connected to the land. To animate him, the Sun blew three gusts of wind into the figure and brought the man to life. Overjoyed by his creation, the Sun made another figure, this one a woman. Into her, he blew four heavy gusts of air, giving her the strength to birth Rarámuri children. The Rarámuri man and woman took care of the earth as the Sun had wanted, planting corn, weaving baskets made of grass, and fishing in the lakes and streams. They had children who joined them in planting and harvesting. Each day the Rarámuri families, which soon numbered many, gave thanks to the Sun, whom they called Onorúame, for giving them life.

A demon of the underworld became jealous of the Rarámuris' beauty and close relationship with the earth. He created his own figure out of ashes to rival the Rarámuris. The demon blew only once into the figure to animate it. The man, light skinned like the ashes from which he was formed, felt a jealousy as strong as the demon's. When the demon put him on the earth, the white man, whom the Rarámuris called chabochi for his blond beard, wanted the corn, rivers, and land for himself. It was not long before he began stealing

3

from and killing the Rarámuris, bringing with him more chabochi men and women to help him become rich.

Seeing that the Rarámuri people were in danger of dying out, Onorúame created a mountain range with tall peaks and deep valleys, where they could hide. He filled the Sierra with caves, pine forests, lakes, and rivers. He told the Rarámuris that the Sierra would always protect them from the chabochis because he had given it part of his spirit. He asked the Rarámuris to care for the land and one another, to keep alive the beauty and love that Onorúame desired for the world.

The Rarámuris left behind their villages beside the rivers that flowed through the desert and walked into the Sierra. Once there, they dispersed throughout the mountains, making their homes in caves and small clearings so as to avoid being found by the chabochis. To show their thanks to Onorúame for his gift, the Rarámuris planted corn, beans, and squash. To help care for one another as Onorúame wanted, they ran across the mountains to share their food.

The Rarámuris named the gifts of the land *korima,* a word that described Onorúame's boundless love and generosity. When they talked of the land, they described the korima it gave them. Korima was the caves and thickets that hid them from invaders. Korima was the cool lakes and rivers filled with fish, and the pine nuts that fell on the forest floor every summer. When they ran across the mountains to deliver food to one another, they said *korima* upon arrival, to acknowledge that the gifts they brought came from this land entrusted to them. Just as the land shared its bounty with the Rarámuris each harvest season, the Rarámuris shared with one another. In giving, Onorúame had promised, they would always receive.

As a young Rarámuri girl in the Sierra, Martina had listened to her mother and father tell their peoples' origin story as they planted corn, bean, and squash seeds each spring. She told the story to her own children as she taught them to dig shallow holes and drop in three seeds. She and her husband, Luis, raised the three children in a one-room stone, wood, and adobe house halfway down the Urique

Canyon, one in the chain of seven canyons that Onorúame created for their people. Just as their ancestors had, they cared for a parcel of land and fished in a stream near their house.

Even though Martina and Luis were raised to trust the promises of their origin story, they often wondered why the stream sometimes sat empty and the dark clouds withheld their rain. The family suffered hunger and thirst during these periods, until a neighbor brought korima or the clouds opened up. Both Martina and Luis had experienced spells of drought throughout their lives in the Sierra, and believed that this was Onorúame's way of keeping the Rarámuri people bound to one another and the land. Martina told her children that droughts were reminders from Onorúame not to grow selfish, and to remember that he intended for the Rarámuri people to take care of one another. Rain, she told them, would come, as long as the Rarámuri continued giving and receiving korima. Yet in times of extreme drought, when neither they nor their neighbors had water and food, they thought that Onorúame was asking too much of them.

In years past, the rain had eventually fallen, fat raindrops that lifted the soil and filled the Sierra with the scent of moist earth. But that summer, the summer Martina's breast milk dried up and her infant, Manolo, cried in desperation, the land turned to dust. Jaime and Lupita, their school-age children, languished outside their home, too fatigued to play. Each day, the sky shone a deep blue, the air stayed silent, and the family and forest solemnly waited for rain.

Then, in midsummer, the wind rushed through the clearing, knocking over clay water jugs, tousling the pine branches until their cones fell to the ground, and muffling Luis's and Martina's excited calls with one long, piercing whistle. Lupita and Jaime jumped at the soft thud of pine cones on the forest floor. Manolo, who spent his days lying on a blanket, staring at the sky, turned his head to look toward the sound. A bright, hand-sewn skirt, laid to dry on a boulder, blew away. Martina dashed after it, laughing as she peeled it off the trunk of a pine. Returning with her skirt in hand, her long black hair blowing across her face, Martina smiled and beckoned Lupita

5

to stand, to meet the wind with yumari. The prayer dance brought the Rarámuri people into conversation with the Sierra, Onorúame, and the sky, and was one of the ways their people lived korima. If the rain clouds were pleased with the yumari, they drifted toward them. Luis, rising from his resting place, brought out the deer-hide drum his father had given him when he and Martina built their home. Jaime sat beside his father, brushing back his shoulder-length hair and blinking into the wind as he nestled a faintly curious Manolo into his lap. At seven years old, he already had his father's agility and a desire to run through the canyons. Strapping the large drum around his thin waist, Luis hit his palms against the deer hide in a slow and steady rhythm. The deep booms, loud as thunder, reverberated through the clearing, and even Manolo kicked his feet in anticipation.

Martina and Lupita, who was only four years old and had round cheeks her father liked to pat, stomped on the ground with each drumbeat, allowing the dirt of the Sierra to cover their feet. Luis let the drum's call mix with the wind, a thunderous boom that stayed its high-pitched whistle. The drum told the wind to coax rain clouds in their direction. Above them, the pine trees swayed and enticed the clouds in a language only they understood. When the drum's voice became silent, Luis's hand poised above it, Martina and Lupita each lifted one foot, then brought it to the ground the moment the drum rejoined the wind. They told the Sierra of their love and devotion, knowing that the land, like the Rarámuri people, was in pain.

Millennia ago, the wind and six rivers—the Urique, the Tararecua, the Batopilas, the Verde, the Chínipas, and the Candameña—carved the Sierra's peaks, gorges, and canyons from volcanos that once lay at the depths of an ocean. In the summer of 2005, those rivers should have carried abundant water into the Río Fuerte, an even mightier one that traversed the canyons and the desert and emptied into the creature-filled Sea of Cortéz. Summer was the season when the wind should have carried dark clouds, when they should have converged to shake the forests with their short, thunderous bursts, releasing a rain dense and pelting. Several times that summer, the wind had blown through the Gutiérrez family's clearing, bring-ing the scent of moist soil. But the rain clouds never followed. The Sierra's lakes, rivers, and waterfalls sat dry, the skeletons of fish scattered along their sandy beds. The guayaba and avocado trees of the low Sierra bore little fruit, and the pine trees of the high Sierra struggled to give nuts to the animals and people. The earth where rabbits and mice burrowed became dust, and the bark on the pine trees began to dry and peel off. Along some stretches of the Sierra, pine forests burned, turning the sky a phosphorescent yel-low. Rarámuri families walked across the Sierra in search of water that did not exist.

Martina and Luis had never before known the water to completely disappear, not in the six harvests since they'd met. They agreed that water was scarce, but that was why the Rarámuris had korima: to share what they had, and, in this way, inspire Onorúame and the land to give more abundantly. Both of them knew Rarámuri fami-lies who were leaving the Sierra for Chihuahua City in search of ref-uge from the droughts, but they believed that leaving only made the land feel alone. This was why the rain didn't fall; too many Rarámuris were abandoning korima by leaving to the city. At a corn-beer drink-ing party, Martina and Luis made a promise to raise their family in the Sierra. At the party, dozens of people gathered to dance yumari, eat corn tortillas and pinto beans cooked over an open fire, drink the corn beer called batari, and celebrate their peoples' health in this sacred land. After several days of honoring Onorúame and the Sierra with batari and prayer dances, Luis tossed a pebble at Martina's feet. Though he had met her at other harvest festivals, that year, Luis, whose parents had begun referring to him as a rejón, a man, noticed that Martina had become a muwiki, a woman. It was time for them to make a new home and have children. Luis found Martina easy to talk to and admired her generosity. She wove baskets made of grass, dye-ing some of the threads with the red juice of berries, and gave them as gifts at the party. He'd seen her run in the footraces the communities sometimes held, and admired her endurance and the kindness she showed when she ran alongside other women, shouting *weriga* and *weh-mah* to them to keep up their energy. In Martina, he saw someone with whom he could sit and listen to the sounds of the forest, as he often liked to do, especially after hours spent running through the canyons. It didn't bother him that Martina didn't stay awake dancing until morning, like the others did; he, like her, preferred to meet the day as the sun burst from the mountains.

Martina picked up the pebble and smiled so he would know he could sit down beside her. She had never before had a pebble tossed at her, though she knew that her own parents, like many Rarámuri couples, had begun their courtship this way. Their cheeks red with cold and emotion, they sat beside the campfire, talked about their families, and recounted the races that had taken them to parts of the Sierra where the air lingered, heavy and wet, and they picked bananas from trees. It was lovely to visit these places, they both agreed, though it was better still to return to their pine forests. Later that evening, under the glow of batari, which both drank to feel more keenly their desires, Luis asked Martina if she would build and share a home with him, of wood, stone, and adobe. Martina laughed in delight, and Luis knew her answer. Overjoyed, the new couple spent several nights celebrating with their families. Luis, who was an only child, received his parents' well wishes. Martina's parents shared in their joy, as did Martina's married sister, María José.

One morning, about a year later, Martina welcomed Jaime into the folds of her long, floral-printed skirt. Six harvest seasons passed, and Lupita and Manolo joined them. Each spring, they planted the corn, squash, and bean seeds they had saved from the previous year's harvest. Sometimes they planted new seeds that friends and family gave to them. The harvests were never abundant, but both Martina and Luis knew how to parcel out food so everyone had enough. This was how they had been raised—to give thanks for what they had, because it was exactly what they needed.

In late afternoon, the clouds, seeming to hear the calls of the trees and the family, swelled and turned into soft gray pouches that held the promise of rain. Luis continued to beat the drum, speeding up the rhythm to communicate the urgency of their need. Martina and Lupita were still stomping, strands of hair coming loose from their braids as they matched his pace. At times, Martina looked up at the clouds impatiently, her frustration rising in her chest. Luis stared straight ahead, concentrating on the insistent rhythm the wind and clouds needed to hear. But the clouds passed over them, bright and empty.

Why were the clouds empty? The question weighed on Martina every moment of that year: while she collected grasses for weaving baskets, boiled pinto beans for her children, sat beside the campfire with Luis. The elders, who had witnessed logging companies piling train cars high with pine and oak starting in the 1900s, blamed the mestizos, the people of mixed Indigenous and European blood who made up the majority of Mexico, for cutting down and silencing the water callers. Over the centuries, the chabochis had, often by force, had children with Rarámuri women, and thus a new people, the mestizos, were born. The mestizos had skin of varying shades; some were the color of the earth, others were ashen, and others were shades in between. The mestizos retained some memories of korima, but mostly, they continued the chabochis' theft of land and hoarding of wealth. Some Rarámuris believed that Onorúame was punishing the Rarámuri people for aiding mestizos in the cutting of forests, the mining of gold and silver, and, most recently, the cultivation of marijuana and poppies. Still others insisted that Onorúame would never punish the Rarámuri people, whom he formed out of clay to signify their bond with the earth. Onorúame, they said, withheld the rain to help them remain close to him and the mountains.

As the clouds remained empty and the land was scorched, it became ever more important for the Rarámuri to listen, to figure out why the squash leaves yellowed and withered, the animals died on the forest floor, and their own people sought help from the mestizos instead of the mountains. Without an answer, the Rarámuri couldn't be sure how to help restore balance. Since the birth of their first child, Martina and Luis had closely watched the rows of seeds they planted, praying every day for enough food to carry them safely through the winter. Some years, it felt less urgent to find the cause of the clouds' anger. Those were the years of relative abundance, when the rains visited with enough frequency to allow the plants to bear fruit. And in the years when the rains gave them less, there was still the korima that passed between families. Korima had allowed Martina and her sister to grow even when their parents' bean and squash plants yielded only a few fruits. Now, when their own garden produced too little, Martina and Luis depended on korima to nourish their three children. And when other Rarámuris emerged from the pine forests into their clearing, hungry and thirsty, Martina and Luis invited them to eat beside their campfire, even if what they had was not enough for themselves.

As much as Martina and Luis trusted that water scarcity served the purpose of keeping Rarámuri people reliant on korima, they worried that the rain patterns themselves were becoming much less reliable. This break in patterns, which the Rarámuris tried to mitigate by dancing yumari and enacting other forms of korima, was all the more disturbing because it challenged the Rarámuri notion of circular time. Beyond guiding the Rarámuri people to care for one another through reciprocity, their origin story reflected a circular notion of time: the land itself described life and death as a continuous cycle with no end, and Onorúame made time follow the cycles of the seasons so the Rarámuri people would have no fear of death; the end of a season always brought the promise of renewal. Every year, the Sierra returned to its own beginning as a cold, barren landscape. In the spring, Onorúame brought light and beauty once again. The Rarámuri people saw themselves as part of that never-ending cycle of growth and decay, believing that their own souls traveled to the clouds to live with Onorúame after their physical deaths. Their children, too, were a signal that life was continuous.

Luis and Martina had not heard many of the stories of the Spanish conquest, nor had their parents and grandparents, likely because their ancestors wanted to emphasize the beauty and knowledge of their origin story rather than the many defeats their people had suffered. That origin story gave the Rarámuri people the resilience to continue resisting the invaders, and to maintain their autonomy as settler colonialism sought to decimate their people.

Both Martina and Luis agreed that the cycles of the land had been broken, though they did not understand the cause. Martina strongly believed that the cycle could be restored through yumari and other manifestations of korima. Luis suspected that their peoples' resilience had a breaking point and knew that it had been tested many times throughout his and his parents' lives. The few times he had walked through one of the scattering of mestizo pueblos in the Sierra, he had felt resentment at the sight of the adobe homes, the stores filled with food, and the clean drinking water. Though he didn't know the story of the conquest as it was told in textbooks, he recognized the injustices of centuries of colonization. At first, his resentment was small. He focused on the messages of the origin story: the mestizos had achieved their wealth through theft; the land and the Rarámuri protected one another and would live forever. Then, as he watched his wife become frail and his children suffer from lack of water, the resentment grew into rage. That feeling was in direct conflict with his values, which taught Rarámuris to be at peace with the cycles and left no room for anger. Luis didn't know how to reconcile the origin story with the poverty of his people, a poverty that brought them to the brink of death and went against the continuity they'd been promised.

To tell of the history of colonization is to succumb to linear time. Because linear stories have a beginning and an end, they leave no room for continuity. In the linear story of colonization, there is no other possible end than the Rarámuris' defeat. To tell the story of colonization, then, is to admit that the Spaniards conquered the Rarámuri people and millions of Indigenous peoples throughout the Americas. Scholars' opinions on the success of the conquest vary, though most popular stories about the Rarámuri people are told in its shadow. The result of this is a widespread perception in Mexico that Indigenous peoples are dying out. But Rarámuri people don't experience their own story through the linear narrative of the conquest. The Rarámuris' origin story has no beginning, middle, or end. Their people, like the land, exist in all times. The story of the conquest only shows how linear time serves the colonizers' goal of decimating Indigenous peoples. A counternarrative of Rarámuri resistance may be better understood as the living history. Their origin story is their peoples' retelling of the conquest in circular time. In the Rarámuris' origin story, they are not defeated by the conquistadors; instead, they live forever.

An understanding of the conquest is nevertheless necessary as a frame through which to view this counternarrative. Before the conquistadors invaded, Martina's and Luis's ancestors relied on rain to overflow the rivers and nourish the crops they grew in the Chihuahuan Desert, the largest desert on the continent. For two thousand years, the Rarámuri, Apache, Tepehuan, and Seri people lived on those floodplains. They worked the soft earth with sticks and relied on flood deposition to maintain soil fertility. In this landscape of unforgiving heat, the peoples of the Chihuahuan Desert cultivated an abundance of corn, beans, and squash by adapting to the cycles of the land.

The history of colonization in the Chihuahuan Desert and the Sierra is told in linear time, because the conquistador Hernán Cortés utilized linear time when he began his invasion of the Aztec capital of Tenochtitlán in what he called 1521. Linear time allowed the conquistadors—and all colonizing powers—to view themselves as actors in a quest that had to be fulfilled. Cortés envisioned his story ending with the conquering of Indigenous peoples and the creation of New Spain. Under linear time, the conquistadors justified all measures to achieve their goal, including genocide.

Cortés and his army fought the Aztecs for control of Tenochtitlán in the first phase of the so-called conquest. As he overtook the Aztec capital, Cortés looked for opportunities to expand his claim to lands that yielded valuable resources. When he learned that the Aztec royalty traded dyes for gold and silver jewelry from a region far to the north, an unforgiving landscape interrupted by tall gray mountains and made arable by rivers, Cortés sent an expedition to steal the precious metals from the Indigenous peoples there. It was during a second expedition in 1540, led by Francisco Vásquez de Coronado, that the conquistadors found gold and silver in the mountains in the southern portion of the Chihuahuan Desert.

In order to gain control of those mountains, the conquistadors established their own settlements and forced Indigenous people to mine for them. They used their guns and horses to murder and displace tens of thousands from eighty-nine culturally distinct Indigenous groups, even stealing the floodplain techniques that had been developed over thousands of years.

The story, however, didn't progress as neatly as Cortés had planned. The Rarámuri, Apache, Tepehuan, and Seri peoples resisted, raiding Spanish settlements and killing Spaniards in an effort to protect themselves. Then, in 1642, the conquistadors discovered large deposits of silver and gold in present-day Parral, in southern Chihuahua. The conquistadors, still driven to fulfill their quest, enslaved experienced mine workers from the south, including the Tarascans, Aztecs, other Nahuatl speakers, and Africans. Over the course of the seventeenth century, hundreds of populations of Indigenous peoples in the Chihuahuan Desert—the exact number is unknown—were murdered as mines caved in and they inhaled radon and other fumes that stymied their breathing.

In conflicts with other Indigenous peoples, the Rarámuris had often employed passive resistance, in the form of noncooperation, to achieve their ends. Nonviolence was central to korima, so the Rarámuris relied on tactics of avoidance and retreat to protect themselves. During Spanish raids, for example, Rarámuris would disperse, hiding in rock formations and remote caves until the Spaniards had moved on. They moved quickly across the land, having developed a knowing of the desert across many centuries. But as European diseases and the conditions of slavery decimated Indigenous peoples, the Rarámuris broke their long-standing practice. Now, they revolted more violently and frequently. They killed to avoid being killed.

So strong was the Indigenous peoples' resistance that in the mid-seventeenth century, the Spaniards changed their approach. Instead of waging war, they sought to assimilate the remaining Indigenous peoples into Spanish ways through a tactic known as reducción, which they recognized as a cultural death. The Spaniards took over the last of the arable land near the rivers and lakes with the aim of starving the remaining populations. As tens of thousands of Indigenous peoples became desperate, the Spaniards offered them a place in their settlements on the condition that they adopt the Spaniards' floor-length dresses and shirts and trousers, the Spanish language, and Catholicism. It was during this century that the Spaniards forced Indigenous women to have their children, producing mestizos. By the end of the century, the mestizos outnumbered the Spaniards and became the main cause of violence against the Rarámuris and other Indigenous peoples. To the Rarámuri, the distinction between chabochis and mestizos didn't matter: both carried forward Cortés's mission to conquer the land and Indigenous peoples.

By the last decade of the seventeenth century, the Rarámuri people who continued to resist assimilation accelerated their retreat into the Sierra Madre mountains, a landscape of plateaus and deep gorges in which Rarámuris and other displaced Indigenous people could live on isolated rancherías, hidden and relatively protected from the Spaniards. The conquistadors followed, establishing pueblos with a Catholic church at their center. Using the reducción tactic, they once again corralled tens of thousands of Rarámuris into the pueblos, where they baptized families and forced them to accept Spanish names. By the middle of the twentieth century, only seventy-five thousand people identified as Rarámuri—less than half of their total population only one century before, and one fourth their number before the Spaniards invaded.

Even though it seemed to the chabochis and mestizos that Cortés would succeed with his conquest, the Rarámuri people grew stronger in their resolve to protect the land and one another. Through the centuries, families continued to pass down their origin story in hopes that the newer generations, too, would hold on to the belief that their people would continue on in the cycle of death and rebirth, no matter how many of their relatives were murdered or assimilated. They also expanded the definition of korima to meet new challenges. Even as stores and money were introduced in the Sierra, the Rarámuri became skilled long-distance runners to quickly deliver their own seeds, food, water, clay pots, and handwoven baskets and blankets to one another. They rejected the notions of backwardness and poverty imposed on them, insisting instead that the chabochis' and mestizos' poverty of the spirit grew from their greed and selfishness. Even today, they continue to share the life-saving gifts of the land. They thank Onorúame for the protection and many blessings these mountains give.

That night, the wind quieted, and the Gutiérrez family felt the same despair they had come to know well that year. The children, lying on the wool blankets Martina had woven on her loom, fell into an uneasy sleep. Martina and Luis sat beside their campfire, looking silently into the flames, their fear too big for words. Luis was already thinking about the freezing winter ahead. Manolo had less nourishment than their other two children had, since Martina's milk had thinned and thinned until finally it ran dry, like the stream often did. When they first built their house, Luis had imagined that winter would be a time for rest, for staying beside their campfire and sleeping warm and snug together under woolen blankets. But now that he had children and was watching them struggle to grow in the same mountains that had sustained him, Luis dreaded the deep cold that forced animals into hibernation. Their family would have to rely on a harvest that never received enough water.

Two years before, Luis had noticed that the stream an hour's walk from their home was running dry more often. With each passing season, watching his children remain small and his wife become weak, he wondered why he couldn't walk to a nearby mestizo town and accept bags of beans and corn from them. Some of the mestizos felt sorry for the Rarámuris and offered them food for free, though

Luis and Martina, and many of their family and friends, didn't accept food from mestizos, because they worried that the food was poisoned. Luis now thought the risk of taking poisoned food was worth it, but Martina refused to accept food from mestizos. Martina had stopped running in community footraces; she rarely had the energy to walk through the forest. Mestizos were known to steal from Rarámuris and sometimes even kill them with their guns, but Luis knew that some Rarámuris took jobs for pay. His parents had never done this, and they had always told Luis that working for mestizos was another way to anger Onorúame. The mountains were meant to protect the Rarámuris from the mestizos so they could keep the ways of korima alive, they reminded him. But the drying stream worried Luis, and he decided that he would risk angering Onorúame to feed his family. When Luis told this to Martina, she, too, warned him that working for money would offend Onorúame. She had once been inside the general store in the old mining town of Creel. She had felt mystified, then appalled by the practice of exchanging money for food. The land gave food directly to the people who cared for the land. Peace came from tending to gardens, and it was in this state of peace that Martina felt Onorúame's love for her, Luis, their children, and all the plants, animals, and people of the Sierra. That was korima: the love that spurred an endless cycle of giving and receiving. Why invent an intermediary between people and the land?

Around the time that Luis noticed the stream was running dry, there was a gathering at Martina's parents' house half a day's walk from where she now lived. There, her sister, María José, had told her shocked family that she, her husband, and their two children were leaving for Chihuahua City, where the mestizo government gave food and housing to Rarámuris who petitioned. Many Rarámuris were leaving the Sierra, she said, walking across a flat, gray landscape bare of pine trees and water. Martina and her mother told María José they disapproved. The Sierra had been entrusted to the Rarámuri people for many generations. How would Onorúame feel if their people abandoned the land that had saved them?

Ignoring their admonitions, María José went on to explain that she and her family would make their way to an asentamiento, the name the mestizo government gave to the settlements filled with subsidized housing for Indigenous peoples. María José urged her family to join her in one called El Oasis, which she and Eduardo, her husband, had chosen because they hoped to receive help from neighbors who had ended up there.

Martina and her parents refused, believing the Sierra would deteriorate if the Rarámuri people abandoned it. But Luis fixated on María José's description of a place with plenty of food for all of them. He'd begun to doubt that the Sierra could provide them with enough, but had not yet considered the possibility of leaving. After the conversation with María José and Eduardo, Luis repeatedly urged Martina to consider moving their family to Chihuahua City too.

Luis had begun to suspect that living by korima wasn't enough to sustain them. While Martina believed that remaining patient and giving continuous thanks would show Onorúame that the Rarámuri people remained loyal, Luis could no longer look past his children's hunger. In his journeys through the Sierra, he sometimes met Rarámuris walking to mestizo towns to visit the food pantries run by the Catholic Church and the mestizo government. Others warned him not to seek food from these mestizos' pantries, because mestizos were known to poison Rarámuris. Others still walked for days to reach the Catholic clinics in Creel, seeking help for babies now too weak to sip water.

But Martina remained firm, and Luis would not make a decision on his own. Rarámuri families relied on consensus to make decisions; the thought of overriding his wife never occurred to Luis. Normally, when he and Martina disagreed, they held many conversations and didn't pressure themselves to make a decision by a certain time. Living under circular time allowed Rarámuris to avoid the pressure and associated stress and anxiety of deadlines. But now, with winter looming and the fear of a clear end to his children's lives, Luis was becoming impatient with Martina for failing to see the suffering and potential death that were about to play out.

It wasn't just out of devotion to Onorúame and the Sierra that Martina didn't want to leave: she feared life among mestizos. She had rarely interacted with Spanish speakers and avoided their pueblos. Her perception of mestizos was, by and large, shaped by her parents' warnings and the stories she heard about their many abuses.

Sometimes Luis wondered if he should sign up for one of the summer marathons that took place in the Sierra each year. These marathons, often hosted by Americans, brought runners from all over the world to compete for cash prizes in the Rarámuris' homeland. But at times they were disrupted by gunfire exchanged between drug growers seeking secluded places to grow marijuana and poppies. The gunfire did not target the marathons themselves, but because they took place on contested land, Luis and many other Rarámuris thought it was best to stay away from mestizos altogether, even if it meant foregoing cash prizes and food.

Luis wavered for weeks between visiting a food pantry, entering a marathon, or continuing to forage in the forests. He was beginning to doubt Onorúame's capacity for generosity, but not for anger and punishment. Perhaps leaving the Sierra would so anger Onorúame that he would allow something worse than hunger to befall Luis's family.

When the days shortened and the air once again cooled, Martina knew it was time to harvest her vegetables. She had left her garden in recent weeks, preferring to collect pine nuts or walk to the streams lower in the canyon instead. Normally, she would spend part of each morning in the garden, believing that her presence, and her family's, helped the plants feel a connection to those they would feed. But with her three children sleeping most of the day, their energy diminished by lack of nourishment, her own fears were growing, and Martina decided it was best to leave the garden alone.

During her walks, Martina often thought about her parents and her sister. Luis had been to see Martina's mother and father twice that summer; Martina, worried that she wouldn't withstand the full day's walk, especially not with Manolo on her back, had stayed home. Her parents rarely left their house, for fear of running into the mestizos who seemed to be in every part of the forest. Martina hoped the food from her garden would give her enough strength to visit them in the coming months.

On the one morning that autumn that Martina spent in her garden, she knelt in the dirt and whispered her thanks to the squash, corn, jalapeño, and bean plants. In giving thanks, she hoped to convey to Onorúame that she wasn't turning away from the mountains' pain. It would do no good to chastise the land for failing to provide food. It was better to express gratitude, to encourage the land to strengthen and support the plants the Rarámuri people and the many animals of the forest needed.

After that, Martina showed her children how to look for the squash leaves, wide and soft. She greeted the leaf, then traced the edges until she found the stem. She followed the winding stalk through other garden vegetables: corn, chiles, beans. But she found only a few small squashes, jalapeños, ears of corn, and handfuls of bean pods—enough food until the first snowfall, if the family ate just once each day.

That night, a black, star-dotted sky spread over the mountains. The children fell asleep inside their house, tucked into a bed of wool blankets. Martina and Luis made a campfire, but the scent of branches burning did little to lift Martina's fear. The first frost was due soon, and it was too late to try again with new seeds.

In the glow of the campfire, Luis once again implored Martina to agree to leave the Sierra. The small harvest had strengthened his resolve. Many Rarámuris migrated to the city during the winter, he said, to escape the cold and earn money selling dried herbs and handwoven baskets. He urged her to think of their children, especially Manolo, who was too small for his age. He couldn't find it in himself to voice what he feared most: that the winter, with the shortage of food and the freezing temperatures, would be too harsh for the infant to survive.

Martina couldn't imagine leaving her garden, the mountain air, the pine trees with soft strips of bark, the grasses perfect for weaving baskets. She didn't want to acknowledge the pressure to make a decision. To live in the Sierra was to live by the seasons' time, a circle of endless returns. Surely, she said, next year's harvest would be better.

A few days before, standing atop a precipice, she had noticed what seemed like a thin veil of rain falling into the canyon where Luis's cousin Antonio lived. Luis could ask him for korima, Martina suggested.

Luis feared that Antonio wouldn't have korima to give. Once again, he didn't voice his concerns to Martina, knowing that this would lead him to bring up leaving the Sierra. He didn't want to feel greater resentment toward his wife, so he agreed to visit Antonio in the morning.

The following morning, as shards of pink light softened into yellow, Luis ran through the pine forest to Antonio's home in the low Sierra. There was no path for him to take; he simply followed the land to where it sloped downward, all the way to the bottom of the Urique Canyon. At times, Luis found himself running along the narrow ledge of a cliff. Before him was a vast expanse of gray canyons reaching deep into the earth and far into the horizon. Luis had always believed the grandeur of the Sierra was proof of Onorúame's love for the Rarámuri people. Now, as he ran against the impending winter, Luis saw the peaks and valleys as desolate.

When the sun had traveled more than halfway across the sky, Luis noticed that the thickets of pines looked sparse, and shorter plants with wider vivid-green leaves began to dot the landscape. He stopped to pick a few sprigs of native rosemary, an herb Martina liked to add to pinto beans. He felt the earth soften and the air turn thick. With these signs of water, Luis began to feel hopeful that he would find korima.

As he descended the final stretch of the steep, rocky path, Luis saw his cousin sitting at the mouth of the family's home, a shallow cave tucked between two canyon walls. Beside him, his wife, Esperanza, sewed, and their three older children, close to Lupita and Jaime in age, arranged sticks for the evening fire. Their youngest child, who should have been propelling himself after his siblings on chubby legs, lay on a blanket, gazing at the sky. When he saw the baby, Luis realized their harvest, too, had fared poorly. The cousins greeted each other with a soft swipe of their palms. Antonio, correctly guessing the purpose of Luis's visit, let him know that they had nothing to offer but water they'd gathered at a stream a half day's walk from their home, though that wasn't the only bad news Antonio had to share.

Two weeks before, two mestizos had appeared at the entrance to Antonio's cave. Rifles slung across their shoulders, they told Antonio they wanted him to use his garden plot to plant marijuana for their cartel. When Antonio told the mestizos that he needed the garden to feed his family, the mestizos said he could use half to grow marijuana, and half to grow his own food. But even his own crops were failing to grow, Antonio had told them. There wasn't enough rainfall to grow marijuana or other crops. The mestizos told him to carry water from the stream near their town, ignoring Antonio's protestation that the stream sat dry for much of the season. They gave him a few small marijuana plants and said they would return to check on the progress of the garden in one month's time. Though they didn't directly threaten his family, Antonio understood that the rifles they carried were meant to scare him into compliance.

It was the first time Luis had heard of a drug grower threatening a Rarámuri in that way, though such incidents were becoming increasingly common. Most of the mestizos claimed to work for either the Juárez or the Sinaloa Cartel, rivaling groups in search of remote land on which to grow their products, hidden from the federal army that scoured the Sierra for drug fields and burned them whenever they found them. Growers pushed farther into the Sierra Madres and targeted Rarámuri people, who had a reputation among mestizos for their knowledge of the land and their ability to tend crops in dry conditions. Sometimes they offered Rarámuris payment for their work, but most often they enslaved them, forcing them to grow drugs until the soil was too depleted for their own food.

Antonio said they were considering leaving the Sierra altogether. But they had also planted the small marijuana plants in their garden, just in case. To Antonio, leaving seemed equally as dangerous as staying. He felt sure that there were other dangers in the city, dangers he couldn't foresee. As long as he kept the marijuana plants alive, and as long as he could gather enough water and food to sustain his family, they might as well continue on there. They loved their home. From the mouth of their cave, they could look up at the canyon walls and see the pine-covered mountain peaks touching the sky.

Instead of reinforcing his loyalty, his cousin's story strengthened Luis's conviction that his family, and perhaps all Rarámuri people, could no longer survive in the Sierra. Before he left, Luis told Antonio and Esperanza that should they decide to leave, they could look for Luis and his family in an asentamiento in Chihuahua City. Then he ran through the night to return to his family by dawn.

Even after Luis arrived home empty-handed, even after he described the dry stream and the children's suffering, Martina couldn't imagine what she would do if they left her mountains. How would she protect her family, as a Rarámuri woman who spoke only her mother's language—the language of the mountains and all the life they gave? What would she tell her children about being Rarámuri if they lived in the city? She didn't want them to learn their beloved Sierra was ill at such a young age; it would make them think they, too, were ill. She didn't want them to see that she was afraid, to see fear overpower her trust. She'd been more expressive before she became a mother, letting her family know when she was joyful, angry, or worried. But ever since she had children—and experienced a thrill when they smiled and walked, and devastation when they languished—she had tried to hide her fears. She believed that only by placing her trust in the Sierra—in Onorúame—could she revive the land they loved. She told Luis they couldn't leave.

In the days that followed, Luis continued to walk the forest, listening for hooves on pine needles. Martina wove baskets while the children played and, often, rested. The air turned cooler by the day, and the family finished the last of the pinole. Martina and the children searched for the pine nuts the squirrels and rabbits had not yet gathered. Luis, angry with Martina for ignoring his pleas, walked in the forest with Jaime, teaching him the names of the plants they encountered. Spending time with his eldest son gave him some sense of peace.

Martina's resolve remained strong. Like Antonio, she felt more at ease knowing what awaited her in the Sierra than she would have if they'd ventured somewhere new. Martina and Luis still sat beside their campfire each evening, but now, they barely talked. Martina, saddened by Luis's anger, urged him to visit other friends and relatives to ask for korima. Luis simply nodded, and Martina knew he would run again soon, when he had recovered his strength.

Martina's story would continue to unfold in the Sierra, as it was meant to. Her children would become protectors of the land, and so would their children. In this way, the Rarámuri people would persist, bound in a circle that promised endless returns.

At least, that's what Martina believed, until her cousin Oswaldo stumbled into the clearing one evening, dehydrated from the long journey across the canyon. After Martina revived him with sips of water mixed with pinole, Oswaldo began to cry as he told Martina and Luis that his father had fallen off a boulder at the edge of a precipice he liked for its view of the canyons. Oswaldo thought that perhaps his father had thrown himself off the boulder, unable to bear the thought of leaving the Sierra. Oswaldo, his father, and his mother had planned to set off for Chihuahua City in search of refuge the morning Oswaldo discovered his father's body. Now, in the wake of his father's death, Oswaldo had a reason besides lack of food to leave the Sierra: he believed the memory of his father would be too much for his mother to bear. They had built an altar to send Oswaldo's father to the sky with Onorúame, and Oswaldo had come to say goodbye to Martina, Luis, and the children.

Grief forced Martina's body to the ground. Her beloved uncle, her mother's brother, had been well at the previous year's harvest festivities. Seeing Martina motionless on the floor of their home, Luis was enraged. That Oswaldo had to carry his father's limp body seemed too cruel a fate for Onorúame to allow. Shouldn't those sorts of punishments have been aimed at the mestizos, who caused the Sierra's pain? All along, Luis had believed that accepting his anger toward Onorúame and Martina would bring terrible consequences for his family. But the worst had already befallen Antonio and Oswaldo, and their families. His voice unusually forceful, he told Oswaldo that his decision to leave the Sierra was the right one, that he and his mother should find solace someplace else.

Martina, too shocked to move, heard Luis's words and, for the first time, began to feel their truth.

Bright, burning light

[June 2009]

What does it mean—physically, spiritually, and emotionally—to exit a system that is bound with the natural world and enter one that is actively working to destroy it?

In the Sierra, the Rarámuri people live by korima, a term that is intimately bound with what it means to be Rarámuri. Across the world, hundreds of Indigenous cultures continue to practice a sharing, or gift, economy, a system in which goods or services are given without any explicit agreement for immediate or future repayment. It is helpful to understand korima as a kind of gift economy; this helps situate the Rarámuris' way of living in direct opposition to the capitalistic market economy that dominates today's world. Central to a sharing economy is the connection between human and nonhuman beings. Humans, plants, animals, land, water, and air rely on one another. In this view, humans are an integral—but not superior—part of the world, and are needed to help maintain balance. To be effective in their role, humans must be in constant communication with one another and the land. The essence is in the idea of continuity. Every being, human and nonhuman, keeps the cycle of life going by giving gifts. The land and plants give food, for example, and the water quenches thirst. In a sharing economy, the giving of a gift implies a relationship. All relationships need to be kept up through words and actions. For the Rarámuris, gifts, or korima, can be manifested in many forms; the dance of yumari to coax the rain clouds, for example, or saying thanks to the plants that give food.

In the circular time the Rarámuri inhabit, there is no need to negotiate for returns, because circles always complete themselves, bringing fruits to all who live by korima. Economics are expressed as a worldview where one's spiritual, physical, and emotional health are interdependent with that of the natural world and other Rarámuris. Gift economies mirror the behavior of the land in that they do not follow a strict timeline for repayment. When Martina gives a basket containing five ears of corn to a neighbor, she doesn't have a set time-line for receiving a gift in return. She doesn't even expect the return to come from the neighbor she's given the corn to, or to receive the same amount of corn or another vegetable. Martina believes that gifts have a way of being returned at exactly the right moment, and she never tries to predict when that moment will come. Sharing econo-mies require every member to participate, though there are never rules about how or when one should give. At the heart of a shar-ing economy is a deep respect for the land and an unmovable trust that the land will continue providing. It is common for Rarámuris to speak to plants as they harvest, asking permission to take the squash, bean pods, or corn. In Rarámuri culture, sharing is more important than accumulating, so much so that Rarámuri families who own too many handwoven baskets or wool blankets are scolded by other members of the community for their selfishness.

In the open-air mercado's market economy system, shoppers bought goods using coins, and the value of each good was preset by the seller. The profit-seeking behaviors encouraged by the mercado were antithetical to korima. Sellers guarded their goods from theft, refusing to accept any form of payment other than money or, on occasion, another good of similar value. Instead of caring for the land so vegetable crops would grow, people within the mercado economy labored for coins. Food was rarely shared, and those who accumulated wealth had a higher social status. The market economy flourished under linear time because participants saw life as a quest to accumulate as much wealth as possible before their deaths.

Even in the 2000s, the Rarámuris in the Sierra had retained their sharing economy to a degree that anthropologists considered remarkable, given the violent attempts to assimilate them. But as more and more Rarámuris migrated to the cities in the 2000s and assumed a work schedule by necessity, korima—the central tenet of Rarámuri culture—began to disintegrate.

As the desert sun rose from the mountains west of Chihuahua City, buses rumbled through the cobblestone streets of a downtown lined with bright colonial homes. Soon, they were joined by cars that clogged the main thoroughfares and narrow residential streets, and the sun, fully emerged, cast its sheen on rows of houses that wound their way toward the gray mountains surrounding the city. Though it was still early, roads, sidewalks, cars, and cinderblock homes were already warm to the touch; in a few short hours, steering wheels would burn the palms of mestizo drivers, and the concrete would scorch the bare feet of the Rarámuri children who walked the city.

Golden rays slipped through the barred windows over the Gutiérrez family's stove and across the cement floor of their home in El Oasis, a compound in the working-class neighborhood Colonia Martín López, at the southern edge of the city. The light splashed the walls of their home, brightened the faded peach paint, reflected off the water glasses lining the kitchen shelf. Shadows and orbs flickered on the ceiling.

The dozens of family-owned shops in Colonia Martín López were unlocking their doors when Luis, asleep on his mattress, felt the warm morning light on his face. He opened his eyes and registered his panic. He was late—very, very late.

In one swift motion, he rose from the mattress he shared with Martina and Manolo, who pressed his sturdy, now four-year-old body against his mother's. Luis pulled on his jeans, T-shirt, and sneakers, the work uniform Eduardo had picked out for him from a donation box four years before, when the family had first arrived to El Oasis. He tucked a white kerchief into his Raiders baseball cap, then pulled it low over his head, making sure to cover the sides and back of his neck. By midmorning, the sun, halfway on its journey to the top of the sky, would scorch every bit of exposed skin. Luis preferred working in the winter, when the wispy clouds at least partially protected him.

Most mornings, Luis raced the morning light to the entrance of El Oasis to join the line of men who waited for mestizo ranch owners and construction site managers to hire them for day labor. He knew who paid the best wages, who overworked laborers, and who withheld money. There wasn't time for a cup of instant coffee or even a glass of water, not if he wanted one of the best jobs, which he feared might have already been taken. Luis disliked the rhythms of the city workday, but he followed them: rising before the sun; hoisting himself into the back of a pickup truck; hammering nails into wood; smoothing cement with a wide knife; sipping Coke and water to hydrate his body, which hardly sweat in that moisture-consuming heat; and, finally, making it home in time to scarf down a burrito and sleep before doing it all again.

It was not like the Sierra, where Luis had taken cues from the land. In the Sierra, it was common for Rarámuri people to be active only when the earth was active. During the spring, for instance, Luis helped Martina and the children plant seeds. During the summer, as the plants sprouted from the ground, he spent his days keeping the vegetables company, sitting next to his parcel of land. Other times, he walked or ran through the forest to communicate to the pine trees and native plants that he, a keeper of the Sierra, was with them. Fall, when the crop fully ripened, was for harvesting and for preparing the plants for winter. During winter, the plants and the Rarámuris rested until the cycle began again. It wasn't until he realized that the worsening drought wouldn't end anytime soon that Luis began to feel the pressures of linear time and understand the ways it could make him feel at odds with the land. He had never known time as anything but cyclical, had never imagined that he would one day resent the sunlight for arriving before he was ready.

In the city, those who didn't work for money didn't eat. This was the contract he'd entered into, he'd come to understand soon after arriving to El Oasis. The minutes, the hours, the days, and the weeks moved relentlessly forward. Life was a race against time to get enough money for food and utility bills. Sometimes Luis wondered why his family continued to struggle to eat three meals a day when he worked for ten hours a day, six days a week. When the pressure overwhelmed him, he reminded himself that at least in Chihuahua City there was always an abundance of jobs. No matter the season, laborers were needed to build cattle fences, patch roads, paint storefronts, and lay cinder blocks for the city's newest hotels and office buildings.

A rooster crowed from his patch of dust, the call rising from the arroyo to mingle with the sounds of buses churning up the hills of Colonia Martín López. A small refrigerator hummed in the second room of their two-room cinder-block house, and Luis could hear a mouse scuttling across the floor. A pile of dirty dishes from the previous night's dinner sat on the gas stove, which Martina had mastered after many weeks of trial and error. The sight of dishes spurred Luis to skip washing his face—he needed to get a job that day so Martina would have enough money to buy food for dinner. They'd finished the last of the beans and corn tortillas the night before, and the family was depending on him to bring home money that same day. Luis grabbed his old sneakers and stepped around Martina and Manolo, Lupita, and Jaime, asleep in one row on the twin mattresses they laid across the floor each night. He pulled open the corrugated metal door of their house, one in a long row of identical government-subsidized houses in El Oasis.

In the first days after the family had arrived to María José and Eduardo's house, fatigued and overwhelmed by crowded buildings and sidewalks packed with people, Eduardo insisted that Luis set aside the loincloth and brightly colored blouse Martina had sewn and instead wear jeans and a T-shirt. *The mestizos will throw stones at you,* he warned. Luis had already noticed that none of the men in El Oasis wore the white cotton loincloths, the loose-fitting printed shirts with their puffy sleeves, or the tire-rubber sandals with leather straps; the day he first walked down the corridors of El Oasis, taking in fifty-two cinder-block homes painted peach with pink trim before coming up against the wall that separated the compound from the wider mestizo Colonia Martín López, Luis realized that the Rarámuri men there had let go of certain customs. He thought it strange that the women continued to wear pleated dresses in floral prints while the men dressed like mestizos. But it didn't bother him being the only one dressed like a Rarámuri. He told Martina he would continue to dress in his Rarámuri clothing. Just because his family had been forced out of the Sierra didn't mean they had to leave it behind completely.

Yet Eduardo insisted, and worried that he was asking Luis for too much too soon. He remembered how confused and frightened he and María José had felt when they arrived to El Oasis three years before. But Luis's livelihood—and the survival of both their families—depended on Luis wearing the right clothes. While the Gutiérrez family was staying with his own, Eduardo was responsible for feeding five additional people. He and María José had two sons: Samuel, eleven, and Alex, nine. He needed Luis to get used to city life quickly, or they might not all have enough to eat. He didn't want to risk misinterpretation, so he told this to Luis in the most direct words he could find, even though he knew Luis, like other Rarámuris, would be offended by the command.

Luis, taken aback, struggled to accept what Eduardo was asking of him. In those first days, as the family settled into life in El Oasis, they'd felt a mix of relief, disappointment, sorrow, and grief. Relief at the sight of children carrying bags of potato chips and apples, which they took as evidence that their children's days of hunger were behind them. Disappointment when they encountered Rarámuri men in drunken stupors, their faces pressed onto the concrete of the corridors, women and children walking around them. Sorrow for the boys who wandered aimlessly through El Oasis and Colonia Martín López, sniffing paint thinner from plastic water bottles. It seemed that the Rarámuris of El Oasis had forgotten that caring for their neighbors was central to korima. They grieved, too, for the way of life they had left behind in the Sierra.

Martina made these clothes, Luis responded, finally. What he didn't say outright was that these clothes were his last physical tie to the long days beside the garden, evenings next to a campfire with Martina, afternoons wading in lakes. He regretted that Eduardo felt pressure to provide for all of them, but Luis was sure there had to be another way to help, one that didn't require him to abandon his clothing. Without those hand-sewn clothes, he would resemble a mestizo, a pillager of the land. Eduardo knew then that Luis wasn't yet ready to let go, to put on jeans, a T-shirt, and boots. For now, Eduardo accepted the extra hours he'd spend working to feed the entire family. Luis would learn soon enough how hard it was for poor, working people to come by food, even in this city filled with grocery stores, their shelves stocked high with the same pinto beans, squash, and corn that the Rarámuri people should have been able to cultivate in the Sierra.

That week, Luis became determined to maintain his dignity in El Oasis, where he saw little evidence of korima, though he was amazed at many of the commodities. The first time María José showed him how to open a tap, he could hardly believe the speed with which the water flowed from the faucet. When María José and Eduardo weren't within earshot, Martina and Luis talked about how thankful they were to have water and food, to be safe with family. They also promised each other they'd live in El Oasis as proud Rarámuris, speaking their language, dressing in their traditional clothes, and treating one another with the respect korima called for. They were appalled by the Rarámuri teens who casually mixed Spanish and Rarámuri: how could they leave behind the language of their ancestors? Martina and Luis didn't understand how men and boys came to use alcohol and paint thinner, but they would keep their distance from these substances and the people who used them.

In those first few days, María José introduced the family to community members and showed them around the asentamiento. There were no asentamientos in the Sierra; the vast majority of Rarámuris lived in isolation, but in some instances, Rarámuris built groupings of homes typically numbering no more than five. In this asentamiento, where the houses were attached to one another and more than five hundred people lived in an enclosed space no larger than a supermarket, Martina and Luis expected the Rarámuris to share their food and care for one another with ease. There were no long distances to travel, and it seemed that food was available as long as the men worked enough hours to buy it. But observing interactions in the community, Luis and Martina were shocked and disturbed to realize that some families in El Oasis had more to eat than others. María José and Eduardo, for example, didn't have a kitchen stocked with food like Eugenia, their neighbor and friend, and the proud owner of one of two full-sized refrigerators in El Oasis, which she kept plugged in at all times. Several families had minifridges that they didn't keep plugged in at all times, to avoid higher electricity bills.

When Martina realized the poorest children looked through the dumpster for scraps of food, nourishing themselves with apple cores and bits of burritos swarming with flies, she furiously asked María José what had gone so wrong with the Rarámuri people of El Oasis that some had to eat from the garbage. Why didn't María José and Eduardo share with these families, since they had so much? The family could rely on Eduardo's day wages to buy food, and they often had a bag or two of pinto beans, a packet of corn tortillas, and squash, corn, onions, and tomatoes. Usually there was food left over for breakfast the following day.

María José had grown indignant at Martina's admonishment. *I do share,* she had said. *But I didn't come to the city so my children could starve as they did in the Sierra. I feed my family first.*

María José, like Martina, had been raised to give korima, to share everything she had. María José and Eduardo must have lost their minds, Martina concluded; their ways were becoming more like those of mestizos. If they continued on so selfishly, they'd one day lose everything. If they had too much food, they would anger Onorúame, and the rain would stay away longer, she told María José, who took a different tactic than Eduardo had with Luis. María José began to scold her sister for showing up and acting like she knew better. *You've always been judgmental,* she told Martina, loud enough for the neighbors to hear. Martina cringed, not wanting anyone to get a bad impression. It was embarrassing for people to know her faults, and Martina had planned to make beaded bracelets as gifts for the women in her corridor. Now, after María José's scolding, she worried they'd think her ungrateful, arriving to El Oasis and immediately criticizing her sister. María José was often hot tempered; her anger poured out in harsh words that people didn't forget.

We'll be different, Martina said to Luis. *We'll show the other families they don't need to leave behind the ways of the Sierra.*

They could wear the clothes they'd brought with them. They could continue to give korima without demanding to receive. Maybe they couldn't protect the Sierra as they once had, but they would find ways to live their origin story even in El Oasis. That alone might have the power to call the rain.

Some of the elderly Rarámuris in El Oasis had lived there since about 1954, the year mestizo neighbors recalled a dozen or so families settling the patch of dust on the edge of Colonia Martín López, then no more than a few houses with no running water. These Rarámuris had fled the Sierra during a peak in mining operations, in the 1940s and 50s, desperate for an escape from the mining engineers who enslaved them. They had pieced together cardboard homes with nails borne through bottle caps. Other families began arriving soon after, and the patch of desert on the edge of the colonia was soon filled with these makeshift houses. The government ignored the Rarámuris for decades, leaving them to struggle for water at a single pump the mestizos controlled. Tuberculosis, cholera, and other diseases spread, causing deaths of dozens of people. In 1957, a mestizo reverend named Ezequiel Vargas criticized the government for bringing water lines to the mestizo homes in the colonia and leaving the Rarámuris to suffer. That year, perhaps because they recognized the risk of disease spreading beyond the collection of cardboard houses, the government built thirty-five two-room homes made of cinder block in two parallel rows. Even years after the mestizo homes were modernized, the homes in El Oasis had dirt floors and no electricity.

To this day, the Rarámuri women complain about the wall surrounding El Oasis: it separates them from the larger colonia and makes the mestizos look at them with disdain. They also complain about the tin roofs, which let in water. They laugh at the official name the government gave their asentamiento: El Oasis de los Indios. *Some oasis,* the younger women say, rolling their eyes.

About three weeks after the Gutiérrez family had first arrived to El Oasis, Eduardo, fed up with Luis's excuses, told him it was time for him to work. He was exhausted and couldn't go on much longer working from morning to night. If they were all going to eat, then both men needed to work together to bring home money. *You're being lazy,* he said to Luis.

Here was Luis, attempting to exemplify korima for the community, and his own brother-in-law was calling him lazy. Luis knew then that the conversations he'd started having with younger men there, about korima and the Sierra, did nothing to help the family, at least not in the way Eduardo needed. Eduardo had once helped Luis with spring planting, and Luis, without being asked, had reciprocated by helping with a portion of the harvest. During those first weeks in El Oasis, and especially during this talk with Eduardo, Luis perceived that sharing was rare in the city, even within the Rarámuri community. Here, every moment had to be used to bring in coins, and every person had to help. Everything was quantified, even time. How long had Eduardo been waiting for him to volunteer to go to work? Why hadn't he realized he wasn't contributing as he should have been?

Martina, too, had felt embarrassed when Luis told her Eduardo saw his behavior as laziness. She told Luis to do as Eduardo instructed, even if it meant wearing mestizo clothing. Seeing his pained expression, she reassured him that the clothing wouldn't change who he was.

He simply needed to wear the clothes because it was what Eduardo had asked of him. Of course they should take direction from the person giving them korima, Martina thought. Later, when they had their own house, they could return to their own ways. Until then, they needed to help Eduardo. Luis was surprised to see Martina taking the changes in stride with greater ease than he was. He was appeased by her logic and calm.

He put on jeans and a T-shirt for the first time the following morning. He found the jeans as stiff as he'd imagined, though the shirt was as comfortable as the ones Martina made for him. Eduardo had not been able to find a pair of shoes for him—they would have to wait for mestizos to drop off another bag of used clothes, which usually happened on Sunday mornings—so Luis wore his tire-rubber sandals for his first day of work. The jeans alone made him feel guilty, as if he were doing something immoral. But he brushed aside those feelings by remembering what Martina had said. The mestizo clothing would only be temporary, until they had a place of their own. Then, they could live as they wished.

He got his first job that same day, building a stable alongside Eduardo and other men from El Oasis, who taught him how to use a hammer and nails. After, Eduardo took him to the Soriana supermarket to buy dinner. In the aisle full of shelves stacked high with dried pinto beans, Luis experienced a relief he had never before known. That day, he exchanged coins for a packet of tortillas and a bag of dried pinto beans, and he began to let go of those silent hours spent in communion with the land. Instead, he went to work.

When Luis began working, the forward motion of time became his default. The break with circular time and the sharing economy was so sudden and clear for him and other Rarámuri men that they rarely had time to reflect on the changes. The pressures to work and provide for their families were so high that the men had no choice but to train their minds on the future. In the city, Luis couldn't rely on korima, even though he didn't need to run long distances to visit neighbors; they lived right next door. It was just as Martina had feared: the introduction of money severed the relationship between Rarámuris. Instead of sharing what they had, Rarámuris in El Oasis behaved more like mestizos, buying food just for themselves and their families. It was a way of life that Luis and other men quickly internalized, especially since it fell on men to make the most money. Construction jobs were the most lucrative option, and were widely seen as a man's job. Luis constantly worried about whether he'd get a job on a given day, whether the mestizos who hired him would pay a fair wage, and whether he'd be robbed of his wages on his way home from work. Theft by the mestizos of Colonia Martín López was common enough that Luis quickly learned to be aware of who was walking near him at all times.

When the stress of providing for his family overwhelmed him, his mind replayed memories of their children languishing in the Sierra. Luis had to acknowledge that they were better fed in El Oasis—the proof was in their bodies and their play. Lupita, now eight years old, looked more like Martina each year, her thick, waist-length hair and toothy smile identical to her mother's. She was chubby now, her cheeks and belly round and soft. He laughed when he saw her frolicking with the stray puppies in El Oasis, wrapping them in a long cloth and slinging them across her back like Rarámuri babies. Manolo was plump and smiled easily, which won him lollipops and mazapanes from neighbors who sold candy on street corners. Though the neighbors often requested money in exchange for the candy, it never bothered Luis to pay. It pleased him, too, to see Martina sewing in front of the chapel with María José and Eugenia. They drank instant coffee whether the day was hot or cold, sharing news and stories about every family in El Oasis. Jaime spent many afternoons with his friends, and Luis didn't see him as much as before, but his son was growing strong. The two of them sometimes ran in the arroyo behind El Oasis, a wide canyon with a stream at the bottom and the closest thing they could find to the Sierra.

Sitting on the stoop, Luis pulled on his sneakers and nodded at the handful of men already on their way to the asentamiento's entrance.

He hurried up the short corridor, ducking under bright skirts put out to dry on the clotheslines between houses. He turned the corner and passed the old sewing workshop, locked up these past fifteen years, since the state government couldn't convince Rarámuri women to work on sewing machines. The government had once thought that teaching women to sew on machines would equip them with a valuable skill for contract work; sewing sheets and gowns for the local hospital was one potential client. But unlike the men, the Rarámuri women refused to gain any skill that would assimilate them into the market economy. They saw their roles as raising children and being the culture bearers for their community: they were a counterweight to the men's forced assimilation. For all that Martina and Luis criticized the Rarámuris of El Oasis for leaving behind korima, there were daily acts of resistance to assimilation. The women continued to sit outside, sewing by hand, and refused to enter the workshop newly equipped with machines. The government workers, exasperated, eventually locked its doors.

Luis crossed the white metal gate between El Oasis and Colonia Martín López. The dead-end street just outside El Oasis was quiet, the only sound the brushing of brooms against pavement as four Rarámuri women swept the street of dust, empty potato chip bags, soda cans, and beer bottles. The elderly mestizo owner of the tiendita across the street, where Martina bought milk and three-liter bottles of Coke, which she loved, sat smoking on his front stoop. The rooster crowed again, and for a moment, glancing toward the wide arroyo filled with sunflowers and Rarámuri boys sleeping off their paint-thinner highs, Luis missed the Sierra.

The soft roar of a truck engine grew louder, filling the desert silence. Pulling his baseball cap tightly over his head, he joined the three dozen men standing in one long row against the cement wall, waiting, as they did every morning, for the mestizos in their pickup trucks to park at the curb and call out the work they needed done. All the Rarámuri men were dressed in jeans, long-sleeved shirts, tennis shoes, and baseball caps to protect against the sun. They ranged in age from thirteen to fifty, and most of the ones sixteen and older were fathers. Luis, who was among the tallest, almost five feet seven inches, still had a lean and muscular build from his days of running in the Sierra. He now wore his hair short, knowing that the chin-length styles of the Sierra could cost him work.

The sky faded from dusty pink to muted yellow, and mestizos continued to pull up to the curb in their trucks. Luis recognized Don Cruz's silver Dorado and readied himself to step forward when the rancher, a wealthy man who owned hundreds of acres in the desert south of the city, offered work. Don Cruz paid well, better than the other ranch owners in the state who came to El Oasis to hire Rarámuri.

I'm looking for eleven men to repair a fence that cattle broke through, at my ranch, he called out from his window, in the rough drawl of desert mestizos.

Starting this morning. Who's coming?

How long will you need us? asked Mauricio, a young man who had to consider the wife and infant he left behind each time he took a job.

Six weeks, said Don Cruz, looking the men who'd stepped forward up and down. It was longer than the jobs other ranchers offered. But Luis and Eduardo had worked for him before, tending the alfalfa fields he irrigated with water from the nearby river, and the conditions on his property were among the best they had known. Don Cruz had given his workers three meals a day, for example. They had slept on bunk beds in dormitories, not blankets on hard wooden floors. And over the past four years, Luis had gotten so used to the church-donated mattress he shared with Martina that he now found it difficult to sleep on the desert floor. Most important, Don Cruz was trustworthy. He had never failed to pay his workers the entirety of their wages, as other ranch owners had done. He also drove them back from his ranch at the end of a job, instead of asking them to walk or take the bus. In Colonia Martín López, it was common for police officers to stop Rarámuri men and extort them of their wages.

Mauricio stepped forward, joining Luis and Eduardo. Several others did too, and soon there were eleven. *Pack up. We'll leave in fifteen minutes,* said Don Cruz.

Back inside the house, where Martina was boiling water for coffee and Lupita was getting ready for school, Luis hurried to tell her about the job, which would pay four hundred pesos a day—more than double what he earned repairing roads and laying bricks in the city. Two days of work would be enough for a week's worth of beans, squash, corn, tomatoes, onions, and maybe even some meat. *Yes, take it*, responded Martina in Rarámuri, nodding to reassure him that she and the children would be fine in his absence. From past trips, he and Martina had learned that she couldn't provide enough for their family on her own, at least not for long. But Martina knew the pay was too good to turn down. She and the children could go to María José for korima, as she had done before, if they found themselves without enough to eat. She left out that sometimes María José didn't have enough to eat herself, a fact that she and Luis ignored for the sake of the money their sacrifices would bring. Luis hastily packed up an extra pair of jeans, a couple of long-sleeved T-shirts, and some bandanas.

Despite Martina's reassurance, Luis left that morning feeling uneasy. This was how life was in the city, he told himself to alleviate his anxiety. Every man in El Oasis with a family had to take the jobs that paid the most. Even Jose, the siríame, was taking the job. No Rarámuri man, not even the one responsible for governing the community, could say no to steady work.

As Don Cruz pulled away from El Oasis that morning, Luis and the men in the back of the pickup truck felt a warm breeze. Several waved to the children who rubbed the sleep from their eyes as they chased the truck to the end of the street, where Don Cruz turned left. As much as he missed his family each time he left, Luis enjoyed getting out of the city. On the ranches, he could walk barefoot on the land, and sit under a star-filled sky each night.

The wind rushed past, crescendoing in his ears. The sun hung on the horizon, a fierce ball in the iridescent sky. Forty-five minutes outside Chihuahua City, Don Cruz reached the fork in the road. One route led to the Sierra, and the other led to the southern part of the state, toward Don Cruz's ranch. When Don Cruz turned onto the road that led back to the Sierra, the men, confused, called out to him, thinking perhaps he'd been distracted and had taken a wrong turn. A young man named Fernando rapped on the window, but Don Cruz didn't look back or pull over. A sense of foreboding came over the men, who began to suspect that Don Cruz hadn't made a mistake after all.

Wind carrying ice

[September 2009]

As it often did in September, the wind crossed the Sierra and brought hints of ice to the desert. It moved like the Rarámuris did, ignoring township borders meant to corral their people into the Spanish-speaking Catholic churches and blowing through villages. It hit adobe homes and rang church bells. It carried the scent of pine trees and morning frost out of the Sierra and across the desert, where ancient ocean currents once made paths for sea creatures.

The Gutiérrez family had followed the wind's path out of the Sierra four years before, walking through the forest and then along the two-lane highway that cut across the Chihuahuan Desert. Martina and Luis believed the wind itself had led them to three Rarámuri women standing at an intersection they came upon soon after they entered Chihuahua City. The women had guided the family down a street lined with squat gated homes and family-owned shops, through the green metal gates of El Oasis, and to María José and Eduardo's two-room house.

Four years later, the wind, once more carrying the scent of pine trees in autumn, and of the snow that would soon powder the forest floor, found Martina on Avenida Periférico, where cars flowed through three lanes and spewed exhaust. It was the end of the lunch hour, close to 3:00 p.m., and mestizos behind their steering wheels drove south, toward the factories and offices of American-owned companies, pressed to return to work. A bronze statue of Diana la

Cazadora stood at the center of a roundabout, her bow and arrow aiming toward the mountains. In Diana's shadow was Martina, resplendent in a blue, ankle-length dress with white and yellow wildflowers that reminded her of ones in the Sierra. She'd chosen it that morning because the shade of blue matched the autumn sky, and she hoped it would make her more visible to the mestizos who might give her coins. Her dress was vivid even after three washes, which both pleased Martina and made her self-conscious, and she tried to push aside the memories of insults mestizos sometimes hurled at her for wearing a Rarámuri dress while korimeando or simply walking through the city. *India sucia,* they sometimes shouted, throwing wrappers and empty soda cans at her.

She hoped to collect enough money for that day's food by late afternoon. The early afternoon hours were usually the most lucrative in the recently developed commercial district of Periférico. Mestizos stopped for coffee at the Starbucks, made grocery runs to the Soriana Súper, ate at the upscale restaurants lining the avenue, and shopped at the newly built Fashion Mall, a two-story building with a Liverpool, the most elegant store in town. But the mestizos offered their change almost as unpredictably as the mineral-depleted, drought-ridden soil of the Sierra used to nourish Martina's vegetable plants.

In Diana's shadow, waiting for the stoplight to turn red, Martina kept her eyes trained on Lupita and Manolo, who were sitting on a blanket in the shade of a mesquite tree across the street. She brought the younger two with her to korimear once Lupita finished her school day at 1:00 p.m., preferring not to leave them alone in the house. Some Rarámuri mothers left to korimear earlier in the day and instructed their children to play in the corridors after school until they returned. Many others gave their children instructions to go out and korimear on their own after school, to increase their family's earnings. Though the majority of mothers expressed that they worried about leaving their children alone, they also felt that they needed to make this sacrifice in order to collect enough coins.

Since she had started korimeando four years before, Martina always had her children with her. By leaving them alone in El Oasis, she worried they would fall prey to the mestizos who came to El Oasis to buy children. This was a risk she was not willing to take with Lupita and Manolo. Unless they were in school, Martina wanted her children with her at every moment. Sometimes mestizos, pretending to be missionaries or NGO workers, stole the infants that trusting mothers let them hold. Other times, mestizos offered to take young children to the tiendita to buy them milk or candy, then made off with them. This happened, at minimum, twice per year, and so far there had been no repercussions. Jaime had started korimeando on his own two years before, when he was nine, a decision Martina initially objected to because she worried about his safety on the streets. Luis had said it was important that Jaime learn how to take care of himself in the city, especially since he would one day have to work for mestizos. After some discussion, Martina had reluctantly agreed. She felt that Luis had a stronger grasp on how to raise a Rarámuri boy in the city, so she had let his decision stand. She didn't express her fears about Jaime's safety very often, trusting that the risk now would put him in a better position to find work when he was older.

That day, placing Lupita and Manolo in the shade of the mesquite tree directly across from a Starbucks, a few feet from where mestizos sipped sugary coffee on a terrace, Martina instructed Lupita to not let Manolo wander into traffic or talk to strangers. She told them they could accept coins from mestizos passing by but never approach a car, even if the mestizo inside waved pastel-colored bills at them. *Mestizos sometimes pull Rarámuri children into their cars, and the mestizo police never find them,* she warned Lupita, who listened to her mother, wide-eyed, the seriousness of her role in protecting her younger brother clear to her even at just eight years old. She knelt on the ground and tucked her pink skirt underneath her; then she pulled up Manolo's sweatpants, which were a couple sizes too big, and nestled him in her lap. She pointed out the birds jumping from tree branch to tree branch to entertain him.

When the stoplight turned red and the lines of cars came to a halt, Martina stepped out of the statue's shadow and walked into the intersection. She kept her head tilted toward the ground so as not to make eye contact with mestizos who might see her gaze as open defiance. Rarámuris in the city relied on mestizos' pity in order to eat, an attitude that was really about maintaining power imbalances. Mestizos saw themselves as superior for their choice to assimilate into the market economy and earn their keep through what they considered honest work. They looked at the Rarámuris as backward and inferior because Rarámuris refused to assimilate with formal jobs. Yet they gave the Rarámuri women their spare change; the sight of a mother with young children asking for money on the street elicited feelings of discomfort, perhaps even guilt. It was perhaps easiest to react with pity; it was a position that allowed mestizos to place the blame of Rarámuri suffering on the Rarámuris themselves while maintaining their status as superior. Only people who considered themselves superior felt pity instead of compassion, which was a sentiment underpinned by respect for others. The mestizos gave the Rarámuris coins only if they felt that their status as mixed-race remained superior. When that status was challenged—through eye contact or a smile, or even by Rarámuris laughing among themselves in the streets—the mestizos might withhold their coins, yell insults from their cars, or throw rocks. Martina had been the target of such actions dozens of times.

She walked slowly along the lane, turning her head from time to time to make sure the children were still safe. Manolo, having realized that his mother couldn't reach him, started running circles around the mesquite tree, giggling as Lupita tried to grab him. Martina's heart leapt to her throat. When Manolo got overexcited, he often forgot to look where he was going. What if he ran out into the street before Lupita could catch him? Martina hurried between two cars to reach Manolo, the bumpers hot against her skin even through the fabric of her skirt.

In the past, the coins she collected while korimeando had been only a supplement to Luis's income, but in his absence, she had to go out every day and face the close calls that came with bringing children along. She preferred to spend her afternoons in El Oasis, sewing in the corridor with her sister and Eugenia, Lupita and Manolo playing nearby. When he had started korimeando at age nine, Jaime's contributions to the family income had helped take pressure off Martina and Luis. But Martina could no longer rely on Jaime to korimear consistently, so she told herself that the family would live off the coins she was able to gather. Luis had left at a time when the concrete, warmed by the summer sun, burned the soles of her feet. Now the wind conjured memories of the desert floor with a sheen of snow. How long would she have to provide for her children with only the coins she collected while korimeando? How long would she have to bring them into the city and leave them alone on the sidewalk, where she might not be able to get to them quickly enough if anything happened?

Lupita realized the chase would never end and caught Manolo in a bear hug. He squealed in delight, and the mestizos on the terrace glanced in their direction. Squeezing him tightly, Lupita lifted him a few inches from the ground and moved him away from the mesquite tree, closer to the Starbucks. They sat at the edge of the sidewalk, beside a decorative bed of small red rocks, with which Manolo immediately occupied himself. Martina took a deep breath and turned back to the line of waiting cars. Still turning her head every few seconds to check on the children, she continued along the lane.

Several cars down, a mestiza woman extended one arm out her window, signaling to Martina that she had coins to give. Just then, the cars started inching forward; the stoplight had turned green. She quickened her pace, walking down the yellow dividing line. When she reached the black sedan with the arm sticking out of it, Martina glanced at the top of the driver's head and held out her open palm.

Korima, Martina said quietly, keeping her eyes lowered. She waited, hoping the woman had coins. A mestizo had once dropped a fresh apple core into her hand and laughed at her surprise. Martina had felt humiliated and thought for a moment of throwing the apple core back in the car. But to do so could have led to a beating, so she'd controlled her impulse and simply walked away.

The woman unclenched her fist and dropped two coins into Martina's hand. Martina closed her fingers around them and felt the cold, smooth metal. She knew by the size of the coins that they were worth just one peso each. The two coins were not enough to buy even one tomato.

Gracias, she said in Spanish, her accent still marking her as recently arrived from the Sierra. Without a word, the woman rolled up her window and drove on.

Martina stepped away from the car, making sure to walk on the yellow line dividing the lanes. Now that traffic was moving forward, she wanted to get out of the street. A mestizo man in a blue sedan slowed his car to a crawl and waved at Martina to pass. Summoning her courage, she darted across the final lane to the sidewalk, where Lupita and Manolo were waiting. Lupita was singing a song she'd learned jumping rope with her friends at recess. Manolo listened, enraptured.

Martina sat down and took Manolo in her arms. He filled the space in her lap, his head resting against her chest. They watched the long chain of cars move through the roundabout, passing under the shadow of bronze Diana.

How much did you get? Lupita asked eagerly. She loved math, though she hadn't yet learned the value of each coin. In the evenings, if Martina hadn't already spent the money on food, Lupita would dump the contents of Martina's purse on the floor and count out the coins, first in Rarámuri, then in Spanish.

Martina sensed the weight of the purse around her waist and realized that it wasn't quite enough.

Forty-three pesos, replied Martina in Spanish. She averaged ten pesos each hour. She needed eighty to buy a bag of pinto beans, a packet of corn tortillas, and a couple tomatoes. She had been korimeando for four hours, and she calculated that she'd need to stay for four more—until nightfall. Now that the lunch rush was ending, traffic would slow.

Lupita patted her mother's shoulder, then turned her attention back to Manolo, who was walking toward the Starbucks terrace, hoping someone would give him a baked good. Lupita didn't intend to stop him—she wanted to go with him to keep him safe. Maybe someone would give her food too. If they did, she'd also ask for something for her mother. She could tell how discouraged Martina felt while korimeando, waiting for the mestizos to share what they had.

While urban Rarámuri men went to work soon after arriving in the city so the women wouldn't have to, the women soon found themselves negotiating the meaning of korima in the market economy. Men, including Luis, lost portions of their wages to police extortions and theft by mestizos, so women had to find ways to add to the family income. The vast majority refused to get the sorts of jobs that required them to adhere to regular work schedules or wear formal uniforms, fearing that they and their people would lose all sense of their identity if they gave in to the mestizos' demands. So they began korimeando, which allowed them to wear their traditional dress and take their children along with them. The definition of *korima* hadn't changed for hundreds of years, passed down to new generations through lessons in gardening and running to deliver aid and gifts. Most Rarámuri women didn't know about this other form of the word, *korimear,* until they arrived to Chihuahua City.

Martina remembered the first time she'd heard *korimear,* a few days after arriving to El Oasis. The children were watching cartoons, and María José was explaining how most Rarámuri women earned money in the city. *You'll need to learn to korimear,* she had said, and Martina had looked blankly back at her, then laughed at the funny word. She thought she had misheard.

Korimear? You mean korima?

Korimear, María José said with the sly smile Martina knew from their girlhood, when her sister had frightened her with stories of mountains that turned into giants and carried away young girls in the night. As soon as María José would see the panic on Martina's face, the corners of her lips would turn slightly upward, forming little wrinkles that gave her away.

You're joking, Martina said with exasperation. Only two days in the city, and already her older sister was trying to confuse her.

Korimeando is how we work, María José said, changing her tone to one she had used as the bossy big sister when they were children. *We go korimeando to make the mestizos see us and give us money.*

Martina looked upward, fixing her eyes on a single fluorescent light bulb that glowed through the thick film of dust that covered its glass. The color irritated Martina, and made her miss the pitch-black night of the Sierra. *Korimear.* The word sounded odd, mixing Rarámuri and Spanish, like some of the words Martina had heard the children say playing games in the settlement corridors. The Spanish ending *ear* turned the word into an infinitive, a verb that gave Martina the impression korima was something that could flee or escape. Martina understood korima to encompass the past, present, and future—it was the reason she saw life as circular. If korima was everlasting, how could it start or end?

We work for korima, said María José, trying to make her sister understand. *Like the men, but different. We ask the mestizos to share. They don't want to, so we ask and ask until some of them do.*

Martina leveled her gaze at María José, a piercing look that told her sister she was preparing to make a moral argument, just like the one she had made earlier that week, when María José taught her to pick ripe vegetables from the large bins at the Soriana. The thought of judging food's worth made Martina indignant. Her sister surprised her with a practical detail Martina had never considered. Once she understood how difficult it was to collect enough coins to buy food, María José explained, she, too, would make sure everything she bought was the best it could be. María José now prepared for a similar sort of statement; Martina was always loyal to her ideas, so much so that she often became sanctimonious.

You don't force people to give korima, Martina said angrily. *Or beg them for it.* She was too mad to express what she felt clearly: that korima was a gift one gave and received, the way the rain clouds shared their water when the Rarámuris danced yumari for them.

María José gave a laugh of uncharacteristic exasperation. *Life in the city requires certain negotiations,* she told Martina. *Sometimes a family has to give one thing up in order to gain something else.* María José and Eduardo had accepted this hard truth soon after they arrived to El Oasis, as many Rarámuri families did. They had found it was the only way to eat enough each day. But Martina's thinking was too black-and-white for her to consider that possibility. She told María José that they needed to korimear only because the mestizos had amassed wealth unfairly, by pillaging the land and enslaving Rarámuri people. María José knew Martina didn't yet understand that Rarámuris could starve even in the city, mere blocks from the Soriana, if they waited for the mestizos to share their food with them: the mestizos' economy didn't allow for sharing, or for giving thanks by way of gifts. Instead, Rarámuris had to demand that mestizos share their wealth, or risk death. *Let her figure it out, then,* María José thought. *She'll learn soon enough.*

Later, as Martina picked up Spanish by watching TV and listening to her children, she learned that mestizos called the practice of korimeando *limosnear,* after *limosna,* the Spanish word for alms. During her first year in El Oasis, Martina thought *limosnear* was a more accurate description of the urban Rarámuris' practice of asking mestizos for money. Like most Rarámuris raised in the Sierra, Martina distinguished between reciprocity and transactions. The lack of care inherent in transactions first confused and later saddened her.

It took some months to convince her, but once Martina saw that Luis's income alone wasn't enough, and began to understand the act as one of solidarity, she joined the hundreds of Rarámuri women korimeando throughout the city. Urban Rarámuris first incorporated *korimeando* into their language in the 2000s, as a way to legitimize the practice as work, even if only in their eyes. They understood it as a system in between reciprocity and transaction: it was a way to obtain money they felt was owed to them by the mestizos, whom they blamed for their displacement and continued poverty. When mestizos offered them jobs, most Rarámuri women turned them down, believing it more important to be the community's culture bearers while the men worked. Korimeando was a way for Rarámuri women to resist their assimilation into the factory jobs that were growing more numerous each year, as foreign companies, most of them American, continued to exploit the country's cheap, vast labor force. Their peoples' cultural survival depended on their ability to resist the schedules that trapped them in near-constant work for inadequate pay, and korimeando allowed them to set their own hours and bring their small children with them. Martina, like other urban Rarámuri women, wanted to communicate to the mestizos that, despite her displacement, she was still a protector of the Sierra—a statement she hoped would inspire some of them to give her coins. She came to believe that to korimear was to infuse the system of money with the possibility of boundless giving and receiving. It was one way in which the women adapted their origin story to urban life, evolving their Rarámuri identity.

In the community sewing circle, Martina learned that dressmaking had also become a way of expressing the Rarámuri origin story. In the Sierra, Martina had sewn dresses by herself, usually in the clearing outside her house. Within a day of arriving to El Oasis, María José introduced her to the gatherings where women sewed, gossiped, and developed ways to subvert the mestizos' economy. Sewing circles happened every day, sometimes several times. There was no set meeting time, nor were they planned in advance. They began when a woman came out of her house and sat, usually in the sunlight outside the chapel, the dress she was working on spread across her lap. A woman looking out her window would notice, grab her own sewing project, and join the woman. The sewing circle often grew to twenty seamstresses, each one working with floral fabrics in different colors.

Martina quickly realized that the dresses she had always sewn for herself were simple in design and more muted in color than the ones urban Rarámuri women wore. Rarámuri women in both the Sierra and the city sewed a pleated design similar to the version the Spaniards had imposed on them in the seventeenth century but with one important variation: today, instead of one dress, they were composed of skirts and pleated, waist-length blouses that allowed women to easily breastfeed. Prior to colonization, Martina's ancestors had worn skirts woven from grass but remained bare chested for greater ease when breastfeeding. The details made the difference between the dresses in the Sierra and the ones in the city. Martina's dresses had usually been two colors, whichever cotton fabrics she had received as gifts. She would stitch the panels together with contrasting piping, and that was it.

Martina marveled at the bright floral fabrics the women in El Oasis wore. When Martina first arrived, María José had welcomed her with a gift: thirty meters of printed fabric she'd bought for herself, forest green with purple hydrangeas. Rarámuri women preferred bright prints in thick cotton that held the color through many washes. The dresses ensured they would be seen when they were out korimeando in the intersections. They were also a form of protest against garments produced en masse in factories, which the women considered symbols of oppression. In the sewing circles, Martina admired the triangle designs many women stitched onto their skirts, always in a color that stood out against the bright florals. Sometimes women stitched one long row of triangles around the skirt; other times they created designs with upright and inverted triangles or triangles stacked three rows on top of each other.

The triangles are the Sierra, Eugenia told Martina one afternoon as she taught her to stitch them onto the fabric. Martina had already likened the designs on Eugenia's boldly colored dresses, so many triangles stitched to the hems of her skirt and blouse, to the peaks, valleys, and gorges of the land they loved, stretching as far as the eye could see. So it was true: the Rarámuri women wore the Sierra. Eugenia went on to explain that the bright piping on which the mountains sat was the path the Rarámuri people followed when they left. The path and the mountains formed a circle around the skirt, signifying the return of blessings.

Martina was moved. She thought she knew the answer to her question, but she asked it anyway. *Why did the Rarámuri stitch the Sierra onto their dresses?*

To tell our story in the city, Eugenia said. Martina understood what Eugenia meant: to tell their story for the younger generations. She'd felt distraught when she noticed young Rarámuri girls and men wearing mestizo clothing. She wanted to make a dress with triangles herself, to show Lupita and her sons that their peoples' way of living was changing in some ways, now that they lived in the city, but by no means was it over.

Over time, Martina came to understand the act of sewing together as one of resistance against the mestizos who verbally and physically abused the Rarámuri women. As she became accustomed to korimeando on her own, Martina found that their abuse stopped making her want to stay at home hiding in fear. Instead, it made her want to sew: dresses printed with flor de Jamaica, sunflowers, peonies, and other big blooms that made her clothing her own.

The wind blew plastic shopping bags and leaves through the corridors of El Oasis the day following Eugenia's conversation with Martina about the triangles she stitched into her skirts and blouses. Martina was sewing on her front stoop when a particularly strong gust twisted the fabric over her hand, breaking her rhythm as she pleated a skirt. She pricked her finger and grimaced at the red that bubbled from her skin.

Eugenia, sitting on her own stoop next door, had turned on her boom box, and they listened to a young woman from the Sierra sing in Rarámuri about pine trees and water and gathering in the village to celebrate the harvest. Both of them were working on monitos, tiny dolls made in the image of Rarámuri women. Martina was almost done with her batch; she needed only to tie strings around the monitos' heads so they could dangle from the rearview mirrors of cars. She planned to take them with her to the intersection that afternoon, to sell to mestizos, in the hopes that she would earn more money than by simply korimeando—a suggestion from Eugenia, who rarely went korimeando because she made enough offering dolls, tortilleros, and aprons to nonprofit workers who bought them for resale. Her dolls and tortilleros stood out for the details Eugenia included: tiny beaded necklaces and earrings on the former, and scenes of mountains and flowers behind the women and children in the latter. Since meeting Eugenia in the sewing circle the week Martina arrived to the city, Martina had admired Eugenia's work ethic, and how she kept her daughters' hair combed and their dresses clean.

Martina had been able to afford only a bag of beans and a packet of tortillas the night before, just enough for dinner but with no leftovers. While Martina cooked, Lupita sent Hot Wheels cars zooming across the kitchen floor, attempting to keep Manolo awake long enough to eat. Manolo perked up; his collection of chipped and broken Hot Wheels, castaways that Martina had retrieved from a donation box, were his most prized toys. Jaime and Lupita had gone to school that morning without breakfast, and Martina had appeased Manolo with a couple of lollipops. Neither Jaime nor Lupita had complained, a fact that made Martina's heart ache. They had grown used to three meals a day but didn't grumble when there wasn't enough food, aware that their mother was doing all she could.

She had thought about asking María José or Eugenia for korima, as she had in the past when Luis left the city. She knew that Eugenia usually had two days' worth of food. María José had to buy her food each day, like the Gutiérrez family and most of the families in El Oasis, but she and Eduardo always seemed to be able to buy enough beans and corn tortillas so everyone in their family could eat well. Sometimes Martina avoided letting María José and Eugenia come inside, not wanting them to see she had nothing to share. She was frustrated, and more than a little ashamed, that she and Luis still couldn't figure out how to earn at least as much as María José. In El Oasis, where even the Rarámuri women worried about collecting enough coins, having enough food for oneself meant being less of a burden for others, and Martina felt the change deeply. She now thought twice about asking María José for korima, knowing that if she did, some Rarámuris in the community would accuse her and María José of burdening them all with the obligation to share, when it should be the wealthy mestizos who did most of the sharing. According to many, all demands for korima were to be directed at mestizos. In Luis's absence, the only saving grace for Martina was the fact that the children received a meal in the school's lunchroom, a plate filled with beans, rice fried in tomato sauce, and corn or flour tortillas donated by the state government.

Lately Martina had been considering sending Lupita out to korimear on her own. Young girls inspired the right level of pity in mestizos, who often gave more coins to them than to women. Most mothers sent their daughters out on their own starting at age seven. Martina thought these mothers irresponsible and vowed she'd never do so. It was one thing for mothers to go korimeando and to send out their young sons, but it was something else completely to make girls shoulder that responsibility. More important, children couldn't defend themselves against kidnappers. She'd rather stay out in the intersection until midnight if it meant keeping her daughter safe. When other women decided it was time for their daughters to korimear on their own, they didn't tell Martina; being on the receiving end of one of Martina's lectures was a headache.

As Martina and Eugenia sat on their front stoops and sewed that windy morning, Martina recalled watching Lupita greet Eugenia's seven-year-old daughter, Lilia, as she came out of her house with a tightly woven braid and a new Cinderella backpack. Lupita, her secondhand My Little Pony backpack in place, linked arms with Lilia, and they skipped down the corridor to the school entrance. Lupita was still a tewecke, a young girl. Martina didn't want to put her daughter in danger, and she didn't want to risk her losing sight of the relationship between their community, the land, and Onorúame.

Yet the idea of sending Lupita out had crept into Martina's mind several times in the past few weeks, as she wondered how much longer Luis would be away. Each time she made up her mind not to ask her daughter to participate, she thought of Lupita and Jaime sitting through their lessons all morning, their stomachs empty. She had grown very tired from korimeando extra hours to make up some of their lost income. She'd started eating less so her children could eat more, but often, there wasn't enough. She wasn't sure how much longer she could go on in this way.

Eugenia, aware of her friend's predicament, tried to find a way to broach the subject of money. Eugenia knew that Martina struggled when Luis was away; she noticed her coming home from korimeando close to midnight, her young children exhausted. They had school the next day, and Martina was usually adamant that her children get enough sleep so that they could be on time for classes. Eugenia had offered korima once since Luis left, but Martina had seemed embarrassed, accepting quietly and giving Eugenia a beaded bracelet a few days later, as a form of reciprocity. The exchange had seemed too stiff to Eugenia, not like the free giving and receiving the two friends usually did. She suspected that Martina was becoming uncomfortable because she had far less. Emboldened by the fact that Martina had taken her advice to sell monitos, Eugenia thought she would coax Martina toward the solution that worked for dozens of families in El Oasis.

Have you thought of sending Lupita out to korimear on her own? Eugenia whispered. She kept her voice low so the young children playing nearby wouldn't hear: they would likely tell their mothers about the conversation later, and Eugenia knew Martina wouldn't want everyone to know that she was struggling.

Martina, self-conscious because Eugenia had read her mind, shook her head no.

Then María José's corrugated metal door scraped the cement, and she emerged from her house with a nonchalant look that Martina immediately distrusted. Recently María José had scolded Martina for failing to patch the holes in her tin roof with steel wool. Wind whistled through these holes, bringing with it mice and roaches, exactly the sort of vermin the mestizo government asked the Rarámuris to keep out of their homes. María José paid close attention to the sanitation lectures government health workers delivered in El Oasis once a month, not because she was concerned about the diseases roaches and mice could be carrying—she believed those mestizo illnesses didn't usually touch Rarámuris— but because she worried the government would stop delivering aid or services to El Oasis if they thought the families there didn't take care of what they had. When Martina and Luis had scrawled a line on the house contract—the first time either of them had held a pen—they'd agreed to follow the asentamiento's rules of cleanliness. Failure to comply could result in eviction, or in the withdrawal of community funds. But when María José had urged her sister to patch the roof herself, Martina had simply ignored her. María José was not the siríame; what right did she have to tell Martina what to do? Lucero was Jose's sister and the acting siríame while he worked in Don Cruz's ranch with the other men. If she had asked Martina to do something about her roof, Martina would have immediately complied. She respected the siríame, since they were always elected by consensus. She saw no reason to dignify her sister's demands with a response.

Calling her sister unclean and stubborn, María José had stalked off to her house and pushed the heavy door shut, and that was what had made Martina angry: in the Sierra, Rarámuris never shut each other out of their homes, not even when there was conflict between friends and family. María José had strayed far from the values of korima, Martina thought. She was becoming someone Martina didn't want Lupita to emulate.

As María José approached, Martina bent her head low over the fabric, pretending to pull out a few crooked stitches. Eugenia glanced at María José's face, trying to detect her mood. She was carrying two mugs of Nescafé, a signal that she was returning to continue her conversation about the roof with her sister. Both Martina and Eugenia knew María José had a habit of bringing food or drinks to those she wanted to sway in one direction or another. She'd given gifts of beans and potatoes to a neighbor who played music too loudly each morning, a time of day when María José relished the quiet of the corridor. With enough food and her winning smile, María José had found that people usually gave in.

But not her sister. Eugenia braced herself; it didn't matter if María José shouted, cried, or sweet-talked, Martina usually resisted her sister. And though Eugenia preferred not to get between the sisters when they fought, she was worried Martina would have to skip meals for days if Eugenia didn't continue the conversation about sending Lupita out to korimear on her own. María José handed the mugs to Eugenia and Martina. Martina accepted hers without making eye contact with her sister. She knew what was coming. But Eugenia, knowing Martina had more pressing problems than water and pests getting into the house, interjected. *I've been telling Martina she should send Lupita out to korimear on her own,* she said. Martina kept sewing. Only a tightening of her shoulders revealed that she was upset by the comment.

María José knew then that her sister was struggling even more than she was. Because Martina hadn't asked her for korima recently, María José had thought she was bringing home enough money by korimeando and selling her crafts to nonprofits. She now suspected that Martina simply didn't want to take from her and her children. And while María José resolved in that moment to check on her sister more often, and to bring her food without being asked, she agreed with Eugenia that it was time for Lupita to help out by korimeando on her own.

Everyone needs to eat, she said, stating the obvious. It was an inescapable fact, and so was the underlying message. All three women had been to talks in the chapel about Mexico's child labor laws. The government workers who gave them told the women they should go to work themselves rather than send their children to ask for coins. But for María José and other women who refused to enter the market economy, who saw assimilation as a kind of death, sending young girls to korimear was a means to an end: the only way to eat was by gathering coins, as many as possible, in as little time as possible. *Girls far younger than Lupita spend hours at intersections and fast-food drive-throughs, unsupervised and in any kind of weather,* she added. And when Eugenia concurred, Martina began to realize she could no longer pretend that she was capable of keeping Lupita safe.

Sunflowers spread across the arroyo
[September 2009]

For two years after arriving to El Oasis, from ages seven to nine, Jaime lived and breathed soccer. He stirred in his bed on weekend mornings, the sunlight warm on his face, an eagerness to kick a soccer ball jolting through him. Seconds later, his feet landed on the cement floor. Wearing the same clothes as the day before, he was out and up the corridor, ducking under skirts hung to dry.

Martina was already at the sink, washing dishes while Lupita and Manolo played with other children in the corridor. *Where do you think you're off to this early?* she called teasingly. He responded with a quick smile.

Martina's amused scolding made Jaime feel a little older: she knew that he, like his father, had somewhere to be. At the end of the corridor, he stopped to greet El Rojo, a black lab who had helped the police force with many drug busts before he retired. Jaime scratched El Rojo's ears, and El Rojo nuzzled back and whimpered. Often Jaime knelt down and hugged him.

Already there was the thump of a soccer ball bouncing off the wall of the chapel. El Rojo in tow, Jaime walked around the corner, staying close to the shadowed wall so no one would notice him. Leaping out to steal the ball from another boy, he kicked it so hard against the chapel that the plastic leather gave off a *pop*. He grinned when the other boys shouted in surprise, then hugged his best friend, Manuel. Soon other boys heard the ball bouncing off the walls of the chapel and the surrounding houses. They flocked to join the game, forming teams by calling out each other's names. Someone always wanted to play on Jaime's team; he was fast and good at scoring points. The space between the chapel door and the corner became one goal, and the wall of the old carpentry workshop was the other. Twenty seamstresses would want to crowd into this same space to sew, but now twelve boys between the ages of seven and thirteen elbowed and kneed one another as they dribbled and passed, shot and blocked.

Dale, dale!

Bloquéalo!

They shouted Spanish words they had learned crowded around a TV to watch Los Rayados. Small children got out of their way, watching wide-eyed as the older boys broke a sweat. Girls the same age looked in the other direction, pretending not to notice.

Pásamelo, yo lo meto! Ándale, acá 'toy!

Feet vied for the ball . . . stepping, kicking, turning, twisting as the shouting got louder. The ball shot out of the jumble of boys, bouncing off the wall and back into the game.

'Ey, you're too big to play here, a mother always shouted, wanting the space clear for the first sewing circle of the day. No one heard her, or no one listened. Grunts and tumbles and cheers . . . everyone covered with a new layer of dust—another goal.

Chhh, take that to the street!

More mothers gathered at the edge of the square, some raising their arms in front of their faces in case the ball came flying their way. Eventually the single mother's voice became a low, complaining chorus.

That was how the games usually ended. The boys would then disperse, and half-heartedly look for another space in the asentamiento where they could continue their play. They didn't want to disrupt the sewing circles, but the sound of a soccer ball smacking against the wall of the chapel was often too much to resist. The school's basketball court would have been a perfect space, but the teachers kept the gate locked after classes let out for the day.

The only place left was the dead-end street right outside the asenta-miento's entrance, where vendors stopped with their carts to sell burritos and tamales to Rarámuris and their neighbors. In the after-noons, men sat and drank beer at its far end, which overlooked the arroyo. There were always cars and pickup trucks pulling up to the curb: mestizos made frequent stops to drop off donated goods, doc-tors and nurses arrived to give health talks, and government work-ers came to meet with José, the asentamiento siríame, or Rarámuri governor, often to discuss solutions to the ever-growing problem of drug use among Rarámuri youth.

Jaime also liked flipping pogs and building castles in the sandy area beneath a mesquite tree, but these quieter games interested him only once he'd expended his energy playing soccer. A few months after arriving to El Oasis, Jaime had started inviting his friends to watch soccer games at his house. They ate bags of habanero potato chips, spilling crumbs on the floor each time they pumped their fists in the air to cheer on Los Rayados. Martina didn't mind; seeing her children with their friends were some of her happiest moments liv-ing in El Oasis. After the games, Jaime rested his head briefly against Martina's waist, his way of thanking her for allowing his friends to crowd into the house. Not all mothers in El Oasis let so many boys into their cramped homes, especially once they were all arms and legs and starting to take up more space.

Then, soon after his ninth birthday, Luis told him to spend his afternoons and weekend mornings korimeando on his own, to help supplement their family's income. Jaime didn't take the news par-ticularly badly; this was a rite of passage that nearly every child in El Oasis experienced, no matter how often their parents swore that they would never send their children to the streets. By her silence and her sorrowful gaze, Jaime knew that Martina didn't like this development. He felt warmly toward his mother for the ways she cared for him, but it was Luis's approval he cared most about. In Luis he had someone with whom he could confide and seek advice. Martina, so wrapped up in korimeando and dress-making, couldn't understand what it felt like to be a Rarámuri boy in a mestizo culture that pressured boys to man up, and also punished Indigenous boys and men who went too far. So when Luis told him to start korimeando, Jaime ignored his mother's gazes and told his father he would start the next day. When Luis told Lupita about the new arrangement that night, he even felt a small inkling of pride in knowing that trust was going to be placed in him to help keep the family afloat. It was this new sense of responsibility that helped Jaime tame his desire to jump into the soccer game each time he walked by on weekend mornings, grinning at the children as he walked toward the iron gates, on his way to korimear at an intersection crowded with Saturday-morning shoppers.

Korimeando accelerated the end of his childhood. Instead of playing, he worried about collecting as many coins as he could. Each evening, Jaime turned over his coins to his mother, who then used them to buy groceries or tucked them away to pay the utility bills. Only once his responsibility was fulfilled did Jaime feel that he could spend some time in leisure. Yet the problem remained that there was not enough space to play soccer. Jaime joined pickup games every once in a while, but he also discovered another interest that he could pursue without interruptions.

A couple months after he started korimeando on his own, Jaime started to join a few other boys his age in spray-painting images of Catholic saints and cartoonish cholos—boys with wide-brimmed hats, baggy jeans, and oversize jerseys—on the cement wall enclosing El Oasis. The first moment he aimed the spray can at the gray wall filled him with almost as much excitement as scoring a goal. Covering his nose with a bandana so he wouldn't get high inhaling the spray paint and make a mess of his work, he pushed down on the valve release and watched the bleak gray wall fill with color. Sometimes it took up to two hours to complete a painting; to Jaime's joy, no one ever interrupted him. No one cared about these walls that overlooked the arroyo, where boys slept off their paint-thinner highs among the sunflowers. Jaime painted whatever he wanted. He chose to imitate other drawings of cholos he saw around the colonia. At first, they were just drawings he was copying off other children.

Then, after a while, Jaime began recognizing himself in his paintings of young men in baggy clothes holding up peace signs; the ones with their arms crossed on their chests, smirking; and even the ones giving the middle finger.

Weekdays, when school let out at two o'clock, Jaime and his friends often wandered around Colonia Martín López to look for inspiration in the work of mestizo boys who marked their territory with their own designs. Mestizo boys spray-painted their messages in bubble letters and incorporated devils and fanged monsters that awed Jaime and the dozen or so boys his age. Their designs weren't better than the ones middle-school Rarámuri boys created, but the mestizos had claim on most of the colonia, filling the sides of stores and entire abandoned walls, while the Rarámuri boys mostly spray-painted in the area immediately outside El Oasis. Wandering Colonia Martín López, with its pop-up mercados, fruterías, and secondhand appliance and clothing stores, Jaime always felt like a tourist, one who might be driven back within the four walls of El Oasis on the slightest whim. Sometimes groups of mestizo boys taunted or beat up Rarámuris when they felt they were getting too close. It didn't matter that he had lived in Colonia Martín López for four years; Jaime had learned long ago that the colonia beyond the four walls of the asentamiento did not belong to his people. He and his friends moved cautiously, not walking too fast or too slow, not making eye contact with the mothers pushing their babies in covered strollers or the men waiting for the bus. Wandering the streets, Jaime felt a mixture of fear and envy, an uncomfortable feeling that they all shared but no one expressed in words, perhaps because it was too confusing and overwhelming. These were the streets the mestizo police patrolled, where Luis and other Rarámuri men were stopped and told to hand over their pay. The streets filled with the violent lyrics of narcocorridos—not the Rarámuri songs about the beauty of the Sierra set to the melody of violin and drums his neighbors played, but the jumble of accordion, trombone, and guitar blaring from boom boxes at shop entrances.

The narcocorridos both frightened and impressed Jaime. He sometimes stopped on the sidewalk to listen to the stories of poor men who moved up in the world by selling drugs and intimidating others with their money and guns. The songs' messages seemed applicable only to mestizo boys, a problem Jaime thought he could overcome by learning to speak unaccented Spanish and wearing the right mestizo fashions. Once he met those unofficial requirements, he thought, the tales in the narcocorridos might be accessible to him, too, as they were to any mestizo boy willing to sell drugs. In that job, boys made a week's worth of construction wages just for running marijuana or cocaine across the city to the next contact, who would take it farther north, toward the border. Most of the marijuana and heroin that came into Colonia Martín López remained there only temporarily, until a drug runner could get it to the more lucrative markets in the US. Neither mestizos nor Rarámuris could afford those drugs, save for a few ounces of marijuana occasionally.

Though Rarámuris were seldom able to afford the drugs, the Rarámuris of El Oasis were sometimes approached by members of the rivaling Juárez and Sinaloa Cartels and asked to pedal them. They knew it brought in more money than working in construction or korimeando, but few wanted to get involved in selling the "bad crops," as Martina and María José called the marijuana and poppies mestizos planted in the Sierra. Luis disapproved, too, though his reasons were more practical. Police officers looked for any excuse to harass and extort Rarámuris; selling drugs was a direct path to making a lot of money, garnering attention, then losing any earnings to the police. At age nine, Jaime already thought his mother and aunt were old-fashioned and his father too fearful. He knew all about the two rival cartels, about how the men who formed them grew rich. They didn't empty their pockets for the police the way his father and most other Rarámuri men did. They owned many of the buildings in the colonia, wore Levi's and expensive snakeskin boots, and dined on steak in the city's finest restaurants, some of which Jaime had peered into while korimeando with his mother;

he'd felt the saliva collect in his mouth at the sight of the steaks, as it did when they passed by restaurants selling fried chicken, pizzerias, and Chinese takeout spots. Catching whiffs of the foods that his family couldn't afford, Jaime began to imagine what it would be like to sit inside those restaurants himself.

In the days after he'd first arrived to El Oasis, Jaime had noticed the boys his age and older sniffing from plastic bottles. He hadn't understood what they were doing, but he had noticed they wore hooded sweatshirts even when it was hot, and they swayed from side to side when they walked, as if struggling to keep their balance. While his parents learned about El Oasis from María José and Eduardo, Jaime learned from his cousins, Samuel and Alex. They told him where to buy small bags of potato chips (the tiendita across the street), how many pogs the children considered a good collection (at least ten), the best place to play hide-and-seek (the arroyo), and which elderly mestiza store owner was the most likely to give away lollipops (the one at the top of the hill just beyond the asentamiento entrance). At some point during their tour in that first week, Samuel had explained to him matter-of-factly that in El Oasis, some Rarámuri children and adolescents sniffed paint thinner. Samuel had tried it a few times, he admitted. He'd been curious about the sensation the older children described: they said they felt their bodies sink into the floor and their minds become empty. It sounded a little scary, but so many children were trying it that he assumed there was something appealing about it. He was about to tell Jaime that it was a pleasant experience, but he stopped when he saw his cousin's curious expression. Samuel didn't want to encourage Jaime to try it. *Paint thinner rots your brain,* he quickly said. That's why he had stopped—he didn't want to end up like Miguel, the boy in their corridor who had started at age seven and kept going until he could no longer hold a bottle up to his nose. *The fumes went inside his brain and turned it to mush,* Samuel said, repeating what his parents had told him. Miguel's mother took care of him day and night. He spent his days sitting on the front stoop, smiling at nothing. That's what happened to boys who sniffed paint thinner, so he should never, ever try it, he told Jaime, a perfect echo of María José. Jaime, bewildered, realized he had much to learn about life in El Oasis. His cousin's ominous words quickly faded, replaced by the joy of having so many friends to play with. He didn't miss the Sierra much after a few days, when he realized how much he liked racing Hot Wheels, watching cartoons, and kicking a soccer ball.

The question of whether they'd one day sniff paint thinner entered the lives of the boys in El Oasis as early as age six. Though José had forbidden paint thinner in El Oasis, slightly older children were already sniffing, so it came up in the boys' conversations. The fact that José forbade it spoke volumes about the damage it caused and how helpless the adults felt to control it: a Rarámuri siríame rarely made hard-and-fast rules, preferring to counsel community members. That approach was more congruent with korima, since it guided rather than forced people to make the best choices for their families and communities. Paint thinner was a fierce new problem for the Rarámuris, one that José thought required a firm ban. That angered some of the mothers, however, who argued that it was safer for their children to sniff in El Oasis, where at least they couldn't be hit by cars or assaulted by mestizos. But others still insisted that children using the drug normalized the behavior for the younger ones, who would likely go on to imitate them. María José, whom others listened to because she had successfully kept her children from becoming addicted, was one of the women most vocal about keeping paint thinner out of the asentamiento, especially since Samuel had first been offered the solvent inside its walls. Within a few weeks of her arrival, Martina also became adamant that paint thinner should be kept out. She wasn't worried that her own children would try sniffing it—she intended to raise them by the values of korima, and dismissed the possibility that they might one day want, or feel forced, to follow in the footsteps of their peers. With the right guidance, she believed, her children would be as horrified by the addiction as she and Luis were. But she agreed that allowing paint thinner in El Oasis only normalized the behavior. Better to keep it out, she thought, and she and her family could model the strength of an El Oasis family living by Rarámuri values.

It didn't matter how much the mothers argued about the rules around drugs in El Oasis; no one could keep the boys from returning to the asentamiento high, or the younger children playing outside from seeing them. Sometimes the children dared each other to run up to the boys who fell asleep on the sidewalk and poke their faces, a game that ended when an angry mother came to defend her son. All the parents and children were aware that the paint thinner caused brain damage; there was more than one young man like Miguel in El Oasis, though most had parents who kept them hidden inside to avoid the pain of hearing other families use them as warnings. Yet, in 2010, nearly half of all the children in El Oasis had gotten high on the solvent by age ten.

Though Jaime was initially curious about the paint thinner, he found that there were more interesting aspects of life in El Oasis. He enjoyed studying math, playing sports, and doing graffiti. But within a year and a half, he realized that his cousin Samuel, who went to the mestizo middle school and stayed away from sniffing, was rebuffed by the Rarámuri cholos. Samuel and Alex were goody-goodies, many of the boys said. They stuck close to home and, especially, to their mother. Jaime heard these comments from his friends, who repeated what their older siblings said. He didn't like the way they talked about his family, but more than that, he hoped they'd never say those things about him. Boys who were mocked, he thought, grew into men the police beat and extorted.

Over time, Jaime came to understand that the easiest way for boys and men to gain social status in El Oasis was by enacting violence against those they perceived to be weaker: women and the men who listened to the women. The Rarámuri men learned this behavior from the mestizos. In the Sierra, Rarámuris did not tolerate violence against women, the consequence for inflicting it being expulsion from the community. In the city, some of the boys and men who were forced to pay dues to the police merely for working, who were robbed and insulted by the mestizos who hired them, returned home and beat their own wives and children; it was a way for them to impose some semblance of hierarchy within and control over their own lives. Some of Jaime's friends suffered violence at the hands of their fathers. He couldn't imagine his own father treating him or Martina and Lupita that way. In those first two years, he joined Martina and Lupita in afterschool excursions to the playground in the colonia and the downtown streets lined with brightly painted colonial homes. Despite his revulsion at the way some Rarámuri men treated women and children, he realized there would come a day when he'd have to leave his mother and sister and join the Rarámuri boys in Colonia Martín López, or risk becoming a target of mockery and, later on, even extortion.

That day came nine months after Jaime started korimeando on his own. He and Manuel were sitting on the sidewalk outside El Oasis after school, comparing baseball cards their mothers had bought them while shopping for fabric downtown. They scrutinized each card, trading information on the players and noting which ones they should look out for on TV. They planned to build their collection together, knowing that it would take years to collect the hundred or so cards they were envisioning.

Manuel's older brother, a middle schooler named Marcos, approached them. Standing over the boys and speaking quietly, he asked them if they wanted to go to the arcade. A group of mothers sewing nearby cast suspicious glances their way. Everyone had seen Marcos walking around the colonia with a bottle of paint thinner tucked into his sweatshirt. Though he wasn't high that afternoon, the mothers kept looking over at the group, trying to figure out what they were talking about. They all watched out for the younger children, reporting back to one another when they thought one was in danger or doing something wrong. Martina was out korimeando with Lupita and Manolo at that hour. Though Marcos was aware that the Rarámuri mothers all tried to protect one another's younger children, he knew speaking to his brother and his brother's friend in broad daylight, where everyone could see, would likely be seen as harmless.

Jaime tried to act nonchalant about the middle schooler inviting him to the arcade, which had opened just two months before. He'd walked by it dozens of times on his tours of the graffiti in Colonia Martín López. The entry was an archway of jagged cement. There was no front door, as far as Jaime could tell, only a deep cave-like space he couldn't quite see into. The bells and dings of eighties-era arcade games filtered onto the street, and he could just make out the shadows of boys crowded around the games. Jaime had been aching to go inside, but he and his friends hadn't dared. It was clear that the Rarámuri middle schoolers had staked a claim on the place, and they never let the younger children join without an invitation.

Manuel was quick to respond to his brother, almost as if he'd known this moment was coming.

Yeah, sure, he said with a shrug. Marcos grinned and ruffled his hair.

Jaime knew he needed to answer quickly, or risk looking babyish, like his cousins. He had thought about this day so many times, he'd planned a response. He would accept the invitation in the same noncommittal manner as Manuel, not wanting to look too eager. He interpreted the invitation as a sort of trial initiation, to see if he was ready to walk the streets of Colonia Martín López as a cholo. If he was, it would mean he could walk around Colonia Martín López with a greater sense of security, but also that he'd need to offer his friends protection. Though none of them had guns, as some of the mestizo boys did, the Rarámuri cholos helped one another: they kept an eye out for police presences, worked together to steal from homes and tienditas, and always shared their bounty.

Though the invitation could change his life, Jaime hesitated. The problem was, hanging out with the cholos entailed sniffing paint thinner, at least on occasion. He suspected that he would be offered some at the arcade. He had already heard some of the mothers talking disapprovingly about the place, saying they thought the owner was selling the solvent to middle schoolers. Jaime knew Manuel would sniff; he'd told Jaime so several times over the past year. *Not every kid gets addicted,* he had repeated. The trick was to know how much to sniff, and when. That's how Marcos enjoyed the highs without letting them take control of him, Manuel had said. Marcos had promised to teach Manuel how to sniff so he didn't get hurt when the time was right. Jaime wasn't sure if Marcos was addicted or not, or if they could even trust him. But Jaime thought going along with Manuel was the safest way to transition into this next phase: he was determined to not end up like his cousins or his father, soft and fearful. Many times, Jaime had told himself he would follow Marcos's lead, if the day should come. But he was still worried he'd get addicted from just one whiff. There was also the promise he'd made to his father.

Luis had talked to Jaime many times about not sniffing paint thinner, even if other boys offered him some. He'd repeated what Jaime had heard so many times: that paint thinner rots your brain. Because these warnings came from his father, who had a way of speaking to him that made him feel both respected and loved, Jaime had promised to never use. He convinced himself he'd find a way to respect his father's wishes even as he shaped himself into a cholo, to gain the protection it offered without using drugs, though he couldn't think of a single person who'd done it.

Perhaps if Jaime had more time to play soccer, he wouldn't have sniffed. It's possible that, if given adequate space to play their pickup games uninterrupted, most of the boys in El Oasis would have focused their attention on soccer and followed their elders' advice about staying away from the paint thinner. It might have made a difference if Luis had been able to stay in town more consistently. It might have helped, too, if Luis didn't spend some of his free evenings drinking beer with other men by the arroyo, something he had started to do to alleviate some of the anger and frustration he felt after police extortions. Without his father to talk to, Jaime had to work through dilemmas about his future on his own. Without Luis, Jaime always came to the conclusion that it was best to be nothing like his father. Years later, Martina would wonder whether things would have turned out differently if she had insisted that Jaime stay with her instead of going out to korimear on his own.

That day, with his father away and Martina korimeando somewhere in the city, Jaime decided that if sniffing paint thinner was the price he had to pay to become one of the cholos and move through the colonia with ease, then maybe it was worth it.

At the arcade, the older boys teasingly asked Jaime and Manuel if they'd had to ask their mothers for permission to join them. *No,* the boys quickly answered, *we just left.* Pleased with their response, Marcos invited them to play two of the arcade games, giving them each three pesos to spend.

The arcade was cold and dank, exactly as Jaime had imagined. The space was shallower than he'd thought, and there wasn't enough room for everyone to see the screens of the machines they were playing on. But it didn't matter: everyone who could was watching as if the games were live sports matches on TV, cheering each time one of the ninjas got knocked over and spurted blood. Jaime was enthralled by the game and pleased that he and Manuel were hanging out with the older boys. He'd been nervous as they'd walked down the road, but now he felt that it wasn't so hard being around the older kids. They ate chips and drank sodas too.

Jaime didn't notice the mestizo man standing beside a folding table at the back of the room. He was so caught up in the game that he didn't see the man pouring paint thinner into two plastic water bottles. He'd just managed to side-kick his opponent—the older boys yelled at him to keep going—when he caught a whiff of chemicals so strong, he almost gagged. He looked in the direction of the smell. Marcos was holding a bottle of paint thinner up to Manuel's nose. Manuel inhaled once, deeply.

Jaime turned his attention back to the game. He knew Marcos would bring the bottle to him soon; it was making the rounds, each boy sniffing once. If he didn't breathe in once, Jaime thought, the boys would make fun of him, and he'd probably end up like his cousins, forever ridiculed.

He didn't want to break his promise to his father. But Jaime didn't think he'd get addicted from just one whiff. No one outside the arcade needed to know.

When the bottle reached him, Jaime pushed his worries aside. Without missing a beat, he inhaled, hoping he looked like he'd done it a hundred times before.

When he returned home hours later, he found a frightened Martina waiting for him. The mothers who had seen him walk off with Marcos and Manuel had reported it to her, adding that they hadn't seen him come back. Martina, with María José's help, had searched every corner of the asentamiento, giving up only when María José said he was probably just playing soccer somewhere in the colonia. She herself had sounded unconvinced, but she was trying to comfort her sister—what more could she do? Martina was about to leave El Oasis to keep searching, but María José stopped her, telling her she'd only anger Jaime and push him away. *He'll come home,* she had counseled Martina, who once again looked to her sister for guidance on how to live in the city.

Jaime thought he could calm his mother's anguish by pretending he didn't notice it, so he leapt into a description of the games he'd played with Manuel. He left out the names of the other boys who had been there, knowing that mentioning them would only worry her more. Martina pointed to Marcos and his friends as examples of boys who weren't living by korima, the kind of boys she didn't want her son to become. What he didn't realize was that Martina already knew everything. Jaime was still too naive to understand that everyone in the community had been watching him and Manuel and the other boys their age, waiting to see what path they'd take.

Though she had temporarily allowed herself to be soothed by María José, Martina had expected much worse—for Jaime to have gotten high and drunk beer in one of the colonia's empty lots, for instance. Now, bewildered, but for the most part relieved, she told him that before she would allow him to go back there, she wanted to see for herself what the games were all about. She had heard other mothers grow outraged, complaining about the mestizo owner who sold paint thinner to their sons, but Jaime wasn't high. His eyes were bright with energy, and he didn't smell like the solvent. She wanted to believe Jaime's reassurances. Her son had never lied to her, as far as she knew. He was happy in school and spent most of his time close by. Martina trusted that everything she and Luis had taught him about korima, and about the dangers of paint thinner, had stuck. Jaime, fearing that Martina would find out the truth, reached for excuses to keep her away from the arcade, but couldn't think of any.

Martina hadn't ventured far into the colonia for some time, so she had yet to see the arcade. The following morning, she discovered that it was a hole carved into the wall of an abandoned building. The cinderblock entrance was jagged with rough edges that could cut skin, and there was no door or sign, only the sounds of the arcade games ringing within. The shop owner wasn't standing out front greeting passersby, as so many others did. When she squinted to try to see inside, Martina discerned a lone man at the back of the room. She wondered why he didn't turn on a light. Was he trying to hide something? Everything she saw seemed to confirm the rumor that the owner sold paint thinner to make extra money.

Martina thought about walking inside and spitting in the man's face, but she knew she would get beat up or worse. She realized that Jaime had likely been offered paint thinner here the day before. She didn't blame her son—she thought the man must have lured him in with the games, then given him a whiff. There were others like the arcade owner, luring children in with candy and cheap plastic toys; the tactic was notorious in Colonia Martín López. But Martina had never seen a store that was such an obvious front. Most at least sold other products, fruit or stationery, to disguise their crimes against children. This man didn't seem concerned that his place looked like the kind the police would raid for drugs, or at least the kind that would give them pause. In her short walk through the colonia, two patrol cars had passed her. Did they not see what this man was doing, right on the main thoroughfare?

Martina knew José didn't like to get the mestizos involved in Rarámuri affairs, but this place was such an obvious source of paint thinner that she thought he might agree to speak to one of the patrol officers about it. They took him more seriously than they did other Rarámuris, since he was the siríame and sometimes cooperated with them, when they needed physical descriptions of children who had gone missing, for instance. In the meantime, Martina planned to tell Jaime that he could not return to the arcade. She wasn't sure if she would accuse him of lying about the paint thinner. Like José, she preferred not to give orders, and she believed there was value in trusting her children. But remembering how thrilled Jaime had looked the night before frightened her. Now that she'd seen the sort of place that excited him, she wondered if anything she and Luis had done to keep him away from the substance had worked. Standing before the arcade, Martina felt this man—hidden in plain view—had some power over her son, and that she'd have to fight it hard. If she didn't act now, Jaime would return. And if he hadn't sniffed the day before, then it was only a matter of time.

That night, Jaime braced himself for the verdict he was sure Martina would deliver, all the while resenting her. His father was away, so it fell to her to tell Jaime whether he was allowed to return to the arcade. Even if Luis had been home, Jaime wasn't sure how he could have explained to his father that spending time with these boys was a way to avoid becoming like him. Even if he couldn't say that, though, he could still have taken a walk with him, and vented about being pushed out of El Oasis by the women who wanted more space for their sewing. They left no room to play soccer, to make graffiti art, to look at baseball cards uninterrupted. What could a Rarámuri woman understand about Rarámuri boys, or Rarámuri men, for that matter? Martina and Lupita had sewing and cooking and friends in El Oasis. The asentamiento was theirs, and the boys and men were forced to wander and work in the streets that belonged to mestizos.

After a day spent ruminating, Jaime concluded he couldn't tell his mother about his frustrations, or about anything else that mattered to him. Martina liked to see her kids happy and bought them things they wanted whenever she could, but when it came to their fears and complaints, she only told them to remember all they had to be thankful for. Then she talked about korima and the ways of the Sierra. She would never understand why the older boys' invitation had been so important to Jaime, or why he needed to go back that very afternoon or risk being labeled weak and unworthy of protection.

He hardly dared glance at Martina's face after school. When he did, he saw anger in her pursed lips, and sorrow in her eyes. He knew then what her answer was. Martina told him, as sternly as she could, that he was not to return to the arcade. Then she sat a glass of water on the table, as if it would wash out the anger he felt boiling up.

Jaime shouted at his mother, a stream of words in Rarámuri that the entire corridor could hear. Like a child many years younger, he said he didn't want to spend his days in El Oasis anymore, and that she couldn't keep him from the arcade. He repeated the words over and over, emotion overwhelming him.

Martina thought she recognized a tantrum she could soothe by putting her hand on his shoulder. This would relax his body and cause the yelling to break. Then she would pull him in for a hug and rock him back and forth until he felt calm enough to accept her decision. She had consoled her children this way hundreds of times, in the Sierra and in the city.

When the palm of her hand lightly touched his shoulder, Jaime turned his face away. Martina felt his shoulders slump. He stopped yelling, and a few tears rolled down his face. She tried to embrace him, but Jaime pulled away. Then he left the house, leaving a shocked Martina to wonder whether following him would only push him further away.

By age eleven, Jaime was sniffing paint thinner on a near-daily basis. Instead of korimeando after school, he now joined other boys at the arcade or the arroyo, taking whiffs until he felt the familiar sensation. The addiction had gripped him fully by his tenth birthday; he had not been able to sniff only occasionally, as Manuel had said. When he was high, Jaime felt like he could approach mestizo cholos and strike up a conversation about graffiti. The effects on his speech and ability to walk felt like minor problems—he was awash in possibility, certain he was paving his way to a new future, one far away from poverty. The stories of mestizo boys murdered by cartels or thrown in jail didn't scare Jaime; he thought the risk of harm was low simply because so many of them committed robberies or sold drugs without any repercussions whatsoever. Anyway, Jaime wasn't looking to become a kingpin. He wanted enough money to eat three times a day, wear the jerseys and baseball caps he liked, and buy colored pencils and paper for drawing. He also thought it would be nice to see his mother and sister in new dresses more often. Their clothes were always stained with car exhaust from so many hours spent korimeando. He wanted his father to stop working altogether and spend his days carving wood figures or running, as he had in the Sierra.

With four or five whiffs, Jaime felt a heavy cloud settle over his mind, a pleasant sensation that dulled his worries and left him content. Yet the feeling lasted only a few minutes, and the arcade owner kept pouring the solvent into disposable plastic water bottles, offering the children whiffs as they played, charging them an extra three pesos for each one. After the high wore off, Jaime felt an anxiety that made him unable to think about anything other than huffing the paint thinner again. Between the ages of ten and eleven, he attempted to quit sniffing paint thinner several times. He feared becoming so addicted that his brain turned to mush, as Samuel had once said. He was also ashamed that he no longer contributed coins. He wanted to stop sniffing, but still retain the social status he had gained with the Rarámuri boys who called themselves cholos. He believed this to be a possible goal; cholos didn't have to use drugs, they only had to look the part and act tough. It was about confidence and being prepared to meet the many injustices that would come their way. Yet each time he tried to quit, Jaime returned to the arcade within a matter of days, always because something in his life had gone amiss.

When he wasn't high, Jaime was preoccupied with an upcoming milestone: he would be graduating from the elementary school in El Oasis at the end of that school year. Rather than excitement, the thought filled him with dread. Jaime cherished the safety of school. He had also discovered a love for math upon moving to the city, and had spent his first years in El Oasis going through his worksheets with great enthusiasm. But those years had come to an end, and that fall, in addition to working up the will to kick his paint thinner addiction, Jaime worried about what was next. To Jaime, sixth grade marked the final year of his childhood, and he prepared himself for the future by trying to look like the older boys. One mid-September afternoon, when his father had been away for seven weeks, Jaime asked his mother for a haircut like the ones worn by kids a few grades ahead of him. He wanted long uneven strands, partly covering his face. He planned to add his New York Yankees baseball cap, a knockoff from one of the small clothing stores downtown, brim pulled low over his face. The other Rarámuri boys in El Oasis wore their hats like that, too, with baggy black jeans and oversize jerseys.

When Martina took the scissors to Jaime's hair, she cut too close to his scalp. He knew she was cutting it that way so he wouldn't get lice and remained silent as he watched long strands fall to the floor. Jaime had promised his father he would no longer yell at Martina when he didn't get his way. His shouts, sometimes so loud they drew a crowd to the door, made Martina cry and Lupita grow hot with anger. When this happened while Luis was in town, Luis would vacillate between consoling his son and forcing him to sit in the back room on his own until his rage subsided. When the behavior first started, Luis would take Jaime to the edge of the arroyo for quiet talks, as he would have done in the Sierra. Jaime, feeling close to his father, would then return home contrite and apologize to Martina. Still young enough to sit in his mother's lap, he would hug her and promise not to lose his temper again. But as Jaime grew older and

Luis lost patience with his temper, which would not soften, Luis opted more often to isolate Jaime.

Resigned to the haircut and feeling guilty about the words he'd imagined saying to his mother, Jaime made up his mind to defend himself against any boy his age who mocked his haircut. With the older ones, though, he'd simply bear it. And in the future, he resolved, he would cut his hair himself.

Starless sky
[September 2009]

At Parque Media Luna, the name for a sliver of land where there was some rusty playground equipment on a corner lot two blocks from El Oasis, Lupita and her two best friends, Camila and Violeta, stood at the top of a skateboard ramp, surveying the near-vertical slope like skiers assessing a mountain. This was the calm before the race, when the girls gathered every memory of the day and harnessed them all into the energy of winners. The ramp was wide enough for them to stand shoulder to shoulder at the top, their floral skirts brushing against one another. It was ten feet tall, but looking down its slope, Lupita thought it might as well have been one of the six-story office buildings downtown. She tried to push that image out of her mind and focus instead on how strong she had become. Her calf muscles didn't burn as they had before, not since she had started running more footraces around the colonia. The girls had scrambled up the ramp, their plastic sandals sliding on cement as smooth as ice. Now they were at the top, hand in hand, palms sweating. They heard their pumping hearts and deep breathing, guard dogs barking madly from the rooftops across the road, and the boom box outside the ice cream shop blaring out narcocorridos.

Lupita and Violeta were waiting for Camila to say the word, but she hadn't yet found the courage. When Camila, who was standing in the middle, dropped their hands a minute later, each girl took a deep breath.

Ya! shouted Camila.

Each girl stepped over the ledge and raced down the ramp as fast as they could, giggling as they tried to keep their footing on the smooth cement. Lupita held her long hair in her hand so it wouldn't fly in her face and took small, quick steps, thinking the less her sandals touched the cement, the less likely she'd be to slip. Violeta jogged sideways and used the outer edges of her feet to keep from sliding. Camila took the biggest strides, facing straight ahead like she was running toward a storm. Sometimes they'd slip and find themselves sliding down into the U of the ramp, laughing so hard they gasped for air as they tried to scramble to their feet. If they made it to the bottom without falling, they steadied themselves, taking deep, even breaths in unison and looking at one another. It was their way of preparing to take on the next challenge together. There was no fun in winning if the others were too far behind, so they always waited until everyone had equally recovered before they went on.

When they had, the girls crouched into a starting position. This time, no one yelled. Camila inhaled sharply, and all three took off at the same time, back up the slope. The first one to slip was Violeta. She slid back down to the bottom and, frustrated, buried her head in her hands. Lupita's blue plastic sandal caught on the polished cement halfway up. She screamed with laughter and slid down on her belly, arms flailing for something to grab onto. When she landed beside Violeta, her friend's frustration had turned to amusement. They turned to see if Camila was still racing, or if her sea-green sandals had made her slip too.

Camila was holding onto the top of the ramp, her belly and legs flat against the cement. She was trying to bring her knees to a crawling position, but her skirt was in the way. Bracing herself with her shoulders, she managed to rise a few centimeters, still trying to get her knees underneath her.

Tu puedes, Camila! cheered Lupita in Spanish. *Tu puedes!* Violeta echoed. The dogs across the street barked frantically. Bolstered by her friends' encouragement, Camila managed to get her knees onto the edge. Then she placed one sandal on the cement, pushed her body upward, and arrived at the top.

After a few minutes' rest, Lupita and Violeta scrambled up. Camila offered her hand to help them get to the top. Then they did it all over again. They raced until their hearts pounded so hard, they couldn't talk. Breathless, they lay in the curve of the ramp, looking up at the sky. It was rare for the three girls to be together on a weekday afternoon, instead of korimeando. Lupita thought the sky must have shone this brightly most days, but that day, she thought it looked like the sapphires Disney princesses wore on their tiaras.

Martina sat on a park bench, keeping a watchful eye and thinking how good it was to see Lupita having fun, especially after Jaime had reacted with sullen silence to the haircut she had given him. During their rare free afternoons, she took Lupita and her friends to the park. The arcade was just a block away, and Martina knew other mestizos in the area also offered paint thinner to young Rarámuri children. Because of that, and the kidnappings that happened frequently enough, Martina didn't let Lupita wander beyond the enclosed street right outside El Oasis without supervision.

When the girls tired of racing, they searched the ground for pebbles of interesting shapes and colors. Jagged pebbles, broken off from larger rocks. Gray pebbles with bits of yellow limestone that glittered in the sun. Rocks with black spots, pieces of crystallized lava from a time when volcanoes had erupted at the bottom of an ocean that had dried up long ago. The girls placed the rocks in the satchels they kept tied around their waists, usually used for carrying the coins they collected. Sometimes they sat in a circle in the middle of the park and admired their findings. *Yours are the prettiest,* Camila always said to Violeta. *You're so good at finding the nice ones,* Lupita added. Violeta smiled proudly, pleased that her friends were admiring her. At home, she kept the rocks in an old yogurt container tucked between her folded dresses. She was afraid her mother would find them and throw them away, to punish her for not bringing home enough coins. When she expressed this concern to her friends, Lupita offered to store the rocks at her house. *I won't mix them up,* she promised. Violeta smiled, appreciative, but she preferred to keep the rocks close to her, so she could take them out and look at them when her parents weren't home. They often went to visit friends and family in other asentamientos, where they sometimes drank heavily for days on end. Violeta looked at her rocks the most on those days, spreading them across the floor of the empty house and admiring them one by one.

Camila, whose hems were always stained with car exhaust, even after her mother had scrubbed them against a washboard, usually had a few spare coins in her satchel, saved from korimeando. A trip to Media Luna was such a special occasion that Camila insisted on treating her friends to some candy on the way back to El Oasis. Martina took them to the tiendita across the street from El Oasis, then sat down to sew in front of the chapel, where she could keep an eye on the girls they sat on the curb outside the asentamiento's gate, eating sticky chile-and-tamarind candy under the golden afternoon sun.

A day off from korimeando was the only time things slowed down enough for them to take stock of the endless, repetitive labor, perhaps because the hours felt extended. There was no rush to gather coins by nightfall, and they could eat dinner at a leisurely pace instead of cramming in a quick meal before bed. But the irony of a day off was that even then, work found a way to creep in. That late afternoon, sticky candy melting onto her hand, mind relaxed, Camila suddenly remembered a recent interaction with a mestiza. The memory buzzed around in her head, a fly she couldn't shoo away. Why did the mestizas find a way to bother her even when she wasn't near them? She tried for another minute to turn her attention to something pleasant—the flocks of birds riding the air currents high above them—but she couldn't. Abruptly, she stood up and faced her friends. Every child in El Oasis needed to vent about the tediousness of customer service sometimes, and they each recognized the signs in one another. Lupita and Violeta, sensing Camila's changed energy, lifted their heads, ready to listen. Camila flipped her hair behind her shoulder and launched into an impression of a mestiza. Perhaps because the girls wanted to feel some semblance of power, they often mocked the mestizas to one another, sometimes by doing impersonations.

I was selling Chiclets at the KFC *drive-through the other day,* Camila said. *A woman pulled up and asked if I had mazapanes. But I only had Chiclets, and I told her so.*

Lupita and Violeta were already shaking their heads.

Do you have blue Chiclets? said Camila in a demanding tone, imitating the mestiza. She rolled her eyes toward the sky, and Lupita and Violeta laughed. They understood this was Camila's internal reaction to the woman. They also knew there was no way Camila would have revealed it to the mestiza, no matter how badly she wanted to.

Do—you—have—white—ones? she said, emphasizing each word. The girls were giggling, and a group of children were looking on now.

Pink ones? Green? Orange? She rattled off colors maniacally. Violeta slapped her forehead. Lupita was still shaking her head. Other children chimed in with colors Chiclets didn't come in: silver, gold, green with yellow polka dots, striped red and white, lime green.

Camila paused and waited for the children to finish their list. Lupita, Violeta, and all the others had dissolved into giggles while Camila looked fiercely at them.

Do you know what she did next? she asked her audience. Several kids shook their heads.

Camila acted out sticking her hand in something. Several children gasped.

She stole the Chiclets, said a girl in disbelief.

Camila paused and pretended to consider the girl's guess. Then, looking at the children, she held out her palm the way they all did when they were expecting coins and delivered her punch line, deadpan.

She paid me with a piece of chicken.

Violeta, Lupita, and the other children howled with laughter at the crude, dumb ways of the mestiza. Each of them had experienced an interaction that insulting. Camila eyed her audience approvingly.

That laughter was a small recompense for the anger she had felt when she'd been handed a piece of oily chicken so hot it almost burned instead of the coins she was expecting. She had eaten it because she was worried it would be the only food she'd get that evening, but she would have liked to have thrown it back at the woman and watched the grease stain her blouse.

As Camila watched her friends laugh, their tongues stained red from the chile and tamarind, she finally lost her composure. For more than a minute, she, Violeta, and Lupita laughed uncontrollably, doubling over to hold their bellies.

That day, Martina had made a calculated risk: she had decided to skip korimeando. Taking Lupita to Media Luna was a way to make up for what she was going to ask her daughter to do. She thought it likely that this would be the last time she would be able to spare an afternoon to bring Lupita to the Media Luna, unless Luis returned soon or Jaime started korimeando again. With Luis still gone, every day of korimeando counted. Martina didn't think she could go on denying herself food so her children would have enough. When she did, she knew that Jaime and Lupita could have eaten more still, a second bowl, a couple quesadillas, because that's how much they ate on the days that Luis and Martina brought home enough money to buy it. Now, nobody had enough, Martina least of all.

Lupita, from now on you'll be korimeando on your own, Martina said when her daughter walked in the door one afternoon, a few days after the trip to the park. All afternoon, she had wondered how to soften the blow of her words, but she didn't know how, so instead, she made herself hard as steel. Her voice sounded strained even as she tried for a command. She busied herself putting a sweater on Manolo to avoid looking at her daughter's face. Once the words were out, she felt a mix of relief and devastation. Finally she would have help collecting coins. But she had never spoken to Lupita in that way about plans that would affect her; reaching a consensus with her children was another aspect of life in the Sierra that Martina hadn't wanted to give up. She knew, though, that if she approached

Lupita in the Rarámuri way, their dialogue could last for days or even weeks, and when she had fully confronted the need for Lupita to korimear, she felt there was no time to waste. She had put it off for as long as she could, and her hunger gnawed at her, making her so dizzy and weak at times that she worried she would pass out. Now she felt her heart breaking, her daughter's silence communicating her shock. Still Martina wouldn't look at her. She didn't think she could bear the surprised and pained expression she expected to see on Lupita's face.

For weeks, Lupita had seen the strain of korimeando affecting her mother, had noticed that she ate less or not at all, and that her legs and hands sometimes trembled. Lupita had offered to join her mother in the intersections before, and also had offered her food from her own plate. Martina always refused, telling her daughter she wanted to keep her safe and fed. But Lupita had known all along that her mother wouldn't be able to hold off on sending her out korimeando for much longer. Rarámuri girls raised in the city had to become sensitive to their mothers' needs from a young age. Men and boys spent so many hours out of the house and often lost their money to extortion or spent it on alcohol and drugs, so daughters had to support their mothers by korimeando, washing, cleaning, cooking, and caring for younger children. Few girls rebelled against these tasks, knowing that without their help, their mother and younger siblings wouldn't eat. That Lupita hadn't yet started korimeando on her own was atypical, no matter how much Martina wished it were the norm.

If Martina had looked, she would have seen watery eyes and trembling lips. As her mother's words hit her, Lupita thought she might dissolve into a puddle of tears. It wasn't the need for her to go korimeando that shocked her, it was the command, a way of speaking to another person that she had never heard from anyone except the mestizos who told her where to stand, what to say, and how to act. Perhaps because she was so practiced at absorbing commands from them, Lupita now hardened herself, at least outwardly. She put down her backpack and went to the bathroom to splash water on her face. When she reemerged, she was expressionless, as if no life-altering words had passed between her and her mother.

It wasn't until the next morning, at her desk inside her third-grade classroom, struggling with equations she normally figured out in a matter of minutes, that Lupita felt scared about being out on her own. The previous afternoon and evening, she'd remained distant from her mother, nodding when she'd delivered her command in that voice that sounded like plastic wrap stretched too tight. She wanted Lupita to start the next day and to buy groceries with the coins she collected. They would meet at home that night and cook the food they had both bought. Lupita was hurt and afraid, but she also didn't want to make her mother's life more difficult by expressing her worries, not when Martina so clearly wanted Lupita to be silent and obedient. Now, as she listened to pencils scratching on paper and worried about the bad mark she would get on her worksheet, Lupita feared she wouldn't be able to hold herself together much longer. She kept her eyes trained on her desk, her fists clenched, determined not to make a scene in front of everyone. Lupita hated appearing weak; like her mother, she wanted others to see her as a strong student, a great runner, and funny. But what if she encountered a rude mestiza, like the one Camila had described? She wasn't sure she'd be able to find the right words to respond to questions. Then there was the matter of defending herself from mestizos who might harm her. How could she stop one of them from pulling her into a car and taking her away to be sold? Martina and other Rarámuri mothers, wanting to preserve their daughters' innocence for as long as possible, didn't explain to young children that some mestizos sold young Rarámuri girls into prostitution. Even without this explanation, when she was out with her mother, Lupita felt men's eyes on her and registered discomfort and vague fear, though the meaning behind their stares was not yet fully clear to her.

At recess, she went over to a corner of the basketball court and beckoned to Camila and Violeta. Lupita knew word of her korime-ando would get around by that afternoon, once others saw her leaving

El Oasis with the group of children who went out every day. She dreaded the whispers that were sure to spread about her and her mother. She thought the biggest gossips, the ones who criticized others just for buying fabrics they thought were ugly, would feel a certain satisfaction when they saw Martina had backtracked on her decision to never send Lupita out korimeando. Every family in El Oasis knew how Martina felt about sending children out alone, but instead of making her a moral authority in the community, as she had hoped, her viewpoint had made dozens of women see her as out of touch and sanctimonious. Once word reached these women, their own children would more than likely tease Lupita at school. Lupita was already resigned to this inevitability, but she thought she could at least delay it by telling only Camila and Violeta at recess. The girls left their places in the line to jump rope and walked to the corner farthest from other groups of children. A canopy covered the basketball court, but at ten in the morning, the blacktop was already too hot to sit on.

Lupita whispered her news to her friends, using her hand to block her face from the other children, who were now glancing up from their games. Even though Lupita tried to hide her fear, Camila and Violeta could tell she didn't quite know what to do. Their mothers had chosen to send them out as soon as the girls were old enough to bite the hand of any mestizo who tried to pull them into a car, as soon as they could run quickly enough to escape. Lucero had relied on Camila to run to the tiendita for her when she was as young as four and had sent her out korimeando by age six. She wasn't exactly comfortable with the latter, but she knew what to be afraid of. Violeta, as a result of her parents' heavy drinking, had learned to korimear and buy food for herself at age five. Camila bent her head close to Lupita and whispered an idea, as if she were sharing a schoolgirl's simple secret rather than planning for their safety and survival.

Walk with us to the roundabout, Lupita, and we'll show you how to yell at the old men who stare at us, she said, smiling conspiratorially to try to ease her friend's worries. *You'll go to the drive-through at the* KFC. *You'll be by the widow where mestizos get their chicken, and no one will touch you or try to carry you off there,* she said, patting Lupita's shoulder. Other children continued to look over and came a little closer, hoping to overhear the conversation. Camila wrapped her arms around Lupita and Violeta and brought their heads closer together. She was speaking hurriedly now.

Violeta and I will be close, at intersections by the roundabout. If anything happens, scream, and we'll hear you. If everything goes OK, *we'll meet at the Soriana when the streetlights turn on.*

After school, dozens of children, most of them girls, rushed home to trade their Disney-princess backpacks for the boxes of Chiclets they would sell that afternoon. Fresh off their final lessons of the day, the children took a moment or two to stretch their legs and drink water. But there wasn't much time to waste, even on a day with crisp air that would have cooled them as they raced around the arroyo or played at Media Luna. Groups of girls between the ages of seven and ten soon had gathered in front of the gate, ready to walk together into the city. Despite the pressure to get to their posts and collect enough coins by dinnertime, some children knelt to watch and comment on tiny black ants swarming on the sidewalk. Others, not wanting to waste a minute, called to their friends to hurry up. As they passed the chapel, a group of women who sat sewing monitos told them to take care. One, the mother of a nine-year-old who was on her way out, stopped her daughter to wipe dirt from her nose with the hem of her skirt. There was a certain balance to achieve in the appearances of the girls. Too tidy and the mestizos wouldn't give them any money. Too unkempt and the mestizos would turn away in disgust, or tell the children to ask their mothers to take better care of them. Lupita and Camila looked just right for korimeando. They had their hair in braids, and their skirts and blouses matched, though the fabric had faded and been permanently stained. Violeta was the one who sometimes looked too disheveled for the mestizos. Her cheeks were chapped from so many hours spent out in the sun, and her hair was tangled and stiff from weeks without washing.

Walking up the avenue toward the KFC and the roundabout, Camila thought of more advice for Lupita.

If a man talks to you, yell "palochi sucio," Camila advised in a mix of Spanish and Rarámuri. She smiled mischievously. *They'll think you're going to curse them,* she said, referencing some mestizos' belief that Rarámuri women could cast evil spells.

If the person at the window is nice, she might give you food, Violeta said. *Say "korima" to her and she'll know what you want.*

Lupita repeated their advice in her mind to calm her nerves. Camila and Violeta hurriedly thought of other tips. *Hold out your hand before the KFC worker comes back to the window with the chicken. The mestizos might give you coins to make you move out of the way. Say "korima," but don't look anyone directly in the face. If someone is rude to you, ignore them. If they grab you, scream.*

At the roundabout, the girls stopped so Lupita could get her bearings. Buses and cars inched forward, and crowds of mestizos and Rarámuris walked in tight groups to and from their bus stops. This hub was always busy, though not usually as lucrative as the upper-class Periférico, where Martina went korimeando. Children tended to stay in this area because it was easy to get to from El Oasis, and they could call on one another for help.

See you when the streetlights turn on, Camila reminded Lupita. Violeta embraced her, and Camila joined their hug. Then they dispersed.

Lupita positioned herself at the KFC, on the thin strip of sidewalk beside the drive-through window, where she had seen other Rarámuri girls stand. Even with her friends' encouragement, Lupita felt apprehensive about dealing with mestizos on her own. And what would Martina say if she didn't collect enough coins to buy even a bag of beans? Lupita wondered if she would take another cue from mestizos and scold her for it. Some parents did that so their children would stay out longer, but if her mother tried it, Lupita wasn't sure she would be able to hold back her tears. She resolved to stay until she had collected at least enough for beans, even if that meant being there after dark.

An awning kept the sun from hitting her directly. The KFC worker, a young woman, ignored her, and Lupita wasn't sure if this was a good or bad sign. The true test would come when she first asked a customer for korima. She had heard stories of mestizos who yelled at children for coming between them and their customers, so Lupita thought she would ask for korima only after the customers had paid.

The first cars rolled through the drive-through, but Lupita couldn't bring herself to extend her palm and say *korima*. Her heart pounded as she imagined a mestizo grabbing her wrist and yanking her into a car. Mestizos glanced at her as they exchanged wads of pastel bills for buckets of fried chicken and containers of mashed potatoes and mac and cheese, and Lupita hoped they would offer her food. But two hours in, no one had given her anything, not even a piece of chicken.

As clouds moved across the sky and the shadows in the drive-through lane lengthened, Lupita began to panic. A new worry materialized: what if the cars stopped coming at a certain hour? She'd never noticed if there were fewer cars later in the day, but from korimeando with her mother, she knew traffic slowed once the mestizos made it home from their offices.

Lupita began to encourage herself, the way she did when she wanted to give up on particularly hard math problems, or when she felt her heart bursting in her chest as she ran a footrace. *Be stronger,* she said to herself, just as the runners said to one another. If she only tried, she might get what she needed.

Heart racing, Lupita watched as the next car pulled up and the exchange of bills for chicken took place. Before the driver could roll up her window, Lupita extended her hand. *Korima,* she said firmly, looking at the door handle. To her surprise, the mestiza dropped two one-peso coins into her palm—her change from the transaction. Lupita realized that she should ask for korima after the worker delivered change to the customer; the customer would be more likely to give her a few spare coins then. Elated at her breakthrough, she willed the next driver to pull forward so she could try again.

Lupita used the same strategy for the next hour. Some mestizos gave her a few pesos, others gave her nothing. Each time she received coins, Lupita felt triumphant, and that much closer to buying the dinner she envisioned for her family: ground beef tacos topped with diced tomatoes, onion, and cilantro. When the mestizos ignored her open palm, she wanted to sigh and tell them to get on their way, but she restrained herself.

Lupita wondered if there was something else she could try to get the mestizos to give her more money. Though mestizos had trained Lupita to be quiet and still in their presence, Lupita recalled a story Martina had once told her about an elderly Rarámuri woman who sat directly in front of a convenience store door, essentially confronting mestizos for not giving. She'd shouted *korima,* and the mestizos, shocked, had opened their wallets. What if she tried the same tactic now?

When the next car pulled up, Lupita stepped in front of the drive-through window before the customer and the KFC worker had even interacted. She looked directly in the face of the surprised mestizo. *Korima,* she said firmly, extending her open hand.

No, the man scolded, shaking his head.

Korima, Lupita said again, not breaking eye contact.

Lupita heard the window behind her slide open. *Stay to the side of the window or you're out of here,* the worker said angrily. She felt something cold course through her body just as she had the day before, when Martina gave her own command. Lupita was frozen in place, an ice statue on concrete warmed by sunlight and car exhaust. The mestizo glared and the worker inhaled, and Lupita willed herself to step aside.

What seemed like hours later, the sky darkened to navy and the streetlights switched on. Mosquitoes swarmed around the hazy glow of the KFC sign, the tallest of all the signs in the roundabout.

Lupita felt as if all her blood had left her body. She mustered the strength to walk across the parking lot to the Soriana and found Camila and Violeta by the front door, just beyond the metal detectors.

They greeted her with tired smiles and asked her how her day had gone. The two had spent their afternoons on different streets that extended from the roundabout, walking lanes of cars just as their mothers did.

Lupita shrugged and said nothing. There was no use pretending everything was fine in front of her best friends; they knew her too well. Besides, she didn't mind too much if they saw her exhausted and lost. They always paid close attention to her feelings and helped her find her way.

They passed the produce section and walked straight to the dry goods aisle. Lupita felt conspicuous in the brightly lit store. Though she had been inside the Soriana with her mother hundreds of times, Lupita had never come on her own or with other children. She noticed the security guard glancing at them as they walked down the aisle lined with pinto and black beans.

As she took a packet of dried beans, Camila realized Lupita didn't know what to buy. Lupita had taken a bag, too, but Camila noticed uncertainty on her face. *Always buy beans first,* Camila said, *because they are the most filling.* She explained that it was cheaper to buy dried beans than canned. They took a long time to cook, but one bag could feed an entire family. Lupita nodded, appreciative. She wouldn't have known the right order for choosing items if it hadn't been for Camila. At the tortilleria, Lupita again followed their lead and selected a one-pound packet of corn tortillas, enough for that night and the next morning. Then the girls each chose two tomatoes, two jalapeños, and a yellow onion to make a salsa, and four apples as dessert. Lupita felt a sense of pride in knowing that she was going to pay for this food. She noticed the mestizos around her, also selecting food for their families. In that moment, she could almost imagine a trip to the grocery store with enough money to buy anything she wanted, no matter the cost. The hours spent korimeando began to feel worth it.

Before they got in line to pay, Camila explained to Lupita how it worked. *We always put our food on the conveyor belt,* she said. *Then we give the cashier our money. If there's not enough, the cashier will take away some of the food.*

All afternoon, Lupita had taken coins from mestizos and tucked them into the satchel around her waist. She'd felt the weight of the coins but hadn't counted them, not wanting to draw attention. Now, as Camila told her how to approach the cash register, Lupita realized she hadn't counted the coins once. Lupita hadn't considered that she might not have enough coins to pay for the food she'd chosen. She'd forgotten to check the prices as they shopped and now wondered why Camila hadn't checked for her either. It didn't matter, Lupita realized, her nervousness once again growing. She wouldn't remember the value of each coin even if she counted them right then.

Camila hadn't checked the prices as she shopped because walking through the grocery store was too nerve wracking. Lupita had been too engrossed in her first experience shopping alone to notice the security guards wandering the aisles, keeping an eye on the girls. Nor had she noticed the baby formula locked in a plexiglass case, or the dozen or so security cameras set up throughout the store. Camila and Violeta were frequently stopped by the guards so they could check that the girls hadn't stolen anything. As a result, they bought nearly the exact same items each time they came to the store, hoping that their predictable pattern would make the employees trust them. But Camila hadn't thought to explain this to Lupita, and now, as Lupita got in line behind Camila and Violeta, she worried that she would once again be humiliated, this time by a mestiza telling her to take food out of her basket.

Camila seemed to know the cashier, a middle-aged woman who smiled kindly at her. She scanned the items, then looked through the coins Camila held out in her hand. *This is enough,* the woman said, selecting the right ones. Camila, elated that she'd collected more than enough money for her groceries, darted to the back of the line to offer Lupita more advice.

If you don't have enough for everything in the basket, tell the woman you need all this food because you're very hungry. She might give it to you.

Placing the food on the conveyor belt, Lupita felt her palms grow sweaty. As the mestiza scanned the items and smiled kindly at her, she took three steps forward, her head barely level to the card reader.

Lupita stretched out her hand to offer her coins—a strange sensation after spending hours on the receiving end of this exchange. The mestiza counted the money without touching it, a small gesture of respect.

You're missing eight pesos, she said in the same kind tone she had used with Camila.

Tell the woman you're very hungry and ask if she'll give you the rest of the food, Camila had said. Lupita took a deep breath but couldn't find the words. Instead, she looked straight into the woman's face, trying to communicate that she should let her take all the food: she hadn't been greedy and had chosen only the same things the other girls had, no more and no less than what her family needed that night.

With the same kind look, the woman took away two small red apples Lupita had chosen and set them aside. Then she rang up the rest of the groceries and bagged them as Lupita looked at the floor, trying to hide the tears once again filling her eyes. Bag in hand, Lupita walked quickly to the Soriana exit. Camila and Violeta knew her well enough to give her a few minutes. Under the awning, beyond the reach of the streetlights, she took deep breaths and tried to swallow her tears.

Corn-yellow light

[September and October 2009]

When Martina asked her daughter that evening how her first day went, Lupita shrugged and refused to say more. Martina glanced at Lupita as she chopped tomatoes and onions for a broth. Her eyes were puffy, and her face was stained with sweat and exhaust. She sat down on the floor and half-heartedly hugged Manolo, who wrapped his arms around her neck. Seeing Lupita so fatigued broke Martina's heart, though she recognized that every girl who went korimeando came home blinking back sleep, skirt hem tinged with exhaust—that was the sacrifice they made to have a little more money. It was her daughter's silence that worried her most. Ever since the day before, when she'd informed Lupita that she needed to start korimeando, the girl had acted as if Martina were a patrona, a woman who had hired her for labor. When Martina tried to show her affection, to let her know she still loved her, Lupita stiffened and averted her eyes. Even when Martina called her chickuli, little mouse, a nickname she had given her daughter back when they lived in the Sierra, Lupita remained emotionless. Martina wasn't sure if Lupita was upset about the way her mother had spoken to her, or about the korimeando itself. She suspected, correctly, that it was both. But she didn't want to address the subject directly, fearing Lupita would tell her that she didn't want to go out on her own. She remembered the promise she and Luis had made to each other: to never let their children become like the others, workers trapped in the forward motion of time, the pressure to earn enough always weighing on them. They would continue to live by korima, they'd vowed, and trust that Onorúame would provide for them. Yet Martina had subjected Lupita to korimeando, and that made her feel like she was no better than other Rarámuri women who no longer lived by korima.

Martina remembered the way the Sierra had turned brittle and stopped feeding the Rarámuris. If the land was in pain, no one could eat. She had learned these past ten weeks that just like the land, mothers can be depleted. She still wasn't sure why Onorúame let the Rarámuri suffer, but even amid her guilt for having sent Lupita out to korimear, she also felt relief that the burden to earn money was no longer only hers.

Lupita would become accustomed, Martina told herself, especially once she realized that she was eating better. She might not understand now that korimeando on her own helped bring enough food to her family and lighten the physical and mental burden on Martina, but eventually she would. Her anger would soften. She just needed time.

Over the next two weeks, Martina and Lupita continued with their new pattern: Martina left the house at midday to korimear, and Lupita went to the KFC on her own after school. Lupita had softened toward her mother, hugging her back when they met at the end of the day to cook dinner. She still refused to speak about her days korimeando, though, and Martina, not wanting to further damage their relationship, didn't press her. Lupita wanted to put her mother's command behind her and settle into her new routine. Talking about her experiences would only remind her of that terrible first day. She had gradually become more accustomed to the unpredictabilities of korimeando, and she tried not to become overly excited when the mestizos gave her coins, or too disappointed when they gave her nothing at all. Though she still came home exhausted, she feared the mestizos a little less now that she realized that they either gave her some spare change or, most often, ignored her. She intended to continue to post herself at the KFC, where she felt protected. If a mestizo harassed her or tried to pull her into a car, she could scream, and the workers inside would hear her. She figured that someone would help. One day, she thought, she might feel ready to venture into the intersections as Camila and Violeta did, and perhaps collect more coins that way, but she wasn't there yet.

Lupita's korimeando did give the family more money, but only about thirty pesos each day. It was enough for Lupita to buy a bag of beans and a few vegetables. Martina used what she collected to buy a second bag of beans, eggs, and a packet of tortillas. It was enough food to get the family through two days, especially during the week, when Jaime and Lupita ate lunch at school. Still, the amount they would end up with each day was unpredictable, and one or two days a week, Lupita came home with only two Cup Noodles, and Martina with a bag of beans. On those days, Martina didn't eat, even when Lupita insisted; Martina wanted the food to be enough for dinner and breakfast for the children, at least.

As Luis's absence stretched on, Martina thought about him and the others and wondered what could have detained them for so many weeks. But almost immediately, worries about having enough food, paying for utilities, Jaime's drug use, Lupita's safety, and caring for a four-year-old pushed thoughts of Luis out of her mind. *He will come back when the work is done, just as he always does,* Martina reassured herself, then moved on to the moment's most pressing concern.

The only times when Martina usually had a full meal were on Mondays, Wednesdays, and Thursdays, when she helped cook the children's lunch in the communal kitchen, a single white room with barred windows beside the school, at the back of the asentamiento. On one side of the kitchen, there were two worktables on which the women spread flour and rolled sticky balls of dough into tortillas. A pot of pinto beans boiled on the industrial stove, and in the frying pans, white rice simmered in chicken broth. The communal kitchen, where TV news stations sometimes came to film segments about government aid for the Rarámuris, had newer appliances and furniture, a sink, four wooden picnic tables for the schoolchildren, and white tiled floors. The kitchen, chapel, and school were the only buildings in El Oasis with tile, perhaps because the state government had decided that families should be responsible for improvements to their own homes. At the start of each week, government workers arrived with sacks of beans, rice, and white flour, and cans of tomatoes and chicken flavoring. The state government required Rarámuri women to cook the midday meal for the school, and they did so on a rotating basis. After serving the children, the women were welcome to eat as well.

The kitchen was usually a place where the women talked, laughed, discussed the dresses they planned to make, and asked after each other's children. It was a testament to the stress the men's absence was causing them, then, when the mood in the kitchen grew incrementally tense that fall. It wasn't just the wives and children of the men who counted on their wages to eat; it was also their mothers, sisters, aunts, and cousins. By mid-October, staving off hunger had become the main focus for the dozens of families affected by the absences. Sometimes a woman wondered aloud why the job was taking so long, but her question was usually met with a clipped response about mestizos who extended their projects without any consideration for the families the Rarámuri men left behind. By then, the men had been gone for twelve weeks.

The slightest misstep or provocation could cause the women to argue and cry. Once, Sylvia chastised a younger mother named Natalia for tasking her seven-year-old daughter with taking care of her five-year-old brother, who had been born with brain damage. *The girl deserves a childhood,* she had told an angry Natalia. Factions began to form as other women voiced their opinions, and the community kitchen was filled with animated voices until a teacher came in and told them to quiet down because they were disturbing the lessons.

Martina tried to keep to herself. On days when she worked in the kitchen, she ate a plate of food once the children had filed back to their classrooms and she had finished sweeping crumbs from the picnic tables. But on days when she had to skip meals, she was dizzy by early afternoon. Her headaches became severe enough that she had to lie down at home in the middle of the day. Her wondering about where Luis was turned to impatience and resentment. Why had he and the others put so much strain on the women? They knew how their families counted on them to survive, and yet they remained away, even as the sun's harsh glow faded to a corn yellow.

Sometimes a fissure would open in the forward motion of time, letting in small waves of relief. For the Rarámuri women of El Oasis, it was storytelling while sewing that most often created these fissures. Perhaps the communal kitchen saw tensions rise between the women because the government required them to be there preparing meals. Government mandates were too big an imposition to bear that fall, as the women vacillated between worrying about the men and gathering enough coins to feed themselves and their children. The sewing circles, though, were on their own terms, and they became restorative.

In the light of the harvest sun, the women spent entire afternoons weaving their needles through reams of fabric, stitching paths and mountains onto floral skirts. That month, Martina skipped korimeando about once a week to work on a dress with bright orange lilies against an indigo background. She had chosen the fabric, the cheapest kind at Telas Parisina, one of the chain fabric stores where Rarámuri women shopped, during a time when she didn't yet know how many extra hours she would have to spend korimeando. The fabric was lighter than Martina would have liked—she preferred cotton with more weight, which couldn't be easily lifted by the wind—but the pattern had been too beautiful to pass up, so she had bought it with the intention of completing it in time to wear for the harvest season.

With such a great need for coins, the women could have sacrificed sewing in order to spend more time korimeando. The morning hours, when the children were in school, saw plenty of traffic in the main intersections and were an opportunity for women to gather coins. Martina sometimes went out after she sent the children to school, returned for them once school let out, then went out again. But as the weeks passed that fall, Martina and other Rarámuri women stopped going korimeando in the mornings and instead worked on dresses. They often sewed in silence, letting the hours unfurl into long mornings and, sometimes, afternoons. Martina didn't plan which days she would dedicate to sewing. She didn't always calculate how much money she would lose by staying home. Instead, she simply picked up her scrap bag, a Soriana shopping bag, and either sat on her front stoop, with Eugenia and María José joining her on theirs, or found a sunny spot in the clearing before the chapel. Stretching the fabric across her lap, Martina's fingers worked the needle to make it move like a snake through grass. Under and out, over and over, the needle guided brightly colored thread around the dress, stitching a sliver of blue fabric into the path she and her family had followed out of the Sierra.

Sewing their stories onto dresses was an act of resistance against cultural death. The Rarámuri women couldn't stave off hunger completely, nor could they will the men to return home. When they felt they might not be able to go on korimeando for much longer— when they were tempted to stay home, lie down on their mattresses, leave their children to fend for themselves—they remembered their people existed outside the suffering of linear time. Now, stitching paths and mountains onto their dresses, the Rarámuri women resisted falling victim to the pressures of capitalist society and instead became the makers of their own stories. They reminded themselves that even if the worst happened—even if they couldn't continue collecting coins to provide for their families—the Rarámuri story would continue. It would continue far beyond their individual lives. That month, dressmaking had become as urgent as korimeando, because it sustained their story at a time when they couldn't anticipate a return to greater stability. On the days that Martina couldn't bear to go korimeando, she saved food for her children, ignored her own hunger, and sewed and sewed and sewed.

One morning in mid-October, as she sifted through uncooked pinto beans looking for pebbles, Martina began to ruminate again on Luis's absence. Luis had been gone for thirteen weeks by then, seven weeks longer than he had for any of his previous work trips. Each time she wondered why he was taking so long, she remembered what others had said: that most likely, the timeline for the project had been extended. Perhaps because she was alone at home, feeling for the rough edges of rocks among the smooth beans, a task she could do without fully paying attention, and perhaps because Manolo was napping instead of gliding Hot Wheels cars across the floor, Martina found herself growing concerned for Luis. Then, in a rare moment of mental quiet, she again told herself that bad news would have reached her through the network of Rarámuri men who traveled back and forth between the city, the ranches in the desert, and the Sierra. Rarámuri men in one of the other asentamientos would likely have learned of any tragedy, she thought, and they would have made sure word reached her.

Martina had already turned her attention to the afternoon of korimeando ahead of her when someone rapped on her metal door. She got up to open it and found María José on the other side, holding a bowl of roasted corn. Martina let her in, thanking her sister for the korima. María José earned a steady income cleaning a mestiza's house, and while she struggled without Eduardo's contributions, she generally had enough food for her own family. María José would have liked to give Martina more food, but she sensed that her sister didn't want her to know how much she struggled, likely because she wanted to be seen as capable of caring for herself and her children. María José also knew how badly her sister wanted to be a culture bearer in the community. She put pressure on herself to remain strong, sometimes to the point that she forgot that she, too, could be a recipient of korima. Martina wanted to help others, but she didn't want to be helped. María José kept as close an eye on Martina as she could, bringing meals over as discreetly as possible when she sensed that Martina was struggling more than usual.

That day, María José's gift of corn was a pretext for sharing some important news. She wasn't sure how Martina would take it; she had been shocked herself when she heard the plans. Martina could be emotional in her reactions, especially when she was confronted with hard choices. To avoid feeling her distress more keenly, she often delayed looking at her options in a clearheaded way and postponed making a difficult choice about what to do. Sometimes it was a matter of making the least harmful choice—a lesson María José had long ago accepted, but that her sister was resisting to learn. Martina didn't want to let time become her antagonist by submitting to the pressures of deadlines. She was willing to delay making hard choices, even when the least-bad choice would improve her life significantly. To Martina, the trade-off between giving up circular time for a few material improvements wasn't usually worth it. Martina's decision to keep Lupita from korimeando for so long was a good example, María José thought. Her frustrations with Martina were already crowding her head as she prepared to deliver her news. If only Martina could give in a little to the mestizos' way of doing things, she would save herself the agony of indecisiveness.

Lucero wants to go to the police to report that the men haven't returned, she said. *She wants the police to search for them in the Sierra.*

Martina stopped sifting beans. The police—the same police who charged Luis a quota of his earnings each payday for simply walking home from the bus stop? The same police who bribed girls for sexual favors in exchange for a few pesos?

Martina hadn't thought much about what to do if Luis's absence continued to stretch on. It seemed to her that the only choice they had was to keep korimeando and wait for the men's return. The thought of sending the police to the Sierra to search for them seemed absurd, given the way they treated Rarámuri men. Why would they help the community now simply because Lucero asked them to? Martina told all of this to María José. Her sister listened patiently, not at all surprised by her opposition.

Then it struck Martina that the men weren't supposed to be in the Sierra at all. The morning Don Cruz had pulled up to the entrance of El Oasis, he had said he wanted to hire eleven men to build a cattle fence around his ranch in the desert. *Why the Sierra?* she asked.

That's where they take men to plant bad crops, answered María José, referring to marijuana and poppies. She let this bit of news sink in, watching as Martina came to the realization she herself had come to only an hour before, when Lucero had shared her plan.

Lucero thinks that's what Don Cruz really wanted them for, María José said. *They've been gone for too long. She doesn't think he'll release them until the drugs are harvested and there's no risk of the federal army finding and burning the fields.*

On the nightly news, Martina often heard reports of the federal army targeting drug fields in the Sierra, under the direction of President Calderón. Once they found the drug fields, the federal troops set fire to the drug crops, burning tens of thousands of dollars' worth. It was common for cartel groups to defend their drug crops by opening gunfire on the federal army. Though the reports focused on the deaths of troops and cartel members, Martina knew that Rarámuri people were likely hiding in the forests nearby, afraid of getting caught in the cross fire. She also assumed, correctly, that the cartels were continuing to enslave Rarámuri men. She hadn't worried about this happening to Luis, since his jobs had only ever taken him to the ranches in the desert. She understood that working in the Sierra put the men's lives in far greater danger.

She was filled with fear for Luis and anger with herself, just as María José had worried she would be. It now seemed that she had been reckless in spending weeks pushing Luis's safety to the back of her mind. Why hadn't someone—why hadn't she—considered this possibility sooner? Don Cruz could be depriving the men of food and water, or it could be that they were caught in a cross fire between Don Cruz's men and the federal army. Perhaps the men were starving as they worked, or perhaps they had been shot dead by cartel members or the federal army.

We should search for them ourselves, Martina said, her tone urgent. María José gave her sister a skeptical look.

Where would we begin? María José asked.

We would spread out across the Sierra. We know the paths and the hiding places better than the police.

Martina had a point, María José thought: the Rarámuri people knew the Sierra better than anyone else. For once, she let her sister's emotions override her own process of careful calculation.

Lucero wants us all in front of the chapel when the sun is going down, so we can talk, María José said. *Tell them what you're telling me, Martina.*

Lucero stood near the chapel as the sun bathed the asentamiento in warm afternoon light. It was the same harvest light that shone in the Sierra, a light that conjured handwoven baskets filled with corn, squash, and beans. It was the light of plenty, the light of security.

Word about Lucero's plan and the meeting had quickly spread throughout the community as María José and others went door to door to inform other families. Reactions were mixed, and community members had already begun to argue among themselves. Leaving behind their washing and cooking, about fifty people, most of them women, formed a circle in the clearing in front of the chapel. The circle, a symbol of consensus and korima, was the only formation in which Rarámuris conducted important meetings. Though the state government had tried to instill the practice of voting in the community—it was faster—the Rarámuri continued to prioritize unanimity. Cooperation was a way to keep community members engaged and close-knit. Voting, which relied on a majority win, left some in the position of having lost.

Lucero wore a yellow frock with three rows of white mountains on the skirt, an elaborate design that signaled to the community she was taking her role as interim siríame seriously. When she spoke, her voice was clear and steady.

Many of us have husbands, brothers, uncles, and friends among the group that left in the summer. No one has heard from them since then, and they've been gone for much longer than they said they would. I think it's time we go to the police. I don't know if the men are in the desert or the Sierra; I only know they've been gone too long, and the police need to help us find them, she said.

She stepped back to take her place in the circle, a signal that she was done speaking and that someone else should now come forward to express her views.

There were several seconds of silence as the community allowed her words to fill the space.

It's the harvest season, said María José, who didn't want to counter Lucero directly. *Another rancher may have hired them to pick apples.*

All afternoon, María José had wavered. Martina's suggestion had initially moved her, but throughout the afternoon, she had talked with others and found their opinions more measured. She had concluded that even if the men were being detained to harvest drug crops, the community shouldn't worry too much, since it was likely the men would be returned. María José thought she understood how mestizos' minds worked: they measured how much money and time people could earn them and based every decision off those calculations. By that logic, it didn't make sense to her that Don Cruz would kill the men; he needed them to finish whatever labor he'd hired them for. She reminded the group that the men were often kept on to start new projects.

But not for this long, Lucero immediately responded. It was the first moment a hint of fear had entered the conversation. During community meetings, everyone allowed a few seconds of silence between voices, as a sign of respect for the wisdom of each individual. It wasn't that they couldn't express their emotions during the meetings; rather, each attendee tried to remember that their individual concerns were less important than the well-being of the community. It was crucial that no one person take up more space than any other during a meeting. That's why hearing Lucero's quick reply, with its defensive undertone, felt almost like slicing a finger while chopping vegetables. Martina cringed internally. She had arrived resolved to speak, but only once others had received a chance to express themselves.

Eugenia allowed nearly a full minute to pass before she spoke. She said she thought the men had been gone for too long and that the community should search themselves, since they would put more effort in than the police. She delivered her words calmly, and the balance of the meeting felt restored. Silence.

A middle-aged man named José Luis spoke next. He also often took construction jobs. There was no reason for the police to harm the men, he said, to counter Eugenia's argument. He believed they would be best equipped to find the men and bring them home safely, since they had recently had some success in curtailing drug trafficking in the state.

Perhaps because of the pressure to make a decision, even if it was the wrong one, Martina grew hot with panic. In the hours leading up to the meeting, she had been filled with remorse. She recognized her inaction in the face of the men's disappearance as the same stubborn response she had shown in the Sierra years before, when she refused to leave despite Luis's attempts to convince her of imminent dangers. Only her uncle's death had revealed to Martina the risks her attitude posed. If she had waited much longer, Manolo may not have survived the winter. Now, as they deliberated, the men's lives could very well be in danger. She didn't want to make the same mistake this time.

We should find them ourselves, Martina declared, surprising even herself as she heard her voice sound through the circle. *If the police find them, there will be a shoot-out. Rarámuris die when mestizos take out their guns, no matter which side they're on,* she said. She tried to keep her voice steady, though the words felt as if they were coming from someone else.

Martina's willingness to state outright the threat of violence against the men spurred a discussion that lasted well over two hours. As the afternoon dimmed, the streetlights cast a fluorescent glow over the circle and the white chapel. Though half the group agreed with Martina, few were willing to go to the Sierra themselves, the logistics of the trip being too complicated to orchestrate with limited money and urgent daily responsibilities at home. Most of the mothers couldn't leave behind children who were struggling with paint-thinner addiction. The men who remained were needed to bring in income so families, and often neighbors, could eat. And then there were the challenges of the search itself. How would the women get to the Sierra? What would they eat on their journey? What would they tell people who asked why they had returned? And what would they do if they actually found the men? The community reviewed their options again and again, each time arriving at the same conclusion: trusting the police would be dangerous, yet leaving El Oasis themselves might not yield results and would endanger the children left behind.

Lucero stayed mostly quiet during those two hours, not wanting to repeat her earlier mistake. She had learned from her brother that a strong siríame needed to preserve the process of reaching consensus. Sometimes that meant stepping back and letting the community carry on with discussion for as long as was necessary: the wisdom of the community was greater even than the siríame's. The role required humility and respect for their culture, which is why many people had proposed José take it on. Lucero had imagined herself taking her brother's place one day, and she saw this community meeting as crucial not only for making a decision about the men, but also for her to show that she, too, could guide her community with grace and wisdom.

Yet as she listened to community members going back and forth, Lucero couldn't help but feel that the men and their families would never have been in this situation had the community lived by korima. If only they had focused more on sharing what they had, dancing yumari, and being considerate toward one another, they wouldn't be in the position of having to ask the mestizo police for help. Lucero felt Onorúame wasn't protecting the missing men because the community had grown too distant from korima.

Her peoples' origin story had taught Lucero that balances existed for a reason. If a Rarámuri person died, it was believed that Onorúame carried them to the next world, where they continued living. Death of the body was never a finality; it was a return to equilibrium. Perhaps Onorúame was trying to restore some sort of balance by keeping the Rarámuri men away. Perhaps he wanted the Rarámuris of El Oasis to use this hardship to come together in prayer. As she followed this line of thought, Lucero realized that involving the mestizo police wouldn't restore balance but would only further disrupt their community. Yet going to the Sierra to look for the men on their own was risky for all the reasons that had emerged in the last two hours. Lucero became more and more convinced that there was a solution Onorúame wanted them to find.

The taut desert air relaxed into a cool breeze. The colder months were coming, Lucero thought absentmindedly. Soon it would be time to prepare for the feast day of the Virgen de Guadalupe, December 12. The moment she remembered the Virgen de Guadalupe, the mother of Onorúame, Lucero realized what the community needed to do.

In five weeks is the feast day of the Virgen de Guadalupe, she began. *If we wait until then, we can ask the Virgen to bring the men back, and she will,* Lucero said. *We only need to dance for her and work together to buy her a cow, and she'll help us.*

Rarámuris and mestizos alike believed the Virgen was more generous on her feast day, because she was pleased with the food and dances made in her honor. The Rarámuris would ask the Virgen to provide for them, sacrifice a cow, and dance matachines for her. Like the land, she was a mother who wanted to be close to the Rarámuris, and who was willing to perform miracles for them as long as she felt loved. As Lucero spoke of the Virgen's feast day, the other community members realized that it was coming just when they needed it most.

When quiet rain showers came to the desert, the kind that filled the city with the scent of freshly turned soil, Martina thought the Virgen must have made Onorúame happy. She was his mother, after all, and mothers knew how to get their children to smile. If Onorúame withheld rain, or allowed hunger and abuse by mestizos of the Rarámuris, the Virgen could fix it by talking with her son, perhaps on a stroll through the quiet woods. She could convince him of anything with her motherly instinct, coaxing him into doing right.

Since deciding to send Lupita out to korimear—the first major decision she had made on her own, and a break from consensus-based decision-making—Martina had found a certain feeling of relief in knowing that she could at least attempt to fix her problems directly. Relief was a feeling that Martina hadn't known before leaving the Sierra. To live by her origin story had always brought her a sense of fulfillment, and of closeness to her community, to the land, and to Onorúame. But living strictly by korima, whether in the Sierra or the city, didn't make life easier, not in the short term, at least. The sense of relief she felt now that Lupita was sharing in the burden of collecting coins was a revelation to Martina. She didn't have to do as korima required; she could make adjustments based on her individual needs. The individualistic nature of this thought process was uncomfortable; Martina felt that she was acting selfishly. But the sense of relief was stronger; it was like water washing over her on a hot day.

She had always believed that the origin story told her to fulfill her duty to korima, and Onorúame would provide the rest. But now, as she stitched paths out of the Sierra onto her dresses, Martina was coming to suspect that Onorúame wanted the Rarámuris to be the makers of their own stories, the solvers of their own problems. This belief was similar to Lucero's, only Martina saw it leading in a different direction. To her, going to the Sierra to search for the men remained the best solution. The thought of Luis suffering during the next five weeks pained her. There was no telling whether the Virgen would succeed in convincing Onorúame to help. So far, she hadn't convinced him to bring the rain clouds to the Sierra.

Martina remained silent as others in the community began to voice their approval of Lucero's plan. Despite her fear and her reluctance to agree, Martina marveled at the way the circle had allowed them to converse and arrive at what was clearly becoming the consensus. There was an inevitability in the act of closing a loop that had always brought peace to Martina. When she sat in the sewing circle, completing a dress, she felt that even the small mistakes— imperfect stitches, uneven triangles—were beautiful, because they had led her around the entire skirt. The decisions they arrived at during community meetings felt the same way. She had always wanted to restore imbalances, to take the cooperative path. It was harder now, though, because she knew too well the dangers of linear time, how the passing of just a few hours could mean the difference between life and death. To the Rarámuri people, death was not something to be feared, since the border between life and death was not rigid. Death was simply a passage into life in the sky with Onorúame. The souls of the dead could return to visit with their living relatives and friends once a year, when they were called to the altar built for them by their loved ones. Death came at the right time, usually when a person had reached an elderly age. The possibility of violent death was one of the main reasons Rarámuri people avoided contact with mestizos in the Sierra. Mestizos killed when they felt their ambitions to get rich were threatened. The Rarámuris recognized that they were at odds with their capitalist time, always in a race to get rich before they died. Since coming to the city, the pressures of linear time made Martina feel that death could arrive through violence. She didn't want Luis and the other Rarámuri men to die at the hands of mestizos. She wanted them to experience death as Rarámuri people were meant to experience it: as a passage into a more peaceful existence.

Even though Martina still felt hesitant, even though she herself would have chosen a different path, she decided to place her trust in the community's wisdom.

Let's ask for the Virgen's help, said Martina. Lucero, pleased, smiled at her, and Martina smiled back.

Corn moon

[October 2009]

After the community meeting, Rarámuri families returned to their homes with a renewed sense of purpose. Four hours after leaving for the chapel, Martina and Manolo returned home, and a little later, Lupita entered the house carrying beans and tortillas in a plastic Soriana bag. Jaime was sleeping off his high in the back room. Martina set water to boil and explained how the community had reached a consensus. She had told her daughter the origin story enough times that she trusted her to understand that their cooperative effort to raise money for a cow now was simply a continuation of their shared efforts to cultivate corn, beans, and squash in the Sierra. Cooperation was what had enabled the Rarámuri people to survive since colonization, and it was how they would now make sure that the missing men were brought back.

Martina asked Lupita if she could start staying out longer to korimear. She sought to remedy her previous command by including her daughter in the decision-making this time, just as Lucero had governed by consensus earlier that evening. She told Lupita her efforts would please the Virgen de Guadalupe and ultimately help bring her father home. Even as she said the words, Martina felt herself hoping they were true. She hid her doubt from Lupita by speaking with the confidence she had felt back when she was so sure Onorúame would forever protect them from drought and mestizos.

Lupita didn't feel that her father's safe return hinged on her cooperation, yet she wanted to spend more time korimeando because she hoped that once this sacrifice was over, her mother would once again have time to take her to Media Luna or on an excursion downtown. Where they went didn't matter much to Lupita; she wanted only to feel that her mother could set aside time for her, just as she was doing for the Virgen. Lupita had gone korimeando on her own nearly every day since the beginning of September and had enjoyed time with her mother only when their time at home happened to coincide. She didn't expect or even hope that Martina would tell her she could stop korimeando—it had become engrained in her mind as an unavoidable part of her life, something she had to do because there was no other option. Dozens of girls in El Oasis had hardened themselves to this reality by age eight; now, Lupita had too. But that didn't dull her desire to feel her mother's attention focused solely on her. Lupita missed playing at the park, knowing that her mother was on a nearby bench looking out for her. She missed walking down the streets of downtown Chihuahua City, sucking on a lollipop her mother had bought for her. She hoped that if she kept korimeando, her mother would come to feel that they had enough money and that she could take time for Lupita. Maybe, Lupita thought, that day would come after the sacrifice of the cow, whether or not her father returned home as a result. So when her mother asked her to consider staying out late, Lupita, politely attentive, nodded at her explanation. She said she would stay out as long as she needed to.

The fifty-three households in El Oasis had each agreed to give Lucero two hundred pesos by the end of November, to help pay for the cow and twenty kilos of corn for tortillas and batari, their home-brewed corn beer. Lucero thought this would give families enough time to collect the funds in time for the purchase of the cow, which needed to take place the first week of December to ensure its delivery by the afternoon of December 11. The amount she asked from each family was just shy of what most households of five spent on one week's worth of groceries. A cow large enough to feed the community cost eight thousand pesos, and Lucero used past years to estimate that she would need two thousand pesos to buy enough corn. The goal was to have enough food to feed the entire community, about five hundred people. Rarámuris in El Oasis were accustomed to giving money for the cow each year, though never before had they felt so much pressure to come up with the exact amount Lucero requested. In the past, families who had more gave more, and those who had less were thanked for whatever they could contribute. It was a fluid process, rooted in koríma, so there were no expectations for repayment. Even so, families with less money to give found other ways to help, offering to make the tortillas on the night of the feast, for example. This year, however, Lucero had made clear that she expected each family to contribute the full amount requested, to ensure they would have enough for the cow and to show the Virgen that the men's safe return was urgent.

Though it had been decades since deer were plentiful in the Sierra, Martina and other women knew the stories of Rarámuri men who used to run alongside them until the animals, exhausted, collapsed to the ground. A Rarámuri man would then swiftly slice the deer's jugular, and the runners would carry it back to the site of the sacrifice, where the women offered it up to the Virgen and prayed. They asked that she continue to watch over their people and to urge Onorúame to do the same.

In the city, Rarámuri people tried to replicate the act of chasing the deer by pooling their money to buy a cow. Many Rarámuris, including Martina, felt that the money tarnished the gift, since the transaction was far removed from the practice of reciprocity. Running to chase down a deer allowed them to feel the earth coating their skin and the pine-scented air filling their lungs; the land, in turn, felt love in the touch of Rarámuri feet. Running was an intimate act they shared with the Sierra, and the deer's collapse was the Sierra's way of expressing its gratitude. The Rarámuris then offered the land's gift to the Virgen de Guadalupe in thanks. The exchange of coins for a cow lacked that intimacy, and therefore, many thought, it cheapened the gift. Yet Martina and most others had come to accept the gathering of money to buy a cow as an acceptable alternative in present times, so long as their people demonstrated unity in the process of gathering. Rarámuris in the Sierra often sacrificed cows, too, as deer became rarer, though purchasing one was rarely necessary, since some Rarámuris owned livestock and were expected to give one of their animals from time to time. In these cases, the cooperative labor came in the form of raising and butchering the cow, preparing the batari, and doing prayer dances. Both in the Sierra and in the city, Rarámuris viewed this adaptation as yet another form of resistance to total assimilation.

The women's motivation stayed strong for one week before they began to wonder whether letting their children go korimeando until they fell asleep on sidewalks late at night, living without gas and electricity at home, and giving their toddlers tap water instead of milk were truly the kinds of sacrifices that would please the Virgen and eventually bring home the men. Lucero, aware of the dangers many women and children were facing, thought about going downtown to ask the government for help. She was hoping someone from the Coordinación Estatal de la Tarahumara would visit El Oasis, as they sometimes did, with a voucher to help them pay for the cow, or at least the corn, but so far no one had come. With all the time she was spending korimeando alongside Camila and reassuring the women that their sacrifices would bring blessings later, she was never able to make the trip downtown.

Lupita, Camila, and Violeta began staying out until ten o'clock at night. The KFC was closed by then, so Lupita stood outside the shopping mall where the Soriana was located and asked for korima by the front door. Since there was little traffic at that hour, Camila and Violeta left their places near the roundabout and went instead to Elektra, an appliance store. Martina had told Lupita to buy a bag of beans each night and nothing more; the extra coins would be put toward the cow. On Saturdays and Sundays, Martina, Lupita, and Manolo stayed at the Diana la Cazadora monument from midmorning until late at night, collecting enough money to buy a cup of corn with mayonnaise, a bottle of Coke, and bags of chips from the street vendors. The traffic flowed until four in the morning on weekends, as partiers hopped from one club to another. Martina was afraid of the men who yelled drunken insults at her, but she stayed out to collect additional coins. On her back, she carried Manolo, who fell asleep with his head resting in the crook of her neck. She and Lupita split up, each of them taking a lane in the same intersection, where Martina could keep an eye on her daughter as Lupita walked, head down, alongside cars.

Other families applied similar strategies. Many children arrived late to school, if they went at all. Their mothers let them sleep in so they would have energy to spend afternoons and nights korime-ando. Tensions began to rise once again as everyone strained to eat less and save more. In the communal kitchen, a woman named Estela complained about María Cruz: at the community meeting, María Cruz had agreed they should put their efforts toward buy-ing a cow, yet she refused to go to the intersections like the other women. Instead, she sat on the sidewalk just outside the front gate of the asentamiento, sewing dolls and waiting for nonprofit workers to buy them. *It isn't fair,* said Estela. In addition, María Cruz rarely took her turn in the community kitchen, saying she refused to let the mestizos tell her what to do. For the most part, the community tol-erated her behavior without calling her uncooperative, because as the wife of José, the siríame, she held a position of prestige and was considered a voice of moral counsel. Even so, most Rarámuri women found María Cruz's refusal to korimear too extreme. She and José often lacked the money to feed their six children and relied on korima from community members.

That afternoon, Estela's complaint somehow made its way to María Cruz. As Estela walked out of the asentamiento gates on her way to korimear, María Cruz glanced up from her sewing and chas-tised her even while she kept stitching.

You think you're a better member of this community because you put yourself out on the street so everyone can throw their spare change at you, she said. The words came out in a stream, in the same sharp tone she used to convey the seriousness of her anger to her children when scolding them. A group of young women sitting on the sidewalk in front of the tiendita looked up. Estela quickened her pace, but María Cruz continued her scolding, her needle dipping in and out of the fabric.

That's right, go on, go show off for the mestizos, be a streetwalker. Don't even think about coming back here to criticize me.

The girls covered their mouths and giggled, and Estela turned the corner, pretending not to hear. María Cruz finished the hem and bit the loose thread that hung off the sleeve.

Word quickly spread about María Cruz's berating as the Rarámuri women, as usual, discussed the incident—though always out of earshot of María Cruz. Women raised in the city, most of whom were in their late teens and early twenties, thought Estela had been right to speak out about María Cruz's refusal to korimear. Women raised in the Sierra, like Eugenia and María José, tended to think that María Cruz's insults to Estela, while cruel, were justified because Estela refused to give María Cruz her proper place. Martina cringed inwardly each time she heard María Cruz and other mothers speak harshly to or insult the youth, but outwardly she maintained a demeanor that showed support for María Cruz. Martina saw Estela's grievance as an indicator that korima was crumbling in El Oasis: in Rarámuri culture, elders were considered a source of wisdom and were to be listened to. A young woman calling out an older one challenged the knowledge-sharing relationship between generations. It seemed impossible to maintain the structure of the Sierra, with elders providing counsel and youth listening and asking questions. José, the siríame, for example, tried to curb paint-thinner addiction in El Oasis by sitting with individuals and talking to them about the harm addiction brought to their people and their way of living. María Cruz, his wife, saw that this tactic wasn't working and often told him to take a more firm tone with the youth, especially since many of them brought paint thinner into El Oasis, where toddlers saw their older siblings using and began to get the idea that getting high might be something fun to do. To María Cruz and other women who felt that their elder status was threatened and their community's well-being endangered, speaking firmly to young children, and harshly to young adults, was the only way to instill a fear of authority that would perhaps make them listen to their elders' counsel.

The problem was that too many of the youth didn't understand the purpose of the elders' counsel. They thought the ways of the Sierra were old-fashioned, that they had no place in this new urban Rarámuri lifestyle. Perhaps they were right, but this wasn't a message that any of the elders were ready to receive. Maybe Estela didn't understand, but to Martina, María José, and Eugenia, it was clear that María Cruz was trying to replicate the ways of the Sierra by leaving the hard labor to younger women and providing them with counsel in return. In the Sierra, María Cruz's role as moral guide would have been seen as an integral part of the planting and harvesting, and she would have been revered rather than treated as an impediment. Estela focused on the fact that there was no guarantee that mestizos would share their coins; it was crucial for every Rarámuri woman to go into the streets and demand that mestizos acknowledge them. María Cruz wasn't being moral by making the younger women do the hard work of korimeando, not when it took every single person to have enough money to eat, and not when it exposed them to abuse by mestizos. Estela felt María Cruz was simply trying to impose her outdated values.

While Martina, María José, Eugenia, and the other women their age saw Estela's point, and agreed that María Cruz should be korimeando along with everyone else, they couldn't begrudge the siríame's wife her refusal to do so. Keeping Rarámuri culture intact sometimes meant doing things the hard way. They advised the younger woman to show María Cruz respect by not criticizing her, and by spending extra time korimeando to make up for María Cruz's lack of contribution. They also told her that more than the sacrifice of the cow, the Virgen de Guadalupe needed to see that the Rarámuri people cared enough for one another to keep the tradition of gift giving alive. Estela's refusal to make peace not only caused factions to form, it also endangered the men, who needed the Virgen to intervene on their behalf.

Two of Estela's friends, María Inés and Juanita, felt guilty over their friend's defiance. They, along with many others of their generation, urged Estela to listen to María José, Eugenia, and Martina and to make peace with María Cruz, but so far, she remained firm in her stance that the older woman should be held accountable.

After three days of advising Estela to change her approach to María Cruz's advice, to no avail, María Inés and Juanita decided they needed to find another way to restore harmony to the community. They felt responsible for Estela's behavior, in a way, since the older women saw them as members of the generation losing respect for their elders. The fund for the feast day was slowly growing, but María Inés and Juanita knew that money collected in anger would serve the Virgen no better than money collected by theft.

In a moment of inspiration, María Inés suggested to Estela that they organize a carrera de ariweta, a footrace. Juanita immediately understood María Inés's intention. The footrace was a traditional activity in Rarámuri culture and would shift the focus from the argument to an exciting event that all the women enjoyed. Moreover, a footrace, even one run on concrete, was an act of intimacy with the land that brought the community closer. It was a kind of spiritual event. Normally, the women in El Oasis held footraces two or three times per week, but with everyone spending extra time korimeando, it seemed they had forgotten about running. If ever there was a need to restore peace in the community, to quiet the mind by uplifting the spirit, it was now. Juanita offered to ask her sister Serafina if she would be willing to race. Serafina, at sixteen years old, was sure to capture the interest of the others. In addition to being widely considered beautiful, with her long legs, waist-length hair, and multicolored beaded earrings that swished against the shoulders of her blouse, she was known to run all-night marathons in the desert, races the community camped out to watch.

While Juanita went to find her sister, María Inés racked her mind to find a suitable opponent. Often it was difficult to find someone to run against Serafina, since she almost always won. No one liked entering a race they knew they were likely to lose, and so far, Serafina had an undefeated record. When the school bell rang, María Inés stopped a group of girls setting out to korimear at the gate, all of them between the ages of seven and thirteen, and asked for their recommendations. Younger girls kept close track of the best runners in El Oasis, often advising the older women on which runners should be paired against each other to make for the most exciting races. Sometimes, for the fun of it, the girls suggested pairings in the hope of rekindling old rivalries—a mischief of which María Inés wasn't aware. The girls had been watching the conflict between María Cruz and Estela play out, and thought that this race might be an opportunity for Estela to get even with María Cruz.

Against Serafina? That's a hard one, said a ten-year-old named Ceci, pretending to think about it. She knew that María Cruz would likely place her bet on Serafina, in the hope of winning more dresses. She didn't want to give away what she was hoping to do: suggest a great runner that would beat Serafina so that María Cruz would lose many dresses.

Try Mariza, she said, after a few moments.

Which Mariza? asked María Inés.

The one that lives in the house at the back, with the pit bull tied in front, said a child named Sylvie, catching on to what Ceci was trying to do.

María Inés thanked the girls. *Come back at nightfall,* she called after them as they went off toward the entrance. She heard them speaking excitedly about the potential pairing as they walked to their posts to korimear.

It took an hour of coaxing, but by four in the afternoon, Mariza had agreed to run against Serafina. She didn't want to break her own winning streak, having never run against Serafina, but María Inés had appealed to her sense of duty to the community and promised that if she won this race, she would make a name for herself as a runner. She was eighteen years old with waist-length hair that she braided each day and long muscular legs honed in her many races.

Mariza was aware that Rarámuri girls and women admired her physique, just as they admired Serafina's, because she and Serafina resembled the long-distance runners of the Sierra. Both took care to avoid Coca-Cola and the flour tortillas that mestizos and city-dwelling Rarámuris loved, with the aim of maintaining the physical conditioning that would allow them to run for days. Mariza knew this race was her big opportunity to show that she could beat Serafina, that her practice of daily running and eating mostly beans and vegetables had prepared her not just for this moment, but for the longer, citywide races the women of El Oasis participated in alongside the women of other asentamientos.

After her conversation with Mariza, María Inés found Juanita sitting in front of the chapel with Serafina.

She said yes, María Inés exclaimed, loudly enough for others to hear. A few women who sat sewing in the corridor paused and looked up to take in the sight of Serafina having her legs massaged by her sister, eyes closed, face tilted toward the sun.

Urban Rarámuri women never watched the footraces without betting dresses on them. It was another manifestation of their gift economy, in the sense that they placed their bets knowing they might end up losing items. Running and the betting that accompanied it were a form of wealth redistribution, a way to ensure that gifts were spread equally among the community. In the Sierra, when Martina had participated in the races, which were held less frequently due to the distance between neighbors, she would typically bet seeds or portions of her harvest. In the Sierra, betting had been a way to apportion food and bring the community together around an exciting event. In the city, the women rarely bet food. Rather, the women spent as much time as they could sewing the dresses that they would then bet on the races. By sewing and betting dresses for the purpose of redistribution, urban Rarámuri women were defying the mestizo concept that time should be productive and wealth should be accumulated. Running and dress-betting in El Oasis were an act of resistance against assimilation into linear time and a capitalist market economy. Though the women of El Oasis no longer ran to redistribute food and stave off malnutrition, they were still fighting the cultural death that would occur if their people gave in to the structures of a work life and left behind the belief that all wealth, including one's own time, should be freely shared.

Though urban Rarámuri women could have chosen to bet money, the hand-me-down clothing that mestizos gave them, or any other possession, betting dresses accomplished both practical and symbolic acts. The practice of betting dresses began in the early 2000s, though no one knew in which asentamiento. As the younger generations began adopting mestizo styles and behaviors—hoop earrings and winged eyeliner, for example—the older women saw dress-betting as crucial to their cultural survival. Frequent races with dress-betting encouraged women to sew more frequently, and to get excited about the possibility of a new wardrobe if they won. Racing and dress-betting three times each week meant that a dress could change ownership three times each week. Sometimes, Rarámuri women lost a dress in a bet before they even had a chance to wear it, though most women strove to wear the dresses they won before the next footrace. Martina loved winning new dresses; her wardrobe was refreshed several times each month, nearly always with clothing she was happy to wear.

It was considered poor taste to put forth an old or poorly constructed dress, so Rarámuri women chose ones in beautiful fabrics and bright colors, with perfectly even stitches. This high standard of sewing also encouraged the generations raised in the city to carry forward with the craft of dressmaking, further helping to ensure their culture's continuity. Inside her house that afternoon, Martina selected her favorite: a sky-blue frock with large red roses and yellow piping. She'd sewn the dress herself and had worn it on only a few occasions. It was risky to bet the dress she most prized, since she might end up losing it. On other occasions, she had chosen instead to bet ones she wouldn't mind losing. This time, though, Martina wanted to show Serafina, whom she was betting on, that she had faith in her ability to keep her status as the best runner in El

Oasis. And more than that, she wanted to show the community her faith in reciprocity. Adding her favorite dress to the betting pool signaled her belief that she would one day receive something in return. Giving was an act of courage, one that required belief in humanity's basic goodness. Though it would sting a bit to lose the dress, it would feel good to see another woman enjoying it. That woman's enjoyment itself was a gift; it meant that in the passing along of their dresses, the cycle of Rarámuri reciprocity would continue.

Another important aspect of the process was choosing a dress from the opposing team against which to bet one's own. Members of the winning team would get to keep both dresses. Often, women chose to bet more than one dress, and they then entered into a negotiation with another woman about which dresses would be bet, and how many. Any woman could begin the betting process by initiating a negotiation. In the end, their matches on the other team had to bet the same number. The women on the winning team kept them all, sometimes taking home up to ten in one evening.

When Martina approached the pile of skirts, sky-blue dress in hand, María Inés, the chokeámé, or mediator, asked which of the other dresses she admired. She remembered seeing her friend Marisol in a pink dress with yellow sunflowers and decided to ask if she would be willing to bet it against her own. These kinds of negotiations lasted on average three hours, as the women examined each other's stitches and aesthetic choices and debated the merits of each dress. María José had to return home for another dress because Marisol, whose green-and-white dress she wanted, didn't think the yellow frock María José had put forth was as beautiful as her own. María José begrudgingly brought out her own green-and-white dress, which she'd been hoping to hold on to, but was soon appeased by the prospect of winning both. She, too, was betting on Serafina. Yet when things weren't resolved so easily, the discussions could turn into fierce arguments about aesthetics and skill, and women with hurt egos insulted one another or retreated to their houses to cry. In those instances, it was the chokeámé's responsibility to broker between the dress-betters and find a solution that pleased both.

María Inés formalized the agreements by tying together the skirts that were bet against each other and adding them to the pile by the white metal entrance gate.

Over the course of the afternoon, the pile of dresses grew to be four feet, taller than the toddlers who ran from one end of the sidewalk to the other to leap into it. The children rolled and laughed in the soft fabric while mothers looked on, laughing too. Several of the women had pooled money to buy two three-liter bottles of Coke from the tiendita, and they sipped from plastic cups they had brought from their homes. Some of the youth who inhaled paint thinner sat at the edge of the arroyo, their bottles hidden in their sweatshirts, and watched as the bets continued and the mound of dresses grew even taller. The sun lingered at the horizon, a ball of fire set against an iridescent sky. The heat relaxed into a breeze. It was as if the sky had heard the women's plea for relief.

In early evening, the sun exploded. Oranges bled into pinks and purples, then begin to swirl and twist. Serafina and Mariza stood at the entrance gate, preparing to run up the hill and into the mestizo colonia. At this point, they became the rowéami, the runners of the carrera de ariweta, and their status entitled them to special treatments. A young girl rubbed each of the runners' ankles and calves, warming up their muscles for a race that everyone expected to last well into the night. Another girl lifted a water bottled filled with pinole, the crushed pine nuts mixed with water, which would give the rowéami energy to run through the night. María Inés lined up ten pebbles along the curb. Each time the runners completed a lap, she would remove a pebble. The runners had agreed to run ten three-mile laps through streets that had been chosen to avoid the heaviest traffic.

María Inés nodded, and the racers began walking up the hill. Rarámuri races always began at a walk, as a way to warm up for the hard push that was coming. Each runner carried a chuúrulá, a mesquite branch hewed into a slender cane with a hooked end, and a metal ring, called a rowelá, wrapped in bright fabric. As Rarámuri women ran, they picked up the rowelá with the chuúrulá and tossed

it forward for the entirety of the race. The act of tossing the rowelá, running forward, and swooping it up with a chuúrulá while
keeping stride functioned as a metronome, the constant motion of
picking up and tossing the ring a way to set a rhythm that could be
sped up or slowed. It was a way of keeping time and the runners'
pace steady, as they ran with the aim of winning, an act that could
take place only in linear time. For the Rarámuris, holding a race
in which only one person could be the winner was a way of uti-
lizing linear time for fun. The excitement of the race, of the betting process, brought a good kind of pressure into their lives. The
moment the rowéami set off, the spectators entered into a state of
anticipation as they waited to see which runner would win, and
who among them would gain the dresses that evening. Importantly,
the Rarámuris controlled the pressures of linear time during footraces; instead of racing to get to work on time, they decided when
and how the footraces should be run. Even though linear time
could be manipulated for fun and excitement, it needed to be tempered with a countermeasure, like the chuúrulá and rowelá in the
case of the footraces. The ring, continuously tossed forward during
the race, signified the strength of circular time. Though each race
would come to an end, a clear winner declared and the dresses
distributed, the ring reminded the attendees that there would be
future races, more sharing of wealth, and additional gatherings
with laughter.

Dozens of women and children, and the few men who had
returned from work in time, had settled on the sidewalk, forming
one long row against the cement wall of El Oasis. They sat close
together, holding children in their laps, smiling in anticipation of
a race that was sure to be exciting. Some of the women took out
swaths of fabric, thread, and needles and began sewing, an activity
that was always considered appropriate, no matter the occasion. A
few children now lay in the pile of dresses, looking up at a sky that
changed by the minute. The man who sold tamales came by with
his cart, and so did the one selling snow cones. For a few hours that
night, everyone seemed to forget all they needed to sacrifice to buy a

cow for the Virgen. Mothers gave their children coins and told them to buy the most brightly colored snow cones they could.

She's fast, María Cruz said during the fourth lap, as Serafina ran down the hill. Mariza trailed half a block behind her. *Maybe someone needs to give her a good scolding to get her to run faster,* she added, cracking a smile.

Martina and María José, who were sitting beside her, laughed at her self-deprecating joke. In Rarámuri culture, to laugh at oneself was a way of lightening tension and healing rifts. Though Estela wasn't nearby to hear her, various groups repeated María Cruz's joke. When Estela heard what she'd said, she felt her guard come down. On her way to her house for a glass of water, she passed by María Cruz and said, *If anyone can make that runner speed up, it's you.*

That's right, said María Cruz, grinning as she sewed.

The community kept vigil as the last rays of light sank into the mountains and the navy sky spread like ink. Deep inside the colonia, the runners' feet slapped the pavement. They ran past the closed shops and the dinner smells wafting from kitchen windows. When their lungs burned and ached, and they slowed their pace even slightly, the women and children running with them shouted the rallying cry. During every footrace, women and children accompanied their chosen runner in shifts. They did this so that their runner would never feel lonely, and so that she could draw energy from her supporters. The shifts were never formally assigned; rather, women and children got up and ran alongside their runner as they felt moved to do so. They made sure their runners were always accompanied, even if only by a couple of people. *Weriga! Weh-mah!* they shouted. Serafina and Mariza followed the commands to run faster, be stronger. In the Sierra, Rarámuris who delivered aid usually did so alone. Now, in the city, as Rarámuris ran, they were accompanied by supporters who urged them to keep going, even when the night seemed too dark and the path too difficult. The Rarámuris of El Oasis knew that many of the mestizos considered their footraces a nuisance;

running as a pack of twenty or more sent the message that they were not afraid to reclaim their land. Their ancestors had once run across this desert floor, before their people had been forced to retreat into the Sierra. Now, as Serafina and Mariza ran on ancient Rarámuri land paved over by the mestizos, they reclaimed the desert as their own, if only for a short while.

Sometimes the women ran in the desert just outside the city, where there were no roads, and they could smell the dust turned up by their feet. In the city, Rarámuri runners found it impossible to concentrate fully on their breathing, their posture, and their pace, especially because occasionally, despite being cautious, a runner would be hit by a car. Though the mestizos claimed to not see the runners, most Rarámuris believed that these mestizos hit them on purpose, as a way to threaten them from overtaking the streets. Sometimes mestizos called the police to complain about their calls of *weriga* and *wehmah* at night, and the police once told José that running was banned. The community waited a few weeks, then resumed the races. They ran whenever the spirit moved them, no matter how much traffic filled the streets, no matter how harshly the sun shone. That evening, Serafina and Mariza ran in peace. The few cars that passed through the neighborhood slowed to let the runners pass. Mestizos stopped to watch the race, and some even cheered the women on.

The Rarámuris often extended the invitation to run to mestizo anthropologists, journalists, and medical workers. They wanted to share korima with the world: A basket filled with tortillas meant for everyone. The land on which all people made their homes. The river that ran unbridled, bringing life to the Sierra and the desert. The race that anyone could run to feel the strength of the land and the power within themselves. But few took them up on the offer.

Martina sat on the curb, letting the cool breeze prickle her neck. Lupita and the other girls had just returned from korimeando. They sat beside their mothers, sipping Coke and eating cups of instant noodles they had bought from the tiendita, waiting in quiet anticipation for the runners to crest the hill. Everyone heard the sandals slapping the pavement before they saw the girls. When Serafina appeared, sweat dripping from her face, eyes trained ahead of her as she flew down the hill, Lupita rose. Martina held out one hand for her daughter's noodle cup and nodded for her to move to the street, to get ready to join the run. Camila stood alongside her friend. Butterflies filled Lupita's stomach. She had been waiting all afternoon for this moment. Running was a break from the monotony of school and korimeando. It was also an opportunity for her and other girls to give in to the urge to run at breakneck speed, so natural at their age, after containing themselves in their seats and at their posts, dutifully following rules. When she heard her heart pound and her breath shorten, Lupita felt she was pressing against the constraints of her days. It hurt to push herself, but it also felt good. It was a way of not giving up.

The runners approached, and a current of air hit Lupita like a splash of cold water. She stepped toe-heel and joined them, arms at ninety-degree angles by her sides, skirts swishing against her ankles, sandals one more voice in the chorus. Mariza and Serafina had now reached the bottom of the hill and were turning around to begin the next lap. Lupita inhaled sharply as she raced up the hill, eyes trained on the ground. To look too far ahead would make her want to give up. Better to focus on each step building toward the next.

Three hours passed and the colonia's twinkling lights switched off, casting the runners further into darkness. The night deepened, and the women and children kept watch. Most of the men had returned to their homes to sleep, in preparation for the predawn hustle to obtain a day job.

Serafina descended the hill for the eighth time, accompanied by Lupita, Camila, Lucero, Martina, and three other runners. At the start of the seventh lap, Martina had set down Lupita's noodle cup, still half filled with broth and a few noodles, and taken off with Serafina and the others. Martina's shouts of *weriga* and *weh-mah* filled the others with new energy as they ran alongside Serafina, and they, too, shouted to keep up Serafina's energy. Serafina pushed herself forward, swooping up the rowelá in one quick motion and throwing it out ahead again. There was no joy during this part of the race, only determination to complete the final two laps.

The running abilities of Rarámuri people had long been portrayed by journalists and photographers as romantic, but the slog of pushing forward, of not giving up, was an essential part of this intimate act. In the Sierra, Rarámuri people had not run across the mountains simply to feel connected to their surroundings; they had run to literally save themselves. They had fled to escape conquistadors, loggers, and drug growers, and to continue to care for the land. When Martina described running in romantic terms, saying that she loved the scent of the pine trees, the dim glow of stars that illuminated her path, and the way the dirt of the Sierra coated her feet, she did so because she knew romance was one way to deepen a relationship. She was aware that many Rarámuri people had only ever viewed running as a means of survival, and Martina had always wanted more than survival. She wanted the joy of everlasting life, of connection to Onorúame experienced through running across the land, and she wanted it for her children as well.

Lupita felt the cold air like knives in her chest, each breath more painful than the last. Her heart pounded in her ears and her legs shook. Still, she ran, matching the strides of her mother and four other women and children who formed a half moon around their favored runner, pushing Serafina forward. Lupita focused on the sound of their plastic sandals slapping the pavement, the sound of Rarámuris in the city. Running, she thought, was one of the best parts of being Rarámuri, and each time she joined in a race, she felt a desire to have dresses bet on her, to run against the best racer in El Oasis, and to win. She imagined herself on TV, the victor in one of the citywide races the government sponsored. She would run in a pink dress and pose with her medal on the top tier of a podium, representing El Oasis.

The streetlights spaced far apart from each other cast discrete circles of light. Lupita squinted at the ground, trying to discern potholes and pebbles.

The drive to win would last only as long as the race. Once a winner was declared, she would be celebrated just until the next time, when the playing field was considered equal once again. Though the community had favored runners, every Rarámuri could participate in the race; it was a community event. Competition was a means of improving individual runners, but the Rarámuris valued seeing every runner become their personal best, rather than upholding one or two stars.

Lupita felt Martina's eyes on her. A toothy smile spread across her face. She broke the city's stillness with a shout. *Weriga!*

Weh-mah! Martina and the others shouted back. The trail continued to reveal itself under the moon's guiding light. They ran into the night, feet pounding, chests heaving.

Dim light, long shadows

[November and December 2009]

Through all of November, the pressure of the deadline loomed like a long shadow. By the end of November, Lucero was still waiting on funds from twelve households. She reminded families when she saw them in passing, and knocked on their doors when she had some spare time, but they kept putting off paying, and she wasn't confident that they would give their share. She updated her plan to count the money one final time on the fifth of December, then visit the rancher just outside the city to select the cow. If she didn't have the full amount, she decided, she would simply buy a smaller cow, and each community member would eat less. Or she might buy less corn and make fewer tortillas. Neither option seemed ideal. If the Virgen felt their offering wasn't made in the fullest spirit of korima, she might feel saddened and refuse to intervene on the men's behalf.

Then, on a gray morning on December 2, Luis turned the key to his door and walked into his house. Martina was sitting on the floor, sifting through pinto beans, with Manolo asleep beside her. Luis closed the door behind him, taking care not to let it bang shut. He took off his baseball cap and held it, then stood looking at his family, not saying a word. Seeing Martina's shocked face and Manolo's sleeping figure, he felt the journey of the past few months end.

For a moment, Martina thought she was imagining his presence. Staring back at him, still holding the beans she'd been in the process of separating, she began to realize that what she had feared—that he was lying dead in the desert or the Sierra, his body consumed by animals and his bones left to wither in the heat—hadn't come to pass. Somehow, Luis had returned home. His cheeks looked hollow, and his eyes were bloodshot; Martina could tell he hadn't slept in a long time. His ragged T-shirt hung off his body, and his jeans were now several sizes too big. He was nearly as thin as he had been when the family left the Sierra.

Luis sat down on the floor beside Martina. They didn't touch each other, not yet. They looked at each other for minutes, each enveloped in the moment. There was no future or past, only the two of them and their sleeping youngest son.

After a long while, Luis found words. He told Martina what had happened quickly, the story coming out in one long stream. It was as if he wanted to put the past firmly behind himself so he could begin to look forward again.

From the back of the pickup truck last June, the men had watched dry, low-lying shrubs and cacti give way to dense pine trees. In Rarámuri, they asked one another if they had heard wrong. Had Don Cruz actually said they were going to the Sierra and not the desert? Luis suggested that Don Cruz might have changed his mind during the drive and was now taking them to a different ranch to build a cattle fence. Eduardo and José, who had more experience with the mestizos' tricks, insisted that Don Cruz was taking them to grow drug crops. After all, this had happened to other Rarámuri men many times before, though it had been at least a year since someone had reported it to José.

They would most likely be safe, José said to the other men. If they did as Don Cruz asked, they would eventually be driven back to El Oasis. He sensed that some of them, including Luis, were becoming panicked. He warned them that jumping out of the truck would likely cause injury. José suspected Don Cruz kept a shotgun in the cabin and that he wouldn't hesitate to take aim at any man who tried to escape.

The truck passed through Creel. Don Cruz followed paved roads deeper into the Sierra, traveling through the mestizo towns most of them had avoided when they lived in the mountains. The men, consumed by worry about what might happen to them, paid little notice to the position of the sun, or to whether the air felt cool or hot.

That afternoon, Don Cruz pulled up to a house in a mestizo town. There, without speaking, he handed the men over to someone else. This second man, who appeared younger, told the Rarámuris that they would be building a fence around his property. Then they would spend the summer planting and harvesting small fields of marijuana and poppies. And after that, they would prepare the field, plant the next crop, bring water from the nearby creek, and weed by hand. They were to take great care, so as not to damage the plants.

Among themselves, the Rarámuri men described what they were being asked to do as dangerous work. It was testament to their peoples' familiarity with suffering that they did not characterize Don Cruz's actions as a secuestro, a kidnapping. One of the tools of colonization was to make Indigenous peoples believe that the Spaniards were saviors: colonizers justified their means by telling the Indigenous peoples that the violence of assimilation was part of the journey to "civilizing" themselves. For centuries, the Rarámuri people had contended with violence on the part of chabochis and mestizos, so much so that the men didn't recognize Don Cruz's kidnapping for what it was. They simply considered themselves lucky to have been given any food during the time that they worked, and to have gotten off alive in the end.

That Don Cruz had changed the scope of work at the last minute wasn't the problem—it wasn't uncommon for a rancher to hire men to build a fence, then change the project to something completely different, even without running it by the workers first. The danger was in the fact that the crops were illegal, and the federal army was pushing into the Sierra to burn all the drug fields they could find, attempting to arrest the cartel workers in the process. Even if the federal army didn't get their hands on them, the

Rarámuri laborers could still be killed or maimed by open gunfire if cartel workers resisted arrest and ambushed the federal army, which happened often. Still, the Rarámuri men didn't think they had been the victims of a secuestro. To them, a secuestro involved being blindfolded and forced into a vehicle. It might involve torture—beatings, electrocutions, or the severing of fingers and toes—and was usually tied to extortion. Some of the mestizos they knew had been locked in taxis and taken to ATMs, where they were forced at gunpoint to withdraw large sums of money and subjected to physical abuse if they failed to comply. Others had been plucked off the streets and taken to hidden locations, where the secuestradores held them hostage and called their family members to demand ransoms. Perhaps the Rarámuri men didn't characterize Don Cruz's actions as a secuestro because they didn't have bank accounts or large sums of money for mestizos to steal or extort. This was simply another, more costly tax they had to pay for being Rarámuri.

The men labored in the fields. They carried water for the thirsty plants. The creek nearby was fuller than the one where Luis had lived, though even here, periods of drought forced the men to walk to other parts of the Sierra in search of water. Don Cruz let only a few of them go at a time, worried they would try to escape. They didn't dare falter in their work; the owner of the ranch had made it clear that he would shoot them if they didn't fill enough baskets with yield from the marijuana and poppy crops.

At night, the men lay silent in a wooden shack the owner locked them into. A young mestizo man with a gun stood watch outside. Some, including Luis, whispered their desire to escape, but José counseled the men to continue working and to wait for the day when Don Cruz returned them to El Oasis. In every other instance when Rarámuri men were forced into labor, the mestizo ranch owners had eventually taken them back to El Oasis, usually within two months. If they ran into the forest, José warned, the mestizos would go after them with their guns. It was best to do the work they demanded and to ask Onorúame and the Virgen to keep them safe, José whispered to a room silent but for the men's breathing. They were in the Sierra, the very land from which Onorúame had formed them. The pine trees, the wind, and the land could hear their pain and would call to Onorúame, who would watch over them until Don Cruz delivered them back to their families.

Luis knew that running might cost them their lives. Yet the alternative—to continue working for Don Cruz and to pray for their safe return—made him feel as if he were ceding control to the mestizos. He dismissed José's advice to trust Onorúame and the Virgen, convinced that Onorúame was no longer in the Sierra. As for the suggestion that they wait for Don Cruz to return them to El Oasis because it was the safest option, Luis couldn't make up his mind. In the past four years, he had talked to other men who had been forced to labor in drug fields, and they all said they were frightened by the possibility that the federal army would find them. The cartels themselves didn't harm the Rarámuri men so long as they did their work. José was basing their safety now on the same stories Luis had heard, and though Luis saw the logic in the path José recommended, he began to feel that their physical safety was only part of what they needed to protect. The anger Luis felt, trapped in the Sierra, far from the family who needed his support, was stronger than his fear for his safety. It was an anger that made him feel he might take a gun and shoot Don Cruz, if only he had the chance.

What would happen if Luis did as José advised? He had always listened to José and Eduardo when it came to police extortions in Colonia Martín López, emptying his pockets each time an officer approached him. Often he wished he could defy the police, even fight them if it came down to that, but he knew that if he did, he would get beaten and perhaps killed, and he couldn't risk leaving Martina alone to provide for their family. All along, he had told himself that the tax he paid was worth it because the little money he brought home provided much more food for his family than their garden in the Sierra ever had. He stifled his anger with that kind of reasoning, just as the men who had been forced to labor in the fields now told themselves they were lucky the mestizos always returned them to El Oasis unharmed. Sometimes, controlling a reaction to difficult circumstances was the only way to keep going: they could trick themselves into believing they had some agency over what happened. Luis thought the men who could no longer massage the truth of the abuse they faced were often the ones who drank until they lost consciousness, who then turned that abuse on the women and children in their lives so they could tell themselves that they were in fact capable of exerting control. He recognized that in their pain, they used the same justifications for violence as the mestizos, claiming that women and children needed to be submissive because men were the natural leaders of their people. In the worldview informed by korima, men, women, and children were equally important.

Luis had never allowed his anger to overtake him. He had never harmed Martina or his children, even when his rage became so strong that he felt he could barely control the urge to hit someone, anyone. Now, trapped in the Sierra, he wasn't sure he could labor indefinitely without doing something drastic. Fighting the gun-wielding mestizos would lead him nowhere, but perhaps running as a group would shock them, causing a delay in their reaction.

Just as he was about to break the night's stillness with his suggestion, he remembered the respect he owed José and stopped himself. In the Sierra, the siríame had guided Rarámuris in the passive resistance of chabochi and mestizo encroachments, giving them the encouragement and strength to develop long-distance running once they had retreated into the Sierra, and to share korima with each other. In El Oasis, José had counseled the community through difficult decisions, always steering them toward a solution that preserved korima and Rarámuri ways. He kept up the men's morale so the women could take to the streets to korimear in their brightest hand-sewn dresses. If Luis were to go against José's advice now, he would be diminishing the siríame's historical role in protecting the Rarámuri people.

Each man lay on his blanket, thinking his own thoughts. The Sierra's perfect silence wasn't possible in the city, where even when police sirens were quiet, the men could feel them. Luis had once

rested profoundly in the Sierra at night, his sleep as deep as the canyons. Now, he found that he was unable to turn off his mind.

Every morning of the long, hot summer, Luis intended to speak to
José and the other men about running. He continued to worry that
trusting Don Cruz to return them to El Oasis was too great a risk.
Don Cruz never spoke to the men about when their work would end
or gave any clear indication that he would eventually drive them
back. But José saw the good food they were given—bean burritos
and sometimes even meat—as a sign that they would be returned
home, likely with the expectation that they would again labor in
Don Cruz's fields.

Luis agonized over Martina, knowing she must be struggling to
buy food and pay the utility bills. He worried about Jaime, who he
correctly guessed was using paint thinner more than ever. He felt
the cruel irony of fleeing the Sierra only to be forced to return and
work for a mestizo; it lent a bitterness to his anger that made him
feel sick most nights when he lay awake. Yet he couldn't bring himself to disrupt the patient endurance the other men displayed. Every
day, they rose before dawn to begin their work, then labored until
nightfall. They had little opportunity to talk during that time. It was
only at night that Luis could have spoken up, but by then, he felt
his resolve wane. It seemed no other man felt the way he did. They
all seemed to believe that waiting out their circumstances was the
only way to survive them, both physically and mentally. Luis wondered if something was wrong with him, if he was becoming too
mestizo-like in his impatience and bitterness over the situation. He
willed himself to be thankful that each day found him still alive, still
capable of doing the work that would one day bring him back to his
family. Yet over and over again, no matter how hard he tried to trust
José's wisdom, he thought to himself that he hadn't fled the Sierra
only to return and be enslaved.

It was in the second month, when the marijuana plants were halfway to their tallest height, that Luis learned one of his companions,

a man named Sylverio, also thought about escaping. He and Sylverio spoke as they walked to a nearby stream to collect water. Like Luis, Sylverio hesitated to share the idea with José, worried that if they ran, his personal desire to return to his family could result in all their deaths. Luis told Sylverio he thought it seemed likely Don Cruz would keep them so he could have a labor force year-round. If Don Cruz intended to harvest drug crops each year, he would need workers, and he would never be able to fool another man from El Oasis. Sylverio agreed. Then he asked the question that kept both men from speaking up: what if José was right? What if they needed to simply wait to be returned to El Oasis? What if Don Cruz and his men killed them when they tried to escape?

Ten more weeks passed, and Luis and Sylverio continued to circle their dilemma. Perhaps it was the cooling of the air—it was the same cool air in which Luis and his family had fled the Sierra—that made him feel something needed to happen. The harvest season was coming, and then winter. José told the men he thought Don Cruz would take them back to El Oasis once they finished gathering in the crops, but Luis, his mind unsettled, could no longer see his logic.

All that summer, Luis had remembered what it had been like the summer before the family fled. The thirst and the hunger, the terror that winter would bring death to their youngest child, the guilt at even considering leaving the hurting Sierra to save their own lives. Now, he feared he had been returned to the Sierra to work until he died. It was like being extorted on an hourly basis, and he felt a bitterness he worried wouldn't be dimmed by his daughter's sweet laugh or his sons' hugs. He and Sylverio didn't talk often, not wanting to rouse suspicion in the other Rarámuri men or the mestizos who watched them. Luis became convinced that the others had been lulled into submissiveness, so much so that they would allow themselves to be killed if Don Cruz decided that'd be easier than feeding and housing them through the winter, or driving them back to El Oasis. He came to see their deaths as the only realistic outcome. Onorúame wouldn't protect them, and mestizos had never been known to do anything but kill Rarámuris. He became increasingly convinced that running was the only option.

On a day when the air felt like ice, Luis volunteered to accompany Sylverio for water. *We should run,* he said quietly. The mestizo watching the field had briefly left them alone. He would return within minutes, and then their chance would be gone. Sylverio nodded.

Luis and Sylverio veered off the path and disappeared into the trees. No one noticed, not even the other Rarámuri men who continued to work in the field. They broke into a run, lifting their knees to their waists and pressing with their toes as they had years before, when they had run footraces on this same land. Without a word, they turned left and began descending a canyon that took them away from the road they had traveled to reach Don Cruz's ranch. It didn't matter that neither of them had run in this canyon before; Rarámuri people had a knowledge of the land that allowed them to find their way, even in unfamiliar territory. They kept going until the trees stood farther apart, revealing some of the plants of the low Sierra. Not wanting to lose the protection of the foliage, they turned eastward, toward the setting sun.

They heard no gunfire. It could have been that Don Cruz decided Luis and Sylverio weren't worth pursuing. Still, to be safe, they stayed away from the mestizo pueblos, sleeping instead in the forest and eating only the pine nuts they found there. The two men reached their front doors five days later.

That afternoon, in El Oasis, Lupita greeted her father with a gasp and a smile. When she hesitated to hug him, Luis went to her, wrapping her in his arms. Lupita, fully realizing he had returned, began to cry. Though she hadn't wanted to worry her mother, Lupita had spent her hours korimeando imagining that her father was being held captive by a mestizo. She thought he might be in a place like the jail cells she saw on TV, in darkness, with no food or water. Now, seeing him in the flesh, she felt a strong desire for life to return to normal. Nothing had been easy or good during Luis's absence, but that was about to change. Her caring, quiet father, who worked every day and made her mother laugh with his teasing, was home. Her mother would become lighter now. She would play with Lupita and Manolo, and perhaps she would start playing basketball with Eugenia, María José, and the other women again. Lupita loved watching Martina run, sweat dripping down her face, laughing as she tried to dribble around her opponents and shoot from the half-court line. Sometimes the family sat on the front stoop together afterward, celebrating Martina's games with chilindrinas, sheets of fried dough layered with lettuce, tomato, and cream that they bought from a mestiza down the block.

Remember you promised we'd go fishing together? she asked Luis through her sobs, stepping back from the embrace so she could look at him.

I remember, Luis said, stroking her hair. *We'll go soon.*

Jaime returned home soon after. He couldn't find words to say hello, so he hugged his father, waves of relief passing over him. Though he wouldn't admit it to his family, he had missed his father's guidance. These past weeks, as he struggled to keep his promise to help Martina and Lupita, he thought often about how much easier it was to stay away from the arcade when his father was home. His father's words of counsel felt like the whispers of pine trees. They steadied Jaime. Sometimes, he and Luis raced each other through the streets. Though his father wasn't as fast as he had once been, Jaime admired his agility. Their talks and races would resume now that Luis was home.

Jaime sat down to play with Manolo and invited Lupita to join them. The three of them sent Hot Wheels rolling across the cement floor as their parents watched, smiling.

Luis and Sylverio's return was seen as evidence that the other Rarámuri men were still alive. That they had run without the others became a source of resentment for some of the women, who felt they should have followed José's advice, but relief far outweighed any other feelings. In the days that followed, Luis felt guilt for getting out, even amid his anger with José for not being braver. Though Martina didn't want to burden him with the details of her struggles during his absence, Luis took Lupita's korimeando as evidence that she couldn't get by on her own. Each time he wondered if the other men were safe, he reminded himself that his family's safety was most important. Running had been the right choice. He hadn't made the sacrifice of leaving the Sierra only to be forced back by exploitative mestizos.

On the morning of December 9, five Rarámuri men, José among them, climbed out of the back of Don Cruz's pickup truck and walked toward El Oasis. Their children were in school, and some of their wives were out korimeando. María Cruz, in her usual spot by the front gate, greeted her husband with only a warm look, then got up to get him a glass of water and one of the blue-corn gorditas a government worker had come to hand out. The other men who had traveled home with José walked through the entrance gate and found their wives and children.

José told María Cruz that Don Cruz had brought them back because they had finished harvesting the drug crops, but a rumor about his true reason for doing so spread through El Oasis: Don Cruz, it was said, was afraid Luis and Sylverio would send the federal army after him. In fact, it had never occurred to Luis or Sylverio to inform the police. They simply didn't trust the mestizos to bring them justice.

The four men who were still missing had gotten off out of Don Cruz's truck in the town of Cuahuntémoc, to help with the last of the apple picking. They wanted to return home with at least some wages. José had promised to inform their families so that they would no longer worry.

Luis approached José on the day he arrived, worried he would be angry with him for leaving behind the group. José told Luis he had been worried about him and Sylverio, and angry that their selfish actions had put him and the other men in danger. Don Cruz had been upset, he told Luis, and for a few days, no one was sure if he'd take revenge on the other Rarámuri men. It had been Onorúame's protection that kept them from suffering Don Cruz's punishment. José had responded honestly to his interrogations, saying he hadn't known what Luis and Sylverio were planning. Then he and the men had focused their attention on the work, which eventually appeased Don Cruz.

José remained calm as he recounted the story to the community members. Luis marveled at the way he told it, as if the eventual outcome were inevitable. It was just like the origin story, he thought: their people were always delivered from danger, no matter how terrible the circumstances. Stories like that had once given Luis strength. Now, listening to José, he felt nothing. Though he didn't say so to Martina, who took José's story as evidence that Onorúame would always protect the Rarámuris, Luis thought their safe return was the result of the practicalities he had thought about at the start of the summer. Don Cruz had returned the men because it was better for him to have access to laborers. Perhaps next time he would offer another rancher money to bring them back to the Sierra. There were multitudes of ways for mestizos to trick Rarámuris into giving them what they wanted.

Though Luis never spoke of it, Martina suspected that hearing how Don Cruz's anger had made the men fear for their safety led him to feel that his actions had been rash and irresponsible. She noticed he avoided talking about the events after that day and sensed that it was best not to bring them up. Knowing him, Martina supposed he wanted to focus on what he could control. They were all back in the city again, and it was once again time to work.

As the men returned, Lucero realized the prayer she had intended to say during the sacrifice—a prayer of thanks, following a request that the Virgen intervene to bring home the men—was no longer necessary. The question was, what should she say to the Virgen instead, beyond giving thanks for returning the men?

Lucero believed that the Virgen and Onorúame were pleased with the community's collective effort to gather money for the cow, and because of that had protected Luis and Sylverio during their escape. Lucero didn't see their escape as an endangerment of the other men, as José did. She felt certain the Virgen had intervened because the women were practicing korima by pooling money for the cow. That families had gone without for the greater good of their community was more powerful than any search effort they could have undertaken themselves. By waiting to offer a cow to the Virgen, they showed her they trusted the men would be safe until then, and also that the origin story persisted outside the constraints of linear time. Lucero saw the men's return as proof that the mestizos' quest to become rich by growing drug crops was a story that could not sustain itself. That story would one day end, and the mestizos, with no promise of continuity, would cease to be rich, while the Rarámuri people would continue to live their story across past, present, and future.

Lucero didn't want the community to forget these lessons. She knew there were community members who struggled to believe their origin story was a living one. These Rarámuris, she thought, had allowed the mestizos' abuse to pollute their minds. Lucero didn't blame them; she, too, struggled at times to understand how Onorúame and the Virgen could allow Rarámuris to suffer droughts, hunger, extortions, and kidnappings. Yet time and again, despite the community's seemingly impossible circumstances, Lucero found she believed more strongly in the origin story than in any linear narrative the mestizos tried to impose. She also believed it was the síriame's responsibility to show Rarámuris that their story continued on in the city. She thought José accomplished this well, but the past few weeks, as the community went without to save money for the cow, had shown her that she was capable of imagining new manifestations of korima. One day, she thought, she'd like to be the síriame of El Oasis, if her brother were to decide he didn't want to fill the role anymore and the community were to elect her. She'd never wavered in her conviction that she and the women were doing right by the men, the Virgen, and Onorúame by placing their trust in the sacrifice, and she wanted the rest of the community to understand the power of their own conviction. That way, when hard times fell again, they would be able to come together as they had in these months since the men were taken. Paint-thinner addiction, alcohol addiction, and violence of all kinds wouldn't disappear overnight, but Lucero believed their peoples' story told that they would overcome these challenges.

For five hundred years, as the deer vanished from the Sierra, the Rarámuris sacrificed domesticated animals whenever they could afford them. Though domesticated animals, like the dresses the women now wore, had been given to the Rarámuris by the Spaniards as a way to assimilate them, the Rarámuris made the offerings their own. The fact that the celebration being planned by Lucero centered around the Virgen de Guadalupe didn't mean the Rarámuris had been subsumed; on the contrary, it showed that they had once again adapted to conditions.

The final family delivered their portion of the cow money to Lucero on December 10. That same morning, the remaining four men arrived to El Oasis, one day's worth of wages in hand. They immediately contributed to the fund for the cow. Lucero, moved by their generosity, asked them if they were certain they wanted to contribute; they did. In previous years, some families hadn't contributed to the cow, or Lucero had had to ask them dozens of times. None of that had happened this year, though—further testament to their peoples' love and respect for the Virgen, Onorúame, and the land, combined with the deep gratitude they felt for the men's safe arrival. There was a sense in the community that this had been a close call, and it was only by way of the Virgen's intervention that every man had returned home.

On the morning of December 10, as she appraised dozens of cows at a ranch on the outskirts of the city, Lucero felt overwhelmed with appreciation for the sacrifices her community had made. Her appreciation was tinged with the worry that soon, the other problems of the asentamiento—the lack of money, the drug and alcohol addiction, the neglect of children, and the abuse of women by men— would cause them all to move on too quickly from this moment of celebration. Lucero understood that forgetting was a tool of colonization. Though she wasn't versed in the historical practices of reducción and assimilation, nor how these tactics caused many Rarámuris to forget the power of their origin story, she knew that one effect of the mestizos' abuse was the belief that the Rarámuris' suffering was their own fault. That, in turn, caused some Rarámuris to feel ashamed of their identity and reject their origin story and korima, which Lucero believed was at the root of the paint-thinner and alcohol addiction in El Oasis. It was the same thing so many mestizos experienced—their families had not passed down their Indigenous ancestors' origin stories, so they believed Cortés's linear story of conquest was theirs.

What future was possible if all the Rarámuri people of El Oasis remembered that korima could be practiced in the city? To begin to imagine that future, Lucero believed her community needed to hold on to the events of the past few weeks. In doing so, she believed, the Rarámuri people could begin to shape a new life in the city, one without extortions, kidnappings, and addiction. This future was foretold in the story. They needed only to remember its truth.

A cold wind blew through the desert the morning of December 12, carrying with it a hint of the frost that covered the peaks of the Sierra. The wind encountered barriers that tried to break it. But buildings made of cinder block could not stop the wind. There was nothing static, nothing man-made, that could diminish its strength. The wind moved across the former seabed with the strength of ancient currents.

When the wind reached El Oasis, it swept through the narrow corridors, lifting the skirts hung out to dry and rustling the leaves of the fig tree in front of the community kitchen. Women and children hunched their shoulders when they felt its chill prick their necks. Nearly two hundred adults sat around the perimeter of the schoolyard, tightly packed, their children in their laps, and pulled tight the bright rebozos draped across their shoulders. Beside Martina and Manolo were Lupita, Jaime, and Luis. María José and

Eugenia sat nearby with their own families. That morning, they all had readied themselves for the sacrifice of the cow by dressing in their best clothing. Usually, Martina sewed new dresses for herself and Lupita for the occasion, but she hadn't been able to complete a single one in the months Luis was gone, perhaps due to a lack of time, or an inability to concentrate, or both. That day, Martina and Lupita both wore the dresses they had won after Serafina and Mariza's footrace. Martina's was a blue as deep as dusk, and Lupita's was sky blue. Though she hadn't planned it, Martina was pleased that their dresses were in colors associated with the Virgen: the colors of the sky and the water, where the Virgen dwelled. That day, Luis and Manolo wore bright-red handsewn shirts, loincloths, and tire-rubber sandals Luis had made for them. Jaime wore baggy jeans, an oversized T-shirt, and white sneakers, but Martina and Luis didn't mind. They were just thankful their family was together and safe again.

The cow stood in the middle of the schoolyard, her legs tied together. Two strong men, Sylverio and Luis Fernando, stood beside her, ready to stay her if she balked. José was also nearby, ready to help if needed. They wanted to keep the cow calm so Lucero could perform the sacrifice with ease and offer the prayer in silence. Community members sitting around the perimeter of the basketball court were quiet and still so as not to frighten the cow.

The cow mooed softly when Lucero approached with a cross fashioned from mesquite branches tied together with a thin rope. Lucero placed the cross upright before the cow. With the men standing nearby, ready to steady the animal, Lucero prayed in silence. The community watched as she thanked the Virgen for the gift of land, water, fire, and sky. She thanked the Virgen for continuing to protect the Rarámuri people across all times and offered special thanks to her for delivering the men safely to El Oasis.

Then, in simple words, Lucero asked the Virgen to protect the memory of korima in El Oasis. The request felt more powerful than it would have to ask that she deliver the men safely. She was calling on the Virgen to intercede in all times, not simply in a particular instance. It was a way of resisting the narrative men like Don Cruz tried to impose: that the Rarámuri people were destined to be forced into labor for mestizos' gains.

Lucero nodded at the men, and they stood on one side of the cow, pushing until her knees buckled and she fell on her side. She balked, kicking her legs and arching her neck, mooing loudly. Sylverio and Fernando pushed her head down to subdue her. Martina didn't wince, even though she wanted to; watching the cow struggle always made her feel a bit uneasy. It was important to watch the cow respectfully, without transmitting nervous energy. It helped the animal give herself over to the sacrifice, just as the deer in the forest collapsed when they became too exhausted to run.

Now lying on her side, the cow mooed once, deep and long. Lucero brought a lit match to a tiny dish filled with copal, a tree resin the Virgen loved for its woody scent. A thin wisp of smoke rose above her head and the head of the cow, who watched Lucero.

With the men still holding the cow's head, Lucero poised her large butcher knife over her neck. That moment, just before life began to leave the cow, was one of fervent prayer. That's what it meant to make an offering: closing the chasm between life and death, killing an animal so an entire people could eat, remembering all must give for everyone to thrive.

Lucero dug the knife into the cow's jugular vein. The cow, in silent shock, lay still as Lucero, gripping the knife with two hands, used all her strength to cut one long slit along her neck. It brought Lucero a sense of peace to express, by making this cut, that the Rarámuri people would always offer their thanks and their gifts to the Virgen. So long as she was able to hold the knife, Lucero would continue to slice the sacrificial cow's jugular each year. Blood began spurting out of the vein, then pouring out in a steady stream. José held a bucket at an angle to catch the flow of blood. As the bucket grew heavy with the blood, the cow's frightened eyes began to lose their light. Martina, filled with admiration for Lucero's strength and gratitude for the Virgen, stroked Manolo's hands as he, enraptured, watched the cow take its last breaths.

For the first time in his life, Luis found that he couldn't give thanks to the Virgen. He didn't agree with Lucero that she had aided their escape and thought perhaps they had merely been lucky. Sylverio volunteered to handle the cow to express his gratitude to the Virgen. Luis couldn't bring himself to do the same. He sat there only because he knew it was expected of him, and because it would have hurt Martina if he had been absent, as some of the other men were.

Within a few minutes, the cow's mouth opened slightly, and a long, pink tongue slid out. Her eyes now stared blankly. Blood continued to flow into the bucket, a thick red waterfall that seemed to have no end.

Lucero placed a plastic cup into the stream to catch some of the blood. When the cup had filled partway, she brought it to her lips. Before the entire community, Lucero drank the cow's life, given to her people so they could live.

The men took their own butcher knives to the cow. First, they peeled back the heavy skin. They began slicing through the cow's muscle, lifting slabs of raw meat onto a wheelbarrow. They unearthed the stomach, the heart, the lungs, coils of intestines. Under Lucero's direction, the men wheeled the dismembered cow out of the schoolyard to a large metal vat filled with water boiling over an open fire.

There, an elder named Teresa stood ready with her own knife. She sliced the meat into smaller chunks, then directed younger women to drop the chunks into the vat. She and five others would take turns keeping watch for the rest of the day, until the meat was fully cooked. A smaller fire burned beside the large one, with a comal big enough to fit up to ten corn tortillas at a time. Six other women sat around it, grinding corn with a metate, a slab of volcanic rock their ancestors had been using long before the conquistadors invaded. Once the corn was ground, another two women mixed the dry cornmeal with water, forming a sticky masa. Others patted the masa into disks and placed them on the comal to cook. They stacked tortillas high in a handwoven basket.

Many Rarámuris described korima as a basket of tortillas that all people gave to and took from. That's why cooking the tortillas beside the meat from the sacrifice carried such significance. Here was yet another example of Rarámuri women cooperating with one another to feed the entire community. Once the handwoven baskets were full, community members would take one tortilla each, making sure every Rarámuri in El Oasis, and even those who came from other asentamientos, had something to eat.

In the afternoon, as the meat cooked over an open fire and the scent of burning wood filled El Oasis, Luis Antonio's violin sang inside the chapel, a few feet from the large portrait of the Virgen de Guadalupe. Beside him, another elder named Felix shook two deerskin rattles, and the dried beans inside made the sound of a rattlesnake. The rhythm was insistent but didn't build toward a crescendo. Instead, it represented the constancy of time, alongside the violin's repetitive four-note melody. The Rarámuri women danced matachines for the Virgen in two long lines.

Martina, María José, Eugenia, Lucero, María Cruz, and twelve other women faced Luis Antonio and stepped to the rhythm of the rattles, their skirts, all different colors and patterns, twirling around their ankles. Martina danced matachines each year to honor the Virgen, just as she had danced yumari to call rain to the Sierra. Lupita, still too young to dance matachines, sat in a pew with Camila and Violeta, admiring her mother and wishing she could dance too.

When seen alone on a street in Chihuahua City, a Rarámuri woman in full dress stands out like a single bright flower against a landscape of concrete and dust. Now, together in one long line, they formed a field of flowers swaying in the wind. It was just as the women intended—for their dance to proclaim their love for the land and the gods who lived in it.

Inside the chapel, the Virgen, alive in the portrait to the right of the holy altar, felt the women's love. Dressed in blue robes, pale face upturned toward the sky, hands clasped in prayer, enlivened by the violin and the blood that had been spilled for her, the Virgen de Guadalupe used all her strength to ask Onorúame to continue to care for the land and the Rarámuri people, to bring them rain and food. To keep them together, always.

José lifted the portrait from its place beside the altar. He carried it over his head and out the chapel doors, where a crowd of Rarámuri people were waiting. Now, all together, they marched toward the white metal gates, out the four walls of El Oasis, and into the streets of Colonia Martín López.

PART 2

Snow-covered cacti

[January 2010]

When Martina and María José were children, their mother told them stories of the mountains awakening at night. The mountains were not really mountains but ganockos, giants, who stole Rarámuri children. *Don't wander off on your own,* she warned them, *because the ganockos might wake up and eat you.* Terrified, the sisters lay awake at night, imagining the dark silhouettes of the mountains moving quietly, searching for children to snatch.

The sisters remained frightened until they were young women, when they understood that this story was their mother's way of protecting them from mestizos. Mothers in the Sierra had told stories of ganockos to their children since the chabochis first invaded, as a way to warn them of the dangers of wandering from their homes among the trees. Martina and María José were in rare agreement when they decided they would not pass on this story to their own children. María José's reason was practical; she didn't want to scare her sons with made-up stories when there were many real dangers to fear: mestizos with guns, for example. Martina kept the story to herself because she wanted to protect her children's relationship with the Sierra. She wanted them to see the mountains as tall, silent protectors, to know the land and believe that it would give them the food and water they needed, so long as they practiced korima. For her children to remain Rarámuri, even in the city, it was essential that they understood that living by korima would bring them blessings.

Instead of the stories of the ganockos, Martina told stories that showed the Rarámuris as morally superior to the mestizos. Her own mother had told her stories like these as well. They served as reminders that, despite the chabochis' and mestizos' most violent attempts to assimilate them, the Rarámuri people remained the true keepers of this land and would forever be protected. One story Martina told more frequently after the family moved to the city went like this: Once, she and her mother, father, and sister had left the house to walk in the forest. When they returned, they found that all that they had—a bit of lard, some woolen blankets, and woven baskets filled with beans—was gone. Supposing a thief had entered their home, their parents told them not to be afraid, that Onorúame would provide for them. That night, a thunderstorm tore through the Sierra, and in the morning, a neighbor came to tell them that a mestizo had been struck by lightning and now lay dead on the side of the road. He had with him a satchel in which he carried a bit of lard, woolen blankets, and baskets filled with beans. Martina liked to remind Jaime, Lupita, and Manolo that even if their belongings hadn't been returned to them, Onorúame would have provided for them, most likely by sending a neighbor with korima. She also told her children that though the chabochis and mestizos succeeded in stealing many things from the Rarámuris, they would never be able to steal korima. The Rarámuris would keep korima alive, even if they had to adapt it, as they had through korimeando. But the Rarámuris would have to struggle for only so long. Martina told her children that because the chabochis and mestizos were morally corrupt, they would eventually perish, leaving the earth once again to the Rarámuris, the children of the sun.

Since the onset of winter, the days had been dreary, with wispy gray clouds shrouding the sun most mornings. Inside their home, which now felt like an icebox, the cinder-block walls and cement floor cold to the touch, Martina layered on the children the extra blankets she'd picked up from a donation box. A light snow had coated the desert one recent morning, casting a sheen on the muted landscape for a few short hours, until the clouds faded, and the sun laid it bare once again. Martina had missed this drama, instead focused on walking the slippery sidewalks to the bus stop to korimear. She shivered beneath her cotton dress, refusing to cover it up by wearing the down jacket a mestiza had given her.

On days when she didn't go korimeando, she followed the sun to the chapel, where dozens of seamstresses sat in the warmer afternoon light and glided their needles through fabric. She sipped atole with extra sugar and sewed a fluorescent pink skirt, her antidote to the overcast days. Afternoons spent this way weren't many; to alleviate some of the pressure Luis felt to provide, Martina gave up hours of dressmaking and instead continued korimeando in the busiest parts of the city. Lupita also insisted on keeping her post at the KFC, despite Martina's protests. Dirt and car exhaust fumes caked her feet, her cheeks and lips were chapped from constant sun exposure, and her fingernails stayed black no matter how hard Martina scrubbed them. Martina didn't like the filth that covered her own body after hours spent korimeando, but she hated to see Lupita in this state. When she told her daughter she should join her instead, as she had before, to watch Manolo on the sidewalk, Lupita countered that the money she brought home helped the family eat better food and pay their utility bills. Martina suspected, correctly, that Lupita was worried about experiencing hunger again, and korimeando was her way of making sure she and her family didn't have to go without food.

What Martina didn't guess was that Lupita also thought continuing to korimear would help lessen her mother's worries about money, which hadn't seemed to disappear with Luis's return. Lupita thought that if she kept contributing, then one day soon, she hoped, Martina would grant her request to go to Media Luna. She missed playing in the park while her mother watched; it made her feel loved for the child she was, not for the coins she brought home. Luis hadn't taken her fishing since the week he returned from the Sierra. That day, they'd stood on the lakeshore and cast lines into the water, so at peace being together that neither cared when they didn't catch any fish. Going back to watching Manolo at the crosswalk wouldn't bring back the feelings she was missing, even if it meant she would spend more hours in proximity to her mother. Lupita was convinced that the key to family harmony was more money, just enough so her parents wouldn't have to worry about groceries and utilities. At the very least, she thought, more money might give her mother the space to notice her accomplishments at school. She had brought home a ribbon for placing first in an addition competition, and Martina and Luis had barely glanced at it.

Jaime hadn't sniffed paint thinner since his father returned; the desire to be close to his father again outweighed the withdrawal symptoms. In the past, motivated by Luis's promises of long walks through the colonia or downtown's cobblestone streets lined with shops, he'd managed to stop sniffing for up to a week. After that, he had always returned, the paint-thinner high dulling the rejection he felt when his father drank beside the arroyo with other men instead of spending evenings with him. He felt a sense of shared suffering with the boys who offered him whiffs from their bottles. Usually, it seemed better than suffering alone, though as soon as the high wore off, he found himself feeling rejected and angry again. This time, though, things were different. Luis had pledged to stay in the city and to return home after work to spend time with his family. Even though Martina and Lupita worried when Luis spent one or two days a week drinking by the arroyo—a lapse in his promise that Martina tried to overlook—Jaime remained filled with hope, especially since his father returned home in good spirits on days when he was paid and didn't have to hand over money to police.

Jaime stopped leaving the asentamiento after school, instead locking himself in the house to detox. For the first two weeks, he endured headaches so severe that he had to block out all sunlight. He skipped school to lay in bed with a blanket over his head, sitting up only when Martina coaxed him to sip water and broth and to eat crackers, though he worried he wouldn't be able to keep the food down. Martina and Luis felt anguished seeing Jaime in pain, but they hoped their child's disciplined suffering would finally get him to the other side of his addiction. After those two weeks, Jaime returned to school, seemingly cured. At recess, he played basketball with other children instead of sitting against the wall, fatigued from his late nights. Martina and Luis were tentatively optimistic; they had experienced his relapses half a dozen times. Jaime's health depended on Luis spending time with him each evening, Martina reminded him, a responsibility that made Luis feel nervous. It was hard to not go to the arroyo to drink; it was the only place where he felt he was among others who understood him. He tried to make up for his two weekly evenings of drinking by giving Jaime his full attention when he was home, taking him out for walks or simply sitting and watching telenovelas with him.

Despite their worries, Martina and Luis were moved that Jaime had taken to waiting at home for his father to arrive, passing the time drawing cartoons of boys wearing wide-brim hats and baggy jeans. Jaime offered to share his colored pencils with Lupita and Manolo, a sign of sibling companionship that pleased Martina. On afternoons when Lupita wasn't korimeando, usually because Martina had insisted she stay home to rest, she sat next to her older brother and filled pages with castles, princesses, dragons, and knights. Manolo scribbled happily, then proudly showed off his pictures of towis, little boys, to his siblings and mother. Just before his father arrived, Jaime would go to the tiendita to buy a bottle of Coke for him. When Luis did arrive home, Jaime would switch on the TV and the family would watch a telenovela together, Martina laughing at the absurd romantic problems the mestizos created for themselves. By nine o' clock, they switched off the TV and lay on their mattresses, finding warmth under their many blankets and trying to ignore the questions Manolo posed to the night: Were the people inside the TV real? Where did the stray dogs of El Oasis sleep? Why did people have eyes on their heads and not on their bellies? When no one answered, he sang softly to himself, the same lullaby in Rarámuri over and over, until sleep began to overcome him and his voice became a whisper, then deep, steady breaths.

Then, one day in mid-January, Luis arrived home and didn't greet anyone. Instead, he lay down on his mattress and turned on the

TV. He had come home in this mood on a few occasions since he returned, always after an extortion. Sometimes he would go to the arroyo first to drink beer with other men, then return home, tell Martina what had happened, and settle in to watch TV, resigned. In the morning, he would usually wake up in a better mood. He'd drink a cup of instant coffee, kiss his children, exchange kind words with Martina, and leave for work. María José had told Martina not to worry too much about Luis using beer to ease negative feelings; drinking a can or two with the other men, often including Eduardo, helped him forget his worries, she said. And because it didn't happen all the time, and because Luis didn't come home drunk, Martina tried not to let the behavior bother her too much. That day, though, he had come straight home, sullen. When too much time had passed and he still hadn't spoken, Martina thought she would prompt him. *What's wrong?* she asked in the same coaxing tone she sometimes used with Manolo.

Without hesitation, his eyes still on the TV, Luis spoke in a hard voice. *Leave the house,* he snapped. For a moment, she thought she had misheard him. She remained in place, looking at Luis and waiting for him to turn his head and speak again. When a few moments passed without another word from him, she began to register the spite in his voice, not unlike the tone some mestizos used to address her when she was korimeando. Suddenly, she understood his command. Perhaps because of the same instinct that made her get out of harm's way each time she encountered a mestizo with that dangerous edge in his voice, she turned around and walked out the door, so distraught that she left behind Manolo, who was waiting for his mother to give him dinner.

Her face hot and her hands tingling, Martina walked quickly up the corridor, pretending not to hear her sister and Eugenia calling out to her from a sewing circle in front of Lucero's house. The air was cold now that the sun was setting, and she shivered in her cotton dress, having left behind her rebozo. She walked mechanically, following her usual route out of El Oasis and to the Soriana. There, she wandered the aisles, looking at the packages of food, the strollers, the racks of clothing, her mind numbed by shock. Luis had never snapped at her, had never told her to leave their home. Even in the Sierra, when he was angry with her for refusing to seek refuge in the city, he had walked in the forest to calm down, or had sat alone with his anger, so as not to burden Martina. Rarámuris tried to keep their anger to themselves to avoid doing harm, but this time, it was clear Luis had not been able to control himself. It wasn't until nearly thirty minutes later, after she'd paced up and down the entirety of the store five times, that she felt the numbness leave. In its place was a feeling of hurt and rejection that settled in the pit of her stomach. Martina now asked herself what she had done to anger Luis. Had she missed him saying something to her when he walked through the door? She had been concentrating on her sewing. No, she decided, it wasn't that. Something else was wrong, something that most likely had nothing to do with her, though that realization didn't do much to lessen her pain.

Martina thought his anger was likely the result of having been extorted for a large amount, perhaps a week's worth of wages. She knew he was supposed to be paid that day. As she left the Soriana and walked along the roundabout, she was glad to be hidden among throngs of people getting on and off city buses so Lupita, who was korimeando at the KFC, wouldn't see her and worry. She remembered Luis had mentioned weeks before that he got nervous each time he walked from the bus stop to El Oasis. He had also spoken of the dread he felt each morning when it was time to join the men at the front of the asentamiento to wait for mestizos to hire them. He worried Don Cruz would show up again and insist they take another job with him. Eventually, there would be more marijuana to harvest, and Don Cruz would need laborers again. What would Luis do then? He couldn't hide, and he certainly couldn't stop working. Martina hadn't known how to respond to his worries, so she simply listened, hoping his fears would lessen with time and he and the other men would find a solution if Don Cruz did return to El Oasis. Now it occurred to her that she had never asked Luis if he believed, as she did, that the return of the feast day of the Virgen, of afternoons spent with his family, would cure him of his fears.

Martina felt her heart soften toward Luis as she recalled his stories of laboring in the fields, the mestizos watching his every move, the endless weeks in which he had resisted the urge to escape. His command that she leave the house had nothing to do with her, she now thought. And she would be better about asking him how he felt, even on days when he wasn't extorted, so he wouldn't feel that she worried about him only when something went wrong. For now, though, she thought it might be wise to stay away a little longer, to give Luis space and time. He would seek her out to explain and apologize when he was ready.

Martina wandered the streets feeding out of the roundabout for another two hours, until the streetlights switched on and she knew Lupita would soon step away from the drive-through window. She waited for her daughter in the Soriana parking lot, and when she arrived, they went inside together to buy food. Lupita was pleased that her mother had come to meet her, thinking she had done so because she wanted to spend time with her. As they headed to the back of the store to pick up a bag of beans and a packet of tortillas, Lupita began to sense that her mother was nervous. She kept straightening her blouse and looking around, as if she expected someone to pop out from one of the aisles and accost her. Worried for her mother but disappointed that their shopping trip wasn't the bonding experience she had hoped for, Lupita paid for the groceries and didn't ask what was wrong. Once home, Martina began cooking silently while Jaime, Lupita, and Manolo sat down to watch TV with their father. She passed out plates of food, and they remained silent, the TV a welcome distraction. Later that evening, as Martina settled down to sew in the back room, Luis came to her. Immediately, she felt the tension in her shoulders release; she was sure he was going to apologize.

In a subdued tone, Luis told Martina that the construction site manager had paid him only one-third of what he had promised for five days of work. He and Eduardo had tried to argue with the manager, but he told both men that they would never again be hired by his company, that laborers were plentiful, and that he had no reason to sit and listen to their complaints.

We're back where we were before, he said, staring at the wall.

Luis's words carried a weariness that Martina had never before heard in them. She understood it wasn't the result of the extortions alone—Luis had known that they would once again become part of his life when he resumed work in the city, and that even this unavoidable tax wouldn't prevent him from feeling thankful to be returned to his family. Something more was happening, Martina was sure of it. She stopped herself before she offered any words of comfort, remembering how her gentle inquiries had angered Luis just a few hours before.

When Martina didn't answer, Luis lay down on the mattress. He was asleep by the time she turned off the TV and went to bed with the rest of them.

January 15, the Friday following Luis's wage theft, was Lupita's birthday. The teachers had assigned her this date soon after her family's arrival to El Oasis, since Martina and Luis had never gone to the nearest mestizo town in the Sierra to register their children with the government. Every year since they moved to El Oasis, Lupita looked forward to receiving a birthday ribbon from her teacher. She loved sitting at her desk with her ribbon pinned to her blusa, the entire class serenading her with "Las Mañanitas," the Mexican birthday song. After school, Martina wouldn't go korimeando, and they would instead spend the afternoon and evening playing at Media Luna and eating chile-covered mangoes, Lupita's favorite treat. Later, they would have birthday cake from the Soriana. Lupita would proudly hand out slivers of pieces to the line of children that formed in front of their house.

To Martina, her children's birthdays signified happy returns of blessings, a kind of harvest that yielded a person wiser in the ways of korima. Martina had never seen a birthday before moving to the city; Rarámuri people in the Sierra didn't track age numerically, since that required following linear time. In Rarámuri culture, people passed through three stages of life: child, adult, and elder. The passage between the three was marked by the visible signs of aging instead of numerically, and each person entered each stage at her own pace. Girls passed into womanhood at some point after beginning to menstruate, and became elders around the time their skin wrinkled and their hair turned gray. Martina had learned about birthdays and the celebrations that accompanied them only through Eugenia and María José, who bought birthday cakes for their children when their finances allowed it. Only a few other families in El Oasis had adopted the practice, most thinking it was a mestizo tradition they didn't need to take part in. Martina didn't consider numerical age important and constantly forgot her children's ages. While Lupita adored the attention given to her in the form of ribbons and a song and cake, Martina loved birthdays because she felt that, like other celebrations and rituals, they were a time to restore harmony in the family and the community. Even before Luis had exploded at Martina, there had been minor tensions in the family, the sort that could be fixed by coming together around a campfire or, in the city, a cake.

That year, Lupita's birthday landed right when the family needed it most, Martina thought. Luis continued to act subdued, not speaking much in the evenings. Martina worried he harbored anger he wasn't speaking about and might refuse to participate in the party. Yet now that some days had passed, she hoped he would be ready to celebrate his daughter. Luis, like Martina, loved seeing his children happy on their birthdays, and he had always agreed to buy a cake for the celebrations. On Tuesday, she asked him if he would pick one up on Friday, a small one worth eighty pesos, which was the amount she had saved. She was pleased when he became animated and offered to buy a yellow cake with sprinkles he had recently seen someone carrying on his way home from work. He thought the color bright and happy, the way he wanted to see Lupita.

Lupita was turning nine, according to her teachers; Martina couldn't be sure. Soon after their arrival to El Oasis, María José had enrolled Jaime in second grade. The teachers at the elementary school generally placed children newly arrived from the Sierra with peers their own age, even if they had never been to school. They hoped it would help them catch up in Spanish, so they could start following the math and reading lessons taught in that language. Many times, Rarámuri births, in mountain homes far from any village clinic, went unnoticed by the government. Martina, Luis, their children, and most of the Rarámuris in El Oasis did not have birth certificates, so the teachers did their best to estimate the children's ages, though the fact that they were often small and underdeveloped made doing so difficult.

On Thursday, Martina spent the cost of a packet of corn tortillas on a silver banner that read "Felíz Cumpleaños." She hung it over the stove the next morning, while Lupita watched excitedly. Lupita admired the way the block letters in primary colors brightened the faded peach walls. Luis had left before she woke up but had promised the night before that he would return in the afternoon with a cake, a surprise that had made her hug her father's waist tightly. Since she began korimeando, there had been only one day—the day she and Luis went fishing—when Lupita felt her parents had done something just for her. The feast day of the Virgen de Guadalupe was a special time for the family, a community celebration Lupita loved, but it wasn't the same as her birthday. More than the cake, more than the ribbon and the banner, Lupita looked forward to sitting all together on the floor of their home, each of them with a sliver of cake, her parents smiling and exclaiming as she told them about her school day, the odd mestizos she met while korimeando, and the places she wanted to visit in the city once the weather warmed up.

Lupita didn't know how she would manage her excitement through the entire school day. Martina had told her they wouldn't need to korimear that afternoon and that they could instead spend the time getting ready for Lupita's birthday celebration. María José and Eugenia would come over with their families, and perhaps Eugenia's husband would bring his guitar. No adult in El Oasis knew the words to "Las Mañanitas," but Eugenia's husband had taught himself to play the tune. Lupita loved when he played the song for his daughters.

During recess, she told her friends they should come by her house for a slice of cake when the sun was low in the sky. Camila and Violeta said they couldn't, since they would still be out korimeando, so Lupita promised to save them some. Word spread across the classrooms, and dozens of children told Lupita they would be there. After school, she went home right away to get ready for her party. She found Martina inside, sweeping the dust from the floor, and Manolo playing with his Hot Wheels. Jaime wasn't back from school yet; Martina had given him some coins to buy a two-liter bottle of Coke to go with the cake.

Luis wouldn't be home for three hours, but Lupita didn't want to waste time. She got out her pink dress with purple wildflowers, green piping, and four rows of mountains stacked on top of each other. It was the one dress she never wore korimeando, not wanting to stain the hem. She'd chosen the fabric at the store because the pink matched her My Little Pony backpack. After putting it on, she covered her hands with soap, then scrubbed them with a brush until the water ran clean and her skin felt raw. She tried not to mind that she could still see the car exhaust stains on her skin. Knowing Eugenia and her daughters would look put together, each in a new dress with neatly braided hair, she asked her mother to redo her own braid, which had come loose as she jumped rope during recess. She wanted to look nice, not like she looked when she spent her afternoons korimeando. Lupita sat still as Martina separated her waist-length hair into three strands and sprinkled water on them to stiffen them. She had picked out a pink hair tie to secure her braid.

Lupita spent the rest of the afternoon watching cartoons so as not to mess up her hair or rumple her dress. Finally, she heard the metal door sliding across the floor. She stood up and looked expectantly at her father, who entered the house wearing an expression she couldn't read. He stood in the doorway empty-handed, not bothering to close the door behind him.

Martina bit her lower lip, knowing what had happened. Luis's face was blank, and his shoulders slightly hunched.

Did you get my cake? Lupita asked timidly. There was no cake in sight, but Lupita hoped Luis would say he hadn't yet had a chance to buy it, that they could go now, as a family, to choose whatever one Lupita liked best. Without a cake, Lupita felt there would be nothing to bring the family together. It would be yet another evening in front of the TV. Lupita didn't mind that so much, but she had imagined that today, on her birthday, she would finally be able to ask for the attention she craved. She held her breath as she waited for Luis to answer, even though she didn't quite believe he would say what she hoped he would, as hard as she willed herself to.

Shame stifled Luis. He felt he couldn't form the words to again explain that he had been extorted. The sight of Lupita's expression— hurt and hope in her bright eyes, her furrowed brow, her pout, made the language he used with his family leave him.

Me robaron, he said in Spanish, reaching for the only phrase that encapsulated his impotence. Spanish belonged to the police, and the shame they inflicted on him could only be described in their language.

Jaime and Manolo remained still, looking at the ground. Lupita began to cry, the image of her family sitting happily around a cake and handing slivers to her friends now shattered. It seemed to her that they couldn't celebrate without a cake, though the cake wasn't the center of the celebration: Lupita was. Martina, distressed by her daughter's tears, offered consoling words, the first that came to mind. *We'll get cake*, she said.

It was Martina's impracticality in that moment, her narrow focus, that shook Luis. To him, it seemed she was always worried about the things that were least important. She should have been asking about the extortion, he thought, especially after he'd shared that he felt trapped in an endless cycle of them. She should have asked Lupita to go to the back room, to give them a few minutes. After that, he would have liked for Martina to tell Lupita that they would go to Media Luna as a family to celebrate. They didn't need a cake, she could have said, instead of implying that getting one was still possible.

Where would I get the money for a cake? he snapped. He had been cleaned out, and he knew she hadn't collected enough korime-ando. *Stop crying,* he scolded Lupita. He went to the back room. Lupita, shocked, wiped her face clean and held her breath, her well-practiced method for holding back tears. He had never scolded Lupita, had never dismissed her feelings before.

Martina stroked Lupita's head, torn because she wanted both to comfort her daughter and to get the children out of the house and away from Luis. After a few moments, Lupita stepped away from her mother and again wiped away her tears.

I'm going to tell Eugenia and María José not to come over, she whispered. The afternoon light was fading, and Lupita knew they could arrive at any moment. She would feel more humiliated turning them away at the door. Martina nodded, sorrow for her daughter filling her.

She went first to María José. Her aunt was just stepping out of the house. After hearing Lupita's whispered explanation, she reassured her niece that everything would be OK and that they would celebrate later. She told her not to worry about notifying Eugenia, to go home and be with her mother instead. On her way back, Lupita told the first child she saw to spread the word that there wouldn't be any cake. Others would soon wander over, each hoping to receive a piece. When the child asked why, what had happened, Lupita evaded the question. It was the first time she felt embarrassment over her father's inability to bring home money. She looked away, and simply said, *I don't know.*

Burning wood

[February and March 2010]

The following morning at recess, while Lupita, Camila, and Violeta played jacks on the basketball court, Camila asked why the birthday party had been canceled. Glancing around to make sure no one was listening, Lupita answered truthfully.

The police took my father's money, so he couldn't bring home a cake, she said.

Camila and Violeta nodded sympathetically. Though neither of them had experienced extortions in their own families—Violeta's father rarely worked, and Camila's father had left when she was a toddler—they knew, from hearing Lupita's and other children's stories, that such events not only devastated households economically but also caused fathers to boil over with anger, sometimes to the point that they hit their wives and children. They weren't surprised to hear that extortion was the reason for the cancelation, though they wrongly assumed that Lupita was more upset about the cake than her father's anger. Fathers often got angry, and as long as they didn't cause physical harm, most children brushed aside their outbursts, at least in front of their friends. It was their way of helping one another toughen up, tempering the devastation they felt in the face of parental reactions they couldn't control. Camila and Violeta thought it was logical that Lupita was most upset about having missed out on a rare treat. When the promise of a treat did come around, its failure to arrive brought up the feelings of neglect and resentment children repressed. A few weeks before, a mestiza social worker had promised to return to El Oasis with mandarins for all the children. Word had spread throughout the asentamiento, and they looked forward to biting into the sweet flesh of the fruits their parents never bought, the price being too high for a food that wasn't filling. When the social worker never returned, the children complained bitterly to one another for a few days. Then they stopped talking about it altogether. There would be another broken promise soon enough; if they dwelled on each one, they would feel nothing but pain. Children in El Oasis were resilient in that way; they helped one another move on and find small pleasures in each day.

Noticing Lupita's sadness, Violeta asked what she wanted to play next. Lupita shrugged; then, after thinking about it for a moment, she said she wanted to jump rope. She walked with a little more energy toward the teachers turning the rope, uplifted by her friends.

Lupita didn't want to tell them what had upset her the most: that the opportunity to feel her parents' attention on her and her alone had come and gone, ruined by yet another extortion. She didn't think Violeta and Camila would understand that sort of disappointment, since they rarely had contact with their fathers. It seemed almost cruel to bring it up, so she let them think what they wanted and tried to take comfort in their support.

It didn't matter, Lupita repeated to herself as she stood in line to jump rope. There would be another birthday next year. But somehow the thought of going through another year of buildup didn't help. Lupita wondered if it would be better to never celebrate her birthday again, to save herself from feeling her parents' neglect.

That week, Luis began to spend more time drinking at the arroyo after work. Jaime continued to wait for him at home after school, but when Luis didn't show up, he once again felt he was wasting time alone in their dark house, waiting for something that wasn't going to happen. His mother would always go korimeando; his father would always work and empty his pockets for the police. These thoughts circled his mind as he sat in the back room, filling sheets of notebook paper with drawings of cholos.

He'd broken his cycle of sniffing a dozen times before—if only for a few days—by staying away from the arcade and the arroyo, moving back and forth between the school and his house as if tethered to those places. If he ventured out, it was only to go to the tiendita for Coke or chips. Each time he returned to sniffing paint thinner, he did so with the sense that he was taking vengeance on his father. Two years into his addiction, Jaime was beginning to see that the trap of the paint thinner was more serious than he'd thought. He feared that he would become like his neighbor across the corridor, like so many other Rarámuri boys who lost the ability to talk and walk on their own, their brains too damaged by chemicals. If that happened, his mother would need to take care of him every day, dressing him and helping him to the toilet. He would be forever bound to El Oasis—the very thing he didn't want. As he sat drawing on those afternoons, Jaime told himself he wouldn't go back to the arcade, even if his father never spoke to him again. He knew that if he sniffed once, he would keep sniffing. What his friend Manuel had told him—that they could control how much they consumed—had turned out to be a lie. Manuel now wandered the streets with a bottle of paint thinner tucked into the sleeve of his hoodie and rarely made it to school.

Then, sometimes, Jaime stopped caring what happened to him. It was a feeling that suddenly settled over him, one that made him put down his colored pencils and lie on his mattress, eyes closed. It had come more frequently as the weeks passed, as Luis spent more time at the arroyo and Martina and Lupita continued korimeando.

At the end of the third week following Lupita's birthday, on a Friday when Luis was expecting to be paid, Jaime decided he didn't want to be at home to find out whether his father made it back with all his money. That day, when he reached their corridor, he kept walking, past the house, out the asentamiento gates, and to the arcade. There, he took a few whiffs of paint thinner and felt his mind cloud.

It had been a typical extortion: Luis was walking from the bus stop to El Oasis, following Avenida Zarco, the main artery between

Colonia Martín López and the rest of the city. As dozens of people streamed past Luis, a police officer had beckoned to him and told him to hand over his cash. The whole affair lasted twenty seconds, too quick for Luis to fully register that he would arrive home without a cake. It wasn't until the police car had pulled away that the anger set in. It made him want to find the police officer and punch him. That same officer had extorted him at least three times before: a tall, middle-aged mestizo with a neatly trimmed mustache.

Luis had thought about heading straight to the arroyo, where a friend would give him beer or mezcal. But he hadn't, believing that Martina would comfort him, as she had on so many previous occasions, and that the family would find another way to celebrate. After Martina had thoughtlessly offered another cake, one that they couldn't have bought, he became even more upset. He thought Martina was being selfish, that she was rarely able to see beyond what she wanted. She didn't understand what it felt like to hand over money to the police, day in and day out, when the entire family was depending on him for it.

That night, at the arroyo, Luis began drinking mezcal. He pooled money with some other men and bought a medium-sized bottle from a tiendita up the road for one hundred pesos. With six or seven swigs from the bottle, he felt himself become dizzy and pleasantly warm. The anger and frustration from the extortions remained in his mind, but he found that those feelings were quieter when he was drunk.

Gray clouds continued to hover over the city at the beginning of March. The dim morning light made Martina's eyes feel so heavy that not even a cup of instant coffee could help her feel more awake. After Lupita's birthday, Martina began returning home later in the evenings, not wanting to run into Luis or see him drinking at the edge of the arroyo. This degree of fatigue was new for her; in previous years, she had managed to make the best of the dreary weather by telling herself that winter was a respite from the brutal heat of summer. It didn't take long for her to recognize that her depression stemmed from Jaime's relapse, which she had finally noticed three days after he first started using again.

That it took so little to send Jaime over the precipice caused Martina to break down in tears. The first night she realized he had relapsed, she immediately left the house and went straight to Eugenia's. Luis sat in front of the TV and barely seemed to notice that Jaime reeked of the solvent, that his eyes were unfocused, and that he didn't want to eat dinner.

Eugenia let her in immediately. Her husband and daughters went to the back room to give the friends space to talk. After briefly explaining what had happened, Martina fell silent, even when Eugenia tried to coax her to speak. She thought she should consult a shaman about Jaime's relapse but knew Eugenia would advise her to lock Jaime away, as she had done with her own teenage daughter, Nancy, the first time she sniffed paint thinner, back at the end of December. Eugenia had screamed at Nancy for inhaling chemicals and destroying the future she was trying so hard to build for her daughters. The whole corridor had listened to the screaming for an entire week, until Eugenia finally allowed Nancy to return to the mestizo middle school, on the condition that if she ever sniffed paint thinner again, she would no longer be allowed to leave the house unescorted.

Martina wasn't willing to go that far. It felt too far from the counseling called for by korima. She would rather put away money for the mestizos' rehab center, should Jaime's addiction come to that, than restrict her son as Eugenia had her daughter. The shaman's advice, however, seemed like the best option, though Martina wasn't sure she would be able to complete his suggested treatment, especially since it required a costly animal sacrifice. She remained in Eugenia's house for several hours, simply sitting in her friend's presence. Eugenia badly wanted to counsel Martina, but she bit her tongue, knowing her friend might start to avoid her, as she sometimes did her sister, if she gave unsolicited advice.

A mestizo doctor doing a mental health screening had once explained to Martina that depression could make the body feel heavy and the mind struggle to find hope. Martina had never heard the term *depresión* before, and she had found it difficult to understand what the doctor meant. At the time, she had thought that the ailment was *tristeza*, the Spanish word for sadness. She thought it was a little different from *omóna*, the Rarámuri word for sadness, if only because mestizos experienced sadness for different reasons. They didn't long for the Sierra, for instance, nor did they worry that Onorúame was angry with them. Still, Martina had believed that she understood what the doctor meant, and she felt confident that she had the right antidote: when she felt sad, she always found solace in thinking about the plants and water the Sierra and Onorúame gave her. Now, however, she knew without a doubt what he had been referring to. Depresión was like being in a dark cave with no light. Instead of thinking about what made her happy in her new life in El Oasis, or of fondly recalling the pine trees and rosemary in the Sierra, Martina replayed memories of lying with Luis and her children on wool blankets inside their home, the fire in their hearth keeping them warm on nights when a sheet of frost hardened the forest floor. They had told stories, Martina and Luis recounting runs through the forest, community festivals, and swims in the rivers, and the children making up their own tales, filled with woodland creatures and plants that loved the Sierra just as much as the Rarámuris did. The family spent every moment together, rarely venturing beyond their clearing because of the cold. When a Rarámuri arrived there, whether the Gutiérrez family knew them or not, they offered the person shelter. Just like offering food, offering shelter was central to korima. Never had the Gutiérrez family denied a visitor a place to stay for the night. Never had they heard of another Rarámuri family doing so.

Jaime and Lupita had wanted to stay close to their parents, to sleep against their warm bodies inside the small wooden house that fit little more than the five of them. Even when they had been hungry, Martina and Luis had found comfort in their family and in the knowledge that winter would pass.

For a while, replaying these memories helped Martina avoid feeling overwhelmed by Luis's drinking and Jaime's sniffing. As she realized she couldn't avoid their substance abuse, Martina began to feel that Jaime and Luis were more like an obsession she couldn't rid herself of. Martina tried to focus on finding solutions, but each time she did, she wondered whether there was any point. It was easier to go through the motions of daily tasks and korimeando and let her mind slip away to the Sierra. There, Rarámuris didn't use paint thinner or alcohol. There, they had lived relatively secluded from the mestizos and their vices.

Martina noticed a marked change in Luis's drinking in February and early March. He came home smelling of alcohol and sometimes slurred his words. She was beginning to worry it wouldn't be long before he reached a point where he needed help walking, or perhaps fell asleep on the sidewalk as other men did. She had learned that, in the city, negative events often escalated and led to terrible outcomes. There was no place to be still and find peace in the city, no place for Luis to escape the extortions or the managers who withheld pay. Time mimicked the forward motion of traffic, always moving at a dangerous speed, too quickly for anyone to discern the dangers. Sometimes she hoped the hours Luis spent at the edge of the arroyo, in the company of mesquite trees, would allow him to reflect on his current route. Martina worried about his safety, much like she worried about Jaime's. What if Luis fell asleep on the road and a car ran over him? What if he wandered into the colonia and mestizos beat him up while he was drunk, and he couldn't escape?

Even with the devastation along the way—the onset of Jaime's addiction, Luis's kidnapping, Lupita korimeando on her own—Martina had never doubted that the path she and her family were on would lead them someplace good; it was provided for them by their origin story, and Onorúame had promised that they would one day find abundant rain, seeds spread by the wind, and baskets piled high with tortillas. After Lupita called off her own birthday party because of Luis's anger, however, Martina worried he would never recover from the kidnapping and would continue to cope by drinking. At this point, he continued to get up and go to work every day, but his drinking had grown from one can of beer a day to two, and sometimes three. Martina resented how much he spent on beer; it meant that Martina had less money to pay the family's utility bills and buy groceries. But she didn't bring this up to Luis; she feared he would grow more impatient and angrier with his family, and that he would withhold all money from Martina, like some of the other men who drank heavily. He was straying so far from their path that Martina wondered if he would ever find his way back. Without that path, the Rarámuri people would become mestizos. It was clear to her now that she would be the one responsible not only for keeping her children close to korima, but also for making sure they had enough to eat. With that realization, a new question weighed on her mind: how would she make enough money to support them all on her own?

One morning in early March, Martina sat on the floor, a pile of dried pinto beans spread before her. She was sifting through the beans, feeling for tiny pebbles. Sometimes the pebbles were jagged and her fingers picked them out quickly. But other times, they'd been made smooth from thousands of years spent being caressed by waves. Every so often, Martina missed them and boiled them with the beans, discovering their presence only when someone in the family bit into something hard. It was a small devastation to feel the pain shooting up the tooth and into the gums when one was expecting the soft warmth of a fully cooked pinto bean.

As she separated out the pebbles, Martina thought about how she had rarely before felt she needed to make major decisions on her own. She and Luis had always helped each other. Now, it seemed her path was filled with dangers she couldn't have anticipated, and she was facing them alone. She found herself considering an opportunity to earn steadier wages, though she wasn't entirely sure how to feel about it.

Two weeks after Luis had returned, Eugenia had asked Martina if she was interested in selling crafts with her downtown. They would set up two tables, displaying their crafts side by side. Each one would take the profits for the crafts she made, and they could take turns managing the tables and their children.

When Eugenia had made the offer, the women were sitting on Martina's front stoop, drinking instant coffee while Manolo ran up and down the corridor. Martina was flattered but didn't accept right away.

Eventually we'll be able to buy a tent, and we won't have to sit under the hot sun all day, Eugenia had said in an effort to entice Martina.

It wasn't a novel idea. In the last ten years, dozens of other Rarámuri women, some from El Oasis and some from other asentamientos throughout the city, had made similar arrangements for informal shops downtown, where mestizos gathered to stroll the cobblestone streets lined with old colonial homes and small businesses. Rarámuri women had found that it was far easier work than korimeando, and more respectable, since mestizos were more likely to admire a neatly ordered table attended to by a Rarámuri woman. Eugenia wanted to set up her own store, tired of the NGOs taking a cut when they resold her crafts. She didn't intend to give up selling to them; it was easy money, especially now that they came knocking on her door every week. But she didn't think it was fair that they made any money off her work, and she thought it would be easy enough to sell her wares and keep the profits herself. She intended for her daughters to accompany her, believing that if she left them alone at home, they would likely use drugs and perhaps even become pregnant. She had already experienced one pregnancy scare with her eldest daughter, Nancy, who was now fifteen. Though it was a common age for Rarámuri women in both the Sierra and the city to have their first child, Eugenia wanted Nancy to finish high school and perhaps even attend college, as a few of the other Rarámuri girls were doing. At the moment, however, Eugenia was preoccupied with Nancy's use of paint thinner.

Eugenia and Martina had bonded over their shared love of sewing long before. Martina admired Eugenia's quick wit, not unlike María José's. Eugenia felt protective of Martina, whom she thought loyal and quietly funny. But it wasn't these qualities that would make Martina a good business partner. Eugenia considered her a strong seamstress, detailed and precise in her work, and thought mestizos would be attracted to their crafts simply because of their beauty. She also believed Martina's loyalty would contribute to a strong work ethic. Eugenia wouldn't have to worry about Martina failing to set up a table or leaving her alone to manage the sales and the children.

I don't know, Martina had answered. *Will we be there all day?*

The days will be shorter than they are korimeando, komali, my friend, Eugenia had assured her. *We'll be home by nightfall.*

Eugenia had known Martina was thinking about Jaime. Who would be available to him if he got into trouble? Martina couldn't rely on Luis.

Martina had sipped her coffee and thought about what she would need to fill a table with her crafts. Fabric, Styrofoam balls for dolls' heads, thread, needles, and beads. Though she had a scrap bag, the more lucrative crafts—dolls mestiza mothers bought for their daughters, embroidered aprons, dresses—required a greater investment of fabric and time. Martina tried to calculate how much she would need up front to buy supplies. She knew she could make a dress for herself with thirty meters. With fabric at twenty pesos a meter, she spent six hundred pesos each time she made a dress. She figured that with fifteen meters, she could make ten dolls, three aprons, a few tortilleros, and perhaps an embroidered table runner. She thought those items would fill a table. Though three hundred pesos was a large sum of money for Martina, she thought she could gather it in a matter of weeks if she was strict with her family's spending. She wouldn't rely on the money Luis brought home. It barely covered their food, especially now that he was spending some of it on beer. But what if the crafts didn't sell? She would have lost days of korimeando, and the family would be in a worse state than before.

Though Luis hadn't spoken to her about the pressure he felt, Martina was certain Luis would be relieved if she found a way to bring home more coins on a regular basis. She had planned to discuss the stall with him, but the days had passed quickly, and then Lupita's birthday had come. In the days after that, Martina, deep in her depression, hadn't even thought about Eugenia's offer. Then, when she realized Jaime was using drugs again, she became pre-occupied with that problem. How would she ever get Jaime to quit paint thinner again, especially now that Luis was spending his after-noons by the arroyo, drinking beer and mezcal?

Martina believed her family's departure from the Sierra had affected her children and could be the cause of Jaime's addiction. And yet, as the shaman had said when she went to him, return was impossible. She waffled in her decision about going into busi-ness with Eugenia, causing Eugenia, María José, and others in the community to grit their teeth each time they talked about her. They wanted her to choose a path, even if it ended up being the wrong one.

Everything is getting worse, María José scolded her sister as they washed clothes. *Get a job cleaning houses or set up the store with Eugenia, or you're going to see Jaime suffer even more.*

María José was done speaking gently to her sister. Jaime's addic-tion was as bad as it had ever been. He was skipping school again, spending hours with a water bottle of solvent tucked into his sweat-shirt, breathing in the fumes constantly. María José knew that he would end up with brain damage if he continued, and no shaman could stop it from happening. The solvent was too strong, too good at taking away hunger and pain. Jaime needed to be locked away and broken of his habit.

When Martina had consulted the shaman, he told her Jaime's addiction was the result of his removal from the Sierra. An elderly man who lived in the Sierra Azul asentamiento, he understood that the Gutiérrez family couldn't return. Instead, he advised Martina to take Jaime on walks in the desert. So far, Martina hadn't succeeded in convincing Jaime to take a walk with her even around the colonia.

There was also her grandparents' anger to consider. Martina knew they disapproved of the family's leaving the Sierra. If they continued to be angry, they could curse Martina and her family, potentially even cause their deaths. Angered relatives had been known to do this as a way to keep Rarámuris from straying too far from the path of korima. The shaman had instructed Martina to sacrifice one chicken for her grandparents. She thought she could save up for the chicken and sacrifice it inside her home, which she'd done before. But then she wondered what good it would do to sacrifice just one chicken? Better to go back to the Sierra to sacrifice the animal, where Onorúame would likely feel more connected to Martina and empathize with her pain. Whatever solutions Martina chose to pursue—the shaman's cure and the mestizos' rehab among them—would cost her money.

Martina recognized that setting up a store meant assimilating further into the mestizos' way of living. It meant adhering to the rules of a market economy, which was propelled by the forward motion of time and profit-seeking behaviors, and risking the reciprocity at the heart of korima. She had had similar concerns when she began korimeando, though eventually, she saw it not as a transgression but a continuation of their peoples' origin story. The gift-giving in korimeando wasn't reciprocal, but Martina had come to believe it was fair for Rarámuris to receive recompense from mestizos for their many centuries of abuse. There was also a shared purpose in korimeando. It was a powerful, albeit quiet, protest, standing out on the streets in Rarámuri dress, speaking an ancient word that held the stories and knowledge of the Sierra.

Martina feared that to go beyond korimeando by setting up a table and selling her crafts to mestizos would bring her closer to the money mindset she and the other women resisted. Interacting with others, including mestizos, by way of transactions meant losing something essential about korima: the free exchange of gifts, which always carried meaning beyond the gifts' physical, practical uses. These exchanges were a way of initiating and maintaining relationships, and those relationships were what made Rarámuris care for one another as well as the land, air, and water. What kind of relationship would she form with mestizas who bought her hand-sewn crafts? And how could she be sure that setting up a table to sell her crafts wouldn't put an end to the origin story, at least as far as she and the children were concerned? What if she was pulled further from the ways of the Rarámuri people? What if setting up a table downtown made her a mestiza?

Manolo and three other young children were running up and down the corridor, throwing a plastic ball for a brown-and-white spotted dog that was more interested in leaping on the children to lick their faces. Martina watched from her front stoop, smiling as they giggled, and brushed Lupita's hair. She planned to head to the grocery store soon, to buy a few cups of instant noodles for the family's dinner. Then Lucero approached.

Komali, bring a bag of beans and eat with us, she called. Her voice sounded like the wind that preceded rain, filled with anticipation of good things to come.

Martina felt the impulse to say yes but then hesitated. What if the community pushed her to make a decision about the stall? She was certain her friends would try to talk to her about the storefront; María José had already spread the news in the hopes of enlisting others to help her convince Martina. Some women in El Oasis were going to be glad to see her fall away from her strict interpretation of korima, Martina thought, and that irritated her. She had been trying to avoid those women, but she was getting tired of eating inside the house. Lucero beckoned again, and Martina decided to risk it. She and the children would get to eat beans, tortillas, and salsa if they joined in; that was certainly better than plain noodles. Martina sent Lupita across the street with twelve pesos to buy a bag of pinto beans.

In the clearing beside the community kitchen, where the women had cooked meat and made corn tortillas and batari after the sacrifice of the cow, Marta's boom box played pop ballads in Spanish. Chavela stoked a campfire with a thin tree branch and sipped a Tecate. A metal vat set on four stones held the boiling water where the beans would cook. Beside Chavela, four women sat on the ground with their skirts tucked under their knees, chopping jalapeños, onions, cilantro, and tomatoes to make a pico de gallo. Several others sat nearby, holding their babies or simply watching the others

PART 2

cook. Chavela told a joke, and everyone, including Martina, laughed. She felt her guard come down as her friends greeted her, and she sat under the mesquite tree, comforted by the branches and layers of long, thin leaves that sheltered the women. Manolo joined a group of children who were racing a plastic dump truck against a monster truck down a short cement ramp. Lucero passed out small Styrofoam cups and poured Coke for each woman. Flocks of sparrows swooped across the turquoise sky, riding the late winter winds.

Like the races, communal cooking outdoors was a way for women to pause time and create a space where they could lift one another's spirits. Of course, there was sometimes gossip and meddling, as Martina had feared, but cooking together outside was a sort of medicine for the stress and depression the city caused in the women. They did it often, even though the mestizo government discouraged it: the food attracted stray dogs, they told the women, some of which carried rabies and all of which would defecate in the corridors of the asentamiento. Sanitation was supposedly a top priority for the mestizos, but the women believed that any problems in that area were a direct result of the poor conditions the mestizos had put them in. Why should the Rarámuri people sacrifice cooking as a community, an activity that had brought their people together in the Sierra, simply because the mestizos hadn't built the asentamiento with that need in mind?

Eugenia, as usual, was absent. She was at home, assessing the crafts she had to sell that week. Her small refrigerator contained beans, squash, roma tomatoes, jalapeños, yogurt, milk, and a bottle of Coke. While many families owned refrigerators—most of them donations—few could afford to keep them plugged in all the time, but Eugenia's income allowed her to do so, saving her from having to buy groceries every week and giving her more time to work on her crafts. The efficiency of the refrigerator was something Eugenia prized, but not because she disparaged the practice of cooking outside. Whenever she felt caught up with her work—which was rare—she joined the women to cook over the fire and even contributed more than her fair share of food.

A woman named Lucía returned with several packets of corn tortillas, the only food the women would not make themselves that evening. To make the tortillas from scratch, they would have had to start cooking much earlier in the day or commit to staying up past midnight. They would have begun by crushing the corn against a metate. The evening before them felt long, but each woman still needed to get up to korimear or to go to work the following morning. Buying the corn tortillas from a mestizo shop owner on days like this was another one of the compromises Rarámuri women made to keep alive another aspect of korima.

Capitalist time forced the Rarámuri women to look ahead rather than let the path unfold passively, trusting that everything would be OK. Time, in this system, was always in short supply, and occasionally, it was simpler to accept the efficiencies that gave a little back to them. A few days before, Martina had received a blender as a gift for attending a rally for César Duarte Jáquez, a light-skinned mestizo seeking a second term as governor. María Cruz had chided her for attending, telling her she was dumb for falling for the mestizo tricks that took away Rarámuri souls. At the rally, Martina, María José, and Eugenia had stared straight ahead, hands folded in their laps, as they waited for the governor hopeful to run out of things to say. Later, María José had shown Martina and Eugenia how to make salsa in the blender; she'd done it many times for the mestiza whose house she cleaned. Three roma tomatoes, three tomatillos, two jalapeños, a few slices of onion, and María José pressed the button. The blender whirred and within seconds produced pale-green salsa. Martina felt as conflicted as María José felt pleased. The blender saved time, but Martina didn't care about that. She loved slicing through vegetables with the stainless-steel knife she'd saved up to buy at the Soriana. She especially loved when Lupita helped her and when they cooked outdoors with their community. Martina felt disappointed when she realized the blender changed the way people gathered to cook and socialize. It sped up the process of making salsa, and forced the cook to stay indoors where there was an electrical outlet. She thought María Cruz was right in this instance; the blender stole from the Rarámuris.

Martina was wary of technology, which had brought her nothing but pain. In her view, mestizos invented tools for the sole purpose of disrupting the natural world's balances. The advancements in technology that allowed for the mining of minerals in the Sierra, for example, contributed to the soil's nutrient depletion and made it harder for Rarámuri people to grow their own food. It was the mestizos' need to alter the natural world for the sake of collecting money that had caused her nothing but pain, and she recognized that technology had aided in this. Drought in the Sierra, Jaime's decline into addiction, and Luis's perilous job outside the city were some of the biggest examples of the pain capitalist ambition had introduced into her life. There were smaller pains too: the pressure to earn enough coins before mealtimes, to put the children to bed at a reasonable hour, to get up and fulfill her many responsibilities all over again. Luis's drinking was pushing her only further into the linear system, making her forecast and plan. She had to create efficiencies, because she had less and less time, and the stakes for Jaime were especially high.

Sin Bandera crooned a love song from the boom box. No one paid attention, since María José was telling a story about a mestiza who had stopped her to ask about the triangle details on her dress. All of them laughed when she described how the woman had lifted her skirt almost to her knees, and how María José had worried everyone would see her underwear. Martina felt her anxieties slip to the back of her mind and her appreciation for her community once again grow.

If she took the job with Eugenia, she wasn't sure what dangers she would encounter. She thought they might be like the smooth pebbles that hid easily among dried pinto beans: sometimes she was able to detect them, and sometimes she wasn't. She couldn't foresee what harm might come if she chose to set up the stall, other than the possibility of further angering her grandparents and Onorúame. And yet, Onorúame had shown them the path out of the Sierra.

Perhaps it was most logical to follow it as it continued to unfold before her, and hope she was wise enough to discern the sleek, slippery pebbles that could cause so much pain.

The sparrows had settled in the trees for the night when the beans rose to the top of the vat, declaring themselves fully cooked. Two baskets were piled high with corn tortillas. Martina, Lupita, and Manolo each took one of the thick tortillas and spooned on beans and pico de gallo. The evening stretched before them like an endless sky. In the light of a streetlamp, the smell of burning wood still lingering in the air, Martina ate.

Swirling dust, pale yellow sky
[March 2010]

Each winter, the Rarámuri elementary school teachers began meeting to discuss their students' futures. There was a high completion rate at the elementary school because it was located within the community and admitted only Rarámuri children. It was an anchor for most families, a place where children went to learn in both Rarámuri and Spanish, where they received lunch each day, and where they were safe from the many dangers present outside the asentamiento gates. Once they completed sixth grade, Rarámuri children could find a similar sense of security only at the boarding schools run by Jesuits in the Sierra. While the teachers recommended all the students continue their education, the reality was that only one-third of sixth graders in El Oasis went on to middle school. Nearly every student who attended the integrated middle school in Colonia Martín López dropped out, the pressure to succeed in a system that disparaged Indigenous peoples too difficult to surmount. Most Rarámuri boys then began a cycle of work and drug use, while the girls often became mothers and also struggled with paint-thinner addiction. The option to attend a Rarámuri-only boarding school in the Sierra was open to all, but the privately run schools were cost prohibitive for every family in El Oasis. A limited number of scholarships were available, and the teachers needed to decide which students should receive them.

During the sixth graders' lunch break on the first Wednesday of the month, Jaime's teacher, Miss Ceci, stood outside the Gutiérrez home and called Martina's name. She had seen Martina finish cooking for the children in the communal kitchen, eat a bean burrito, and leave. This was a good opportunity to catch her alone, before she went out to korimear or run errands.

Martina hated it when people called to her through the window; it alerted the neighbors, including her sister, that someone had come to visit, and she preferred to keep her conversations private. Neighbors in El Oasis tended to give unsolicited opinions with little regard for the sensitivity of a given matter. Community members' lives seemed to blend together, a circumstance of city living Martina had never gotten used to. She opened the door and peeked around the floral curtain hanging over the threshold. When she saw that it was Miss Ceci, she knew to invite her inside, out of earshot of the neighbors.

Martina liked the way Miss Ceci talked to the children, in a gentle but firm tone she tried to emulate, though with little success. Miss Ceci reminded Martina of the elders in the Sierra who counseled members of younger generations when they were going astray. Miss Ceci was Rarámuri, though she also spoke fluent Spanish and lived in an apartment instead of an asentamiento. She smiled at Martina whenever she was on recess duty. Though Jaime was known to fall asleep in class, or skip altogether, he respected Miss Ceci and tried to give her completed assignments. She took an interest in his drawings and often asked to see them.

In direct but kind words, Miss Ceci explained that she was concerned about Jaime going on to the mestizo middle school the following year. She knew he joined other boys in sniffing paint thinner after school. The problem would only get worse once he started attending school outside El Oasis, she explained. In the mestizo middle school, he was likely to be teased and bullied. Keeping him there would require a great deal of parental involvement, which she knew Martina and Luis didn't always have time for. She spoke in sympathetic tones, anticipating the defensiveness many Rarámuri mothers felt when a teacher came to talk to them about their capacity to care for their children. But Martina didn't become defensive; she had been wondering if the boarding school could be an option for Jaime and was glad that Miss Ceci had sought her out to discuss it.

Ceci said Jaime was set to graduate from elementary school that May, and he could leave for the Sierra in August. There, he would take classes in both Rarámuri and Spanish, and he would not be allowed to leave the school grounds without supervision. The school had security, and the teachers checked to make sure the children were in bed each night at the same hour. The structured environment would be good for Jaime, and he wouldn't have access to paint thinner or other drugs. He could stay there until he completed the last year of high school and then potentially go on to college. Other Rarámuri girls and boys were going to college; some had even struggled with drugs early on. Why couldn't Jaime turn out like them?

Neither Martina nor Luis had attended school in the Sierra. Instead, Luis had learned to carve figures and pieces of furniture out of wood. Martina wove baskets, made clay pots, and sewed their clothing. Both tended to the garden and ran. Every relationship they cultivated—with their family, their community, and the animals and plants of the Sierra—tightened their bond with the Sierra, and helped them set up the next generation to think and behave in ways that benefited the people and land that surrounded them. Their parents were among those who chose to keep their children at home, believing the schools were, at best, places where Rarámuri children went to forget their heritage and the values of korima.

The government opened the first federally run boarding school in the Sierra in the town of Yoquivo in October 1926. In the decade that followed, they doubled down on their efforts to strengthen the boarding school system in the area and sent teachers to Rarámuri homes to convince parents that their children should attend. But not every mestizo agreed with the government's boarding school project. In the Sierra, mestizos and whites continued to object to education for Indigenous peoples, believing that it would take away their own economic opportunities. Further, if Indigenous people were given a formal education, mestizos and whites would no longer be able to enslave them to work their fields. Some mestizos, however, called for boarding schools as a means of "civilizing" the Rarámuri people and making them part of the mestizo culture that went hand in hand with the country's post-revolution vision of progress. The 1920s saw a Mexico attempting to shape its own identity after the decade-long Mexican Revolution, which officially ended in 1919. This identity was to be characterized by industrialization, overseas trade, the accumulation of wealth, and the whitening of Mexicans. It was around this time that Mexican mestizos began using the euphemism "mejorar la raza," or "improving the Mexican race." The concept of one Mexican race—"la raza"—was popularized by the philosopher Jose Vasconcelos's *La raza cósmica,* a popular book published in the early twentieth century that put forward the idea that the ideal Mexican people had the best traits of their European and Indigenous ancestors. One of these traits, according to Vasconcelos, was lighter skin and the Spanish language. Thus, the idea of improving the Mexican race lent itself to the practice of sending Indigenous peoples to boarding schools, and even marrying them with Spanish-speaking mestizos, with the aim of producing children who would be lighter skinned and who would only learn Spanish. In this vision of Mexico, citizens would retain only traces of their Indigenous ancestry, enough to distinguish them from Europeans but not so much that they would be regarded by the Western world as racially inferior and unworthy of trade. Dozens of Mexico's most famed artists of the time, including the muralists Diego Rivera and David Siqueiros, contributed to the notion that Mexico's future needed to be characterized by industrialization and the assimilation of Indigenous peoples into mestizaje.

The boarding schools provided for by the government separated children from their parents—an important tactic for the erasure of Rarámuri culture. The rural day schools in other parts of the Sierra continued operating sporadically, sometimes closing due to lack of funds, and other times because Rarámuri children stayed home to work alongside their parents. Still, the federal government continued to endorse the boarding schools, seeing the poor mestizos who wanted to continue enslaving Rarámuris as an impediment to the project of assimilation, which was tied to their idea of economic advancement. To achieve economic prosperity, the government wanted the population to become light skinned, and the country, industrialized.

Both Martina and Luis knew Rarámuris who had attempted to escape the boarding schools and return to their homes. Most schoolmasters put bars on the windows to prevent this. The schools provided meals only for the children. Because of this, Rarámuri parents had to leave their children at the schools and go back home in order to eat. Some parents simply chose to retreat farther into the mountains, changing location every so often. Then, beginning in the 1990s, after thousands of families had fled to Chihuahua City, many found they needed to send their children back to the Sierra to protect them from the dangers of the urban life. The boarding schools, some of which were now run by Catholic nuns, were the only places where mothers like Martina could send their children to ensure they would receive adequate nutrition and an education, and remain safe from the droughts and cartels.

After hearing from Miss Ceci that Jaime should return to the Sierra, Martina thought of the many challenges her family was facing, and how those challenges currently felt insurmountable. No matter what promises they made to each other, or how carefully they strategized with their money and time, Martina and Luis hadn't been able to protect Jaime from his paint-thinner addiction, or Lupita from the potential dangers of korimeando.

Perhaps Martina would have made a different choice if Luis hadn't been so absent, if he weren't drinking to escape his worries and leaving Martina to figure out how to care for their children. But that month, she felt that she was on the brink of giving up and staying inside her home all day, hidden from the world. When Miss Ceci offered Jaime a scholarship, Martina said she would take it. Then she asked if Lupita could have one too.

Immediately after Miss Ceci left, Martina regretted telling her with such certainty that the children would go to boarding school. She was sure it was the right choice, but she didn't feel right making the decision on her own; Luis lived in the house with them, and even though he was distant and taciturn, Martina thought it logical that he would have something to say about a decision as big as sending their children back to the Sierra. Then again, she wasn't sure anymore what kinds of reactions to expect from him. Luis might become angry and kick Martina out of the house again, or he might strike her. Martina had already considered the possibility that Luis might one day become violent with her, as some other husbands did with their wives. If he didn't care enough to discuss the children's schooling, or if he became volatile, Martina knew the decision would fall entirely on her, and she had already decided what she thought was best. Yet she wanted to give Luis an opportunity to speak on his children's behalf. She also thought this conversation might lead to another one, and even open up a path of healing. Martina hadn't lost her hope or desire for reconciliation with her husband. Yet she realized that it was in her and her children's best interest not to rely on the livelihood of a husband who seemed likely to turn away from them.

That night, while Lupita was watching TV and Jaime was out, Martina summoned her courage. She stood beside Luis, careful not to look at him directly so he wouldn't perceive her words as a challenge, and told him what Miss Ceci had recommended. Luis kept his eyes on the TV, giving no indication that he was listening. Lupita, hearing every word her mother spoke, didn't dare look away from the TV; she wasn't sure how her father would react toward her if she paid Martina attention. Martina felt her impatience grow, but she kept talking, hoping Luis was in fact paying attention. When she finished and still he said nothing, didn't even acknowledge her words with a nod or a blink, Martina grew angry. If Luis refused to speak with her about such an important matter, he left her no choice but to make the decision on her own.

Jaime will go to school in the Sierra, she said, raising her voice slightly. At that point, Martina wasn't scared of Luis's reaction. She wanted to see her son settled at last, safe in a place where he would no longer suffer from his addiction.

Martina thought it must have been the change in her voice that caused Luis to look away from the TV and directly at her for the first time since Lupita's birthday. She rarely raised her voice in frustration or anger, and never did when she was speaking directly to Luis. In that moment, she felt the smallest sense of power, and a bit of surprise at the realization that her words, spoken loudly, could bring attention even from Luis, who had been determined to avoid her.

After a moment's pause, in which he studied Martina's face, Luis responded, his own voice hard. Hearing his tone, Martina felt a jolt of panic—not shock, as when he had told her to leave the house, but a stinging warmth in her legs and head. It took a few moments for her to register what Luis had said: *Jaime should be working after this year.*

Luis continued, and Martina tried to focus on his words.

Once he starts working, he'll be too busy to sniff paint thinner. It won't be long before he becomes a father. He'll need to make money.

Jaime as a father—the thought hadn't even occurred to Martina. Though now that Luis had mentioned it, she realized Jaime would likely be ready to make his own home; he needed only to grow a little taller before he could marry and begin having children. He would have passed from boy to man by then, and it was natural that at that point, he'd form a family with a Rarámuri woman, just as Luis had with her. Imagining Jaime as a father felt impossible, not because he was still a boy, but because his addiction made him incapable of caring for himself. How would he provide for a family? Would work truly cure him of his dependency, as Luis implied?

Even as she considered Luis's words, Martina felt he was wrong. There were plenty of young men in El Oasis who worked and sniffed paint thinner, or drank alcohol. Work wouldn't provide the stability and peace Jaime needed; only the Sierra could give him that.

Four years before, when Luis was trying to convince Martina to leave the Sierra, she had argued that the Sierra was the only way to find peace. Even after visiting Antonio, when he had felt most strongly that they should leave, Luis hadn't imposed his will on her. Now, Martina found herself wishing he hadn't responded at all so she could make the choice on her own. She held back the words flooding her mind and said simply, *There's no paint thinner in the Sierra.*

Luis didn't respond. In the past, Martina had never expected immediate responses. She'd never felt rushed in the Sierra, never felt that time was against her, at least not until that last year of drought. Now, however, she felt that Jaime's future at stake. Whatever Luis said next could determine whether he ever gained control of his paint-thinner addiction.

If he starts working, he'll only feel more frustrated and angry, she said. *He'll start drinking and harming those around him. Like you.*

There was no flash of anger from Luis, only hunched shoulders and a sadness in his eyes that Martina recognized. Once again, they didn't agree on whether to stay or go. But this time, Luis didn't have the strength to wait patiently until something brought them into agreement. Jaime was growing up.

Jaime will work when the school year ends, Luis said, his eyes fixed on Martina's face, his tone quiet and firm. In that moment, Martina felt a loss even greater than she had when they left behind the Sierra. She knew Jaime would soon be trapped in a cycle of work and extortion, just like Luis.

One evening a couple days later, Martina sewed while Luis, Lupita, and Manolo watched TV. She tried half-heartedly to convince Lupita to sew with her but gave up when she resisted. At ten thirty, Lupita and Manolo fell asleep on their mattress. Half an hour later, Luis went to bed. Martina normally stayed awake another hour, waiting for Jaime to get home. If he'd forgotten his key, he knocked softly, and she opened the door for him. He came in without saying a word, ate whatever food she had set aside for him, and fell onto the mattress she laid out for him each night after Luis went to sleep in the back room.

That night, Martina waited so late for Jaime she fell asleep sitting up. At some point, she lay down on the concrete floor and slept through the night without waking. When Manolo crawled into her lap in the morning and woke her, Martina looked around the room.

Where's Jaime?

Dull morning light filtered through the barred windows. Lupita was still asleep, and so was Luis, in the next room. Martina got up and walked through the house, looking to see if Jaime had somehow fallen asleep in a corner. He hadn't. She checked the bathroom. The door was ajar, and there was no one inside.

Panic coursed through her, making her arms and knees tremble. Her mind jumped to the worst possible explanation—that Jaime was lying dead in the street somewhere in the colonia, hit by a car or shot by a mestizo. She took a deep breath and tried to calm her mind; there was no use jumping to conclusions. It was also possible that Jaime had fallen asleep in the arroyo and was still there. She thought for a moment about waking Luis but decided against it. Coming to him with a problem might lead to another confrontation, which wouldn't help her find Jaime. It would be better to search for him herself. Surely he was asleep in the arroyo, or perhaps in one of the corridors. Maybe he'd lost his house key.

Tiptoeing so as not to wake the family, she went outside and found Eugenia, who was already scrubbing clothes against a washboard.

Have you seen Jaime? Martina asked.

No, said Eugenia, brow furrowed in concern. She kept washing, and Martina moved on to a group of children playing with a stray puppy. They hadn't seen him either. Martina, feeling her panic rise again, decided to stop wasting time asking around. She had set off down the corridor, intent on searching for Jaime in the arroyo, when María Luz, a woman who lived nearby, rounded the corner and walked quickly toward her. Martina wouldn't have stopped, but María Luz reached out an arm and said quietly, so her words wouldn't filter through the open windows of nearby homes, that her son Ángel was missing too. He was in Jaime's class and had started sniffing paint thinner the year before. The children playing with the puppy had already started spreading the word, but Martina didn't mind. What other women might say about Jaime later was the most unimportant thing in the world. The more people who knew, the more people who could search for him.

They might be in the arroyo, Martina said to María Luz. She set off walking quickly, María Luz close behind her.

A few steps from the gate, Jaime and Ángel rounded the corner. Martina stopped in her tracks; María Luz breathed in sharply. Dizzy with relief, Martina reached for María Luz's shoulder to steady herself. She felt her heart pumping against the walls of her throat—a sensation that made it difficult to breathe. Her son was here, before her.

Her body weak with fatigue, Martina registered that the boys were walking as if through a thick fog, heads angled toward the ground to avoid dizziness. It was then that she noticed the women sitting on the sidewalk in front of the chapel, openly watching the scene unfold.

For the second time that morning, Martina felt a sense of urgency. She needed to get Jaime inside as quickly as she could without appearing overly distraught. Already children were gathering to watch the spectacle, and she didn't want the gossiping neighbors to see her son in this undignified state. Children and mothers alike would start telling others what they had seen. Stories—embellished with untrue and unkind details—would circulate until no one knew what to believe, and then they would believe the very worst. Jaime might be accused of theft, like so many boys in El Oasis who stole to buy paint thinner.

Taking Jaime's elbow, Martina patted his back once, firmly, to straighten him. Jaime looked up for a brief moment. Then his head flopped back down.

Martina wished desperately that her son would lift his head and tell her to leave him alone. Then she would know he was OK, and she could begin to believe that this was a temporary condition and not what she feared.

Martina realized Jaime couldn't lift his head, so she slung his arm around her shoulders and let him lean against her. He was already as tall as his mother, a young boy who continued growing even when he didn't have enough to eat, even when the paint thinner suppressed his appetite.

She wanted to get him home as quickly as possible and put him to bed. She would have picked him up and carried him, but he was too big for her now. So she took small steps instead, murmuring to him to keep up with her. He appeared to hear his mother, putting one foot forward and then, many seconds later, the other. The women, with sorrowful looks on their faces, turned back to their sewing and washing, giving Martina some semblance of respect and privacy. They made it to their corridor, where María Cruz, Eugenia, and María José sat on their front stoops. Martina stared at the ground to make sure Jaime didn't trip, and to avoid seeing their expressions. She hated to think that they pitied her. After the years she'd spent trying to prove to herself and her community that she could raise her family in accordance with korima, it made her feel like a failure. She couldn't bear the thought that she was part of another family that had strayed so far from korima they were now as corrupt as mestizos.

Just when she had managed to help Jaime up the two steps, Luis opened the front door and stood in the entrance. In a matter of seconds, he knew what had happened. Disdain spread across his face, and he glared at Jaime.

Leave him out here, he said to Martina, quietly enough, though she knew everyone in the corridor could hear.

He needs to sleep, she said, almost pleadingly. Luis had to understand. Jaime needed to rest, and she also needed Jaime inside the home, away from the community's pitying eyes.

Luis remained in the doorway.

No drunkard would stand in her way, not when her son was falling apart in front of the entire community. Young children were watching the scene unfold. Martina was always so controlled, using silence and flight to protect herself just as her ancestors had centuries before, when the Spaniards invaded. But now her son was being exposed, his life and social acceptance threatened.

Move, she hissed.

Luis remained in the door. He looked through Martina and Jaime, at the wall of the house before him.

Move, she hissed again. But he didn't move. He simply stood in the doorway, denying them entrance.

To deny entrance into a home was an action so far removed from korima that Martina perceived it as downright violent. Luis was refusing to acknowledge his relationship with his son; he was in fact severing it. And though Martina knew he was no longer the husband and father he had once been, she felt anew the devastation of veering off the path of korima, on to an unfamiliar one she didn't know how to follow.

As she stood trying to decide whether to bring Jaime back down the steps or continue to challenge Luis, Jaime lifted his head and looked at the space around his father. Then he looked down the corridor, toward the school and the arroyo beyond. He seemed not to notice the dozen people now gathered around, completely motionless as they waited to see what would happen next.

He shrugged his shoulder, apparently wanting to free himself from his mother's grasp. At first, Martina only held him more tightly, but as he continued trying to move away from her, she worried that he would fall down the steps. She softened her grip and helped him turn, holding his hand as he descended the steps.

Martina thought he would stop and sit on the bottom step. She supposed he'd recognized his father's figure in the doorway and understood that he wouldn't be let in. But Jaime didn't stop. He turned and walked up the corridor with great effort, toward the asentamiento entrance. Martina started toward him, arms outstretched to guide him.

Let him, Luis said.

Partway up the corridor, Jaime, overcome by the effort required to walk, stopped to lean against the wall of a house. With Martina's arms on his shoulders, pressing him to the wall so he wouldn't fall forward, he slumped to the floor. He lay down and closed his eyes.

The wind picked up midmorning, lifting dust and carrying it through the asentamiento. Small tornados formed in the corridor, swirls of air thick with fine, gray particles. The dust stuck to the wet skirts hung out to dry. It got in Martina's eyes and somehow even on her teeth. Eugenia swept her front stoop, but it didn't make a difference. Minutes later, a thin layer had already settled on the steps.

Jaime lay on his side, his cheek against the cold cement. Though his eyes remained closed, his breathing never turned heavy, and Martina knew he was awake. She didn't touch him, not wanting to disturb him.

María José, unable to contain herself any longer, approached her sister with a cup of coffee. She wanted to offer to bring Jaime inside her house but wasn't sure if that would cause more problems with Luis. The best thing to do, she decided, was to reassure Martina that her son would be okay, that this, like every other problem, could be resolved. The first step was making Martina see that not all hope was lost.

Sister, he'll wake up and ask to come inside. You'll see, María José said.

Though her words didn't irritate Martina, she didn't find comfort in them either. She needed more than knowing he would wake up.

Will he do it again? Martina asked.

I don't know. I don't know, said María José.

Martina accepted the cup of coffee. She didn't take a sip. The coffee cooled as she continued to sit beside her son. Dust clouds covered the sun, the sky became pale, and wind gushed through the corridor. Somewhere in the desert, a tornado as tall as a mountain must have been swirling, picking up more and more dust and spreading it over the land.

Later, Martina went inside to help Manolo in the bathroom. When she returned, Jaime was gone.

Yellow brush, dry creek

[March 2010]

During the years when the mestizos pushed Rarámuri people out of line at the water pump, the arroyo had been their only source of drinking water. The summer rains had filled the creek, giving life to the nopales, wildflowers, herbs, and mesquite trees Rarámuri people sought for food, medicine, and shade. It was in the arroyo that the Rarámuri people built altars for their dead and called them to return to this world for one night on their death anniversaries, to laugh and dance with friends and family. It was there that Luis and Jaime, and other fathers and sons, ran the raipachis, the men's foot-races, keeping alive their connection with the land and Onorúame. This piece of land that resembled the Sierra had sustained the Rarámuri people who lived nearby in cardboard shacks and later in the cinder-block homes. Now, it was a place where boys went to sniff paint thinner, hidden away from their families.

Standing before the doorway to his house, Jaime had heard his father's voice as if from across a canyon. He didn't understand Luis's words in the moment, but he could discern a hard edge that frightened him. He wanted nothing more than to go inside and lay down on his mattress to wait till the dizziness faded, but he sensed that Martina didn't want him to move. She stood beside him, her hand on his shoulder, steadying him as the world spun. Coherent thoughts tried to form in his mind, but the chemicals he had inhaled stifled them, leaving him with only a sense of dread.

Before the abduction, Luis had patted his son on the shoulder each morning, a brief moment of affection before he went off to work for the day. Even when Jaime was still asleep, he had sensed Luis's warm hand on his head and had known that his father loved him. In the past month, Luis had only nodded at his son or ignored him entirely. The dread Jaime felt after hearing the harshness in his father's voice made him realize it wasn't the mattress and blanket he needed most, but his father's warmth.

When Luis came down the steps without saying a word to Martina or Jaime, Jaime understood that his father wanted nothing to do with him. Filled with shame, he found he couldn't bear to remain in El Oasis, where he was nothing more than a burden to his family. When Martina went inside, Jaime mustered the strength to get up and walk to the place where he'd gotten high hundreds of times, the place where he had also run with his father. His head throbbed and his vision was still blurred, but he walked as quickly as he could, eager to hide from his mother and the many neighbors whose eyes he felt burning him.

He descended the steep path, trying not to slip on rocks and empty water bottles. At the bottom, he walked through brush and litter until he arrived at one of the spots where Rarámuri boys gathered to sniff. At that early hour, there were a handful of teens on the ground, too high to move.

He sat down. Nausea overwhelmed him, and his head throbbed as the chemicals left his blood stream. Over the next hour, the nausea gradually wore off, and a painful ache settled in his stomach. The paint-thinner high never lasted more than an hour, which is why many boys kept a bottle of it with them throughout the day. Jaime lay on the ground and thought of his mother, who always had food prepared for this moment. His mother, who had tried to bring him home. This time, Jaime had allowed her to lead him like a little boy. The anger he felt toward her for treating him like a small child, not much older than Manolo, faded, and in its place he felt despair.

Eventually, Jaime slept. Around him, boys awoke and inhaled paint thinner from their plastic water bottles, the chemicals seeping through the blood-brain barrier. Their bodies soon felt heavy. They lay down again.

The sun sat at the top of the sky when Jaime awoke. The mesquite trees shaded him and the other boys from its piercing rays. The sun was warm that afternoon, and the air was gentle. The sunflower stalks, half as tall as Jaime, already had small green bulbs at their tips. At the depths of the arroyo, time was as still as a lake. The boys dozed as sparrows flew between mesquite trees, chirping. They couldn't hear the sounds of the cars and buses on the road above, or the boom boxes blaring narcocorridos from storefronts. They couldn't hear the vendors hawking used clothing, old appliances, scraps of metal, or anything else worth selling. Even after the arroyo became a place filled with trash, a place where Rarámuri children hid to get high, other Rarámuris came here to escape the forward motion of the city, and to feel the stillness that had filled their lives in the Sierra.

He woke with the same throbbing headache he had most mornings, and a hunger for his mother's bean burritos. Then he remembered what had happened earlier, with his father. His mind now clear, Jaime thought about what it meant that his father had denied him entry into their home. Even he knew it was something Rarámuri people never did to anyone, and especially not to one another.

Did this mean Luis never wanted to see Jaime again? Jaime lay still, thinking about what it would mean to leave his home and El Oasis forever. He didn't know of any other boy who had been kicked out of his home, so he didn't know where he would go. He would be forced to sleep in the arroyo and search for food in dumpsters, or to korimear and buy bags of chips for meals. He thought about Martina, the worry and fear she must be feeling. He supposed no one knew where he was.

Jaime never spoke in great detail about his struggle that day. Perhaps it was the memory of the Sierra, present in the arroyo, that gave him the strength to resist the paint thinner that long afternoon and evening. Jaime hadn't ever thought he could find solace or healing in land, the way his parents once had. He had hardly begun to learn that the land was a mother who would never give up on him when his family was forced to flee. Yet those early lessons Martina gave her children in the garden must have remained in him.

Jaime cried in the arroyo that evening, quiet tears he hid by burying his face in his arms. None of the other children seemed to notice. He knew only that he needed to return home and ask his family to accept him again. Without them, he was a mestizo, someone who had lost his way.

All day, Martina had prayed that Jaime would return home. She remained on the front stoop, hoping that if he wandered back into the corridor, he would see her and feel welcome to sit beside her. If Luis didn't let him back into the house, Martina would lay blankets outside and sit beside her son while he slept.

María José brought her cups of atole, which she sipped throughout the day. Manolo played in the corridor, falling asleep in Martina's arms in the early afternoon. The women who passed by said little to her, knowing that only her son's return would rid her of pain. Eugenia brought her mint tea and simply sat beside her. Only María José, who had watched everything unfold from her front stoop, was resolved to speak with Martina again about what she must do.

Sister, you're going to end up like María Cruz, she whispered. It was the most direct she had ever been in her criticism of the woman, whom she considered a friend. She hoped none of María Cruz's children would hear and report back to her.

If you don't put him to work, you're going to raise a grandchild on your own.

She was referring to what had happened with María Cruz's eldest daughter, who had abandoned her own child two years before and gone north to Ciudad Juárez with a mestizo. María Cruz was raising her grandson now. Abandoning a child—that's what Luis had done when he wouldn't let Jaime back in the house. Martina's anger toward him was so great, she wouldn't have returned home that night if not for Lupita and Manolo.

Let him work, let him be among the mestizos, or he'll keep turning on you, María José pleaded.

Martina, too tired to think beyond her son's safe return, stared at the floor and said nothing.

The sky turned the color of a pale desert rose, and still Jaime was not home. Luis returned when the cinder-block walls were bathed in pink light. He sat beside Martina on the front stoop, knowing she wouldn't go inside even if he insisted.

At work, Luis had thought about how unlike Martina it was to challenge anyone. Martina loved peace; every decision she made was in pursuit of a life lived according to korima. It was when she allowed this narrow pursuit to block out the realities of the mestizo world that Luis became angry with her. Martina rarely expressed an understanding of the way the mestizo world worked. Luis believed her adherence to korima was dangerous at times, and he felt he couldn't make her see that. But he had begun to wonder if his refusal to talk with Martina was driving her toward a new way of being he didn't know how to handle. She had shown him that morning that she could challenge him, and she might do it again. Luis thought an explanation for locking Jaime out could make her feel less angry, though he wasn't sure.

Jaime needs to understand how good it is to come home to a warm bed and a meal, Luis began, speaking quietly. He looked at the ground as he spoke. It was better to aim strong words at the ground, where they wouldn't hit the person directly. Like a mother shielding her children from pain, the ground could absorb the shock better than a person. Luis hadn't practiced this way of speaking in recent weeks; he'd aimed his harsh words at Martina and his children, not caring whether his anger rushed through their bodies and depleted the breaths Onorúame had blown into them.

He told Martina he had forbidden Jaime from entering because he wanted to scare him into submission. Nothing else they'd tried had worked, not the conversations or saving up for rehab. When Eugenia had locked her daughter inside the house a few months

before, her screams of anger could be heard throughout the asentamiento. Luis had been shocked, just like everyone else. But it had
worked. Eugenia's daughter had emerged too afraid to sniff paint
thinner or drink again.

Luis finished speaking and allowed a silence to sit between them.
He'd always found comfort in the silences he and Martina shared.
They were responsive silences, ones that tightened their bond. They
perfectly matched the stillness of the Sierra.

Martina was quiet now, but not because she was allowing Luis's
words to sink in. She had listened to Luis with the tentative hope
that he would express regret for his actions and offer a plan for finding Jaime. Now Martina was furious with herself for thinking once
again that he would behave in accordance with what they had promised Onorúame on the Virgen's feast day. His logic was dangerous,
Martina thought. She hadn't judged Eugenia for her harsh measures
before, believing her friend knew what was best for her children,
but now, Martina thought Eugenia had set a risky precedent for the
rest of the community. To lock children inside or to turn them away
was to restrict their movement. It made their adherence to korima
an obligation rather than a gift born of generosity. Korima wasn't a
set of rules; it was a spirit of giving that lived within the Rarámuri
people. Yes, Eugenia's method had worked for Nancy, and Jaime's
self-imposed periods of staying home seemed to have worked for
him, but what if another child reacted by leaving the community and
never returning? The point was, korima wasn't just about family;
it was about understanding that one person's well-being was connected to every other person's—and every other living being's, for
that matter. Eugenia's choices often looked like the smartest ones, in
the sense that they accomplished her short-term goals. But they cost
her in terms of relationships and the preservation of korima as the
central principle of her life. Luis's strategy, inspired by Eugenia, was
a breach of korima that didn't try to retain any aspect of their old
ways, as korimeando did. It was a severing of ties that might turn
Jaime away from them forever.

Luis, now sensing the tension in this new silence, spoke again.

Jaime will work with me, he said. *I'll keep him close. I'll be able to guide him better that way.*

For a moment, Martina considered telling Luis her thoughts in hopes that they could arrive at a decision together. Yet in locking Jaime out of the house, Luis had made clear that he was more interested in making decisions on his own. Martina, no longer caring if Luis turned her out of their home too, remained silent.

Martina spent the rest of the day sitting on the front stoop, waiting for Jaime to return so she could give him a bean burrito. She thought he was most likely in the arroyo, sleeping off his high. She wasn't sure searching for him would do any good; she suspected he would be too ashamed, and perhaps afraid, to come home after what his father had done. Martina sat outside so that if he did return, he would see her there, waiting with food. She planned to tell him that he could sleep at María José and Eduardo's house, an invitation that María José had extended after sharing her opinion about what should be done with Jaime. Martina would sit out all night and all day—however long it took. She thought some of the younger children who ventured into the arroyo to play would come upon Jaime and let him know she had food for him.

That evening, while Luis was watching TV and Lupita and Manolo were in bed, Martina got her wish. Jaime turned the corner and walked toward his mother. He moved timidly, head bowed, but Martina could immediately tell he wasn't high because he was walking in a straight line. She wanted to get up and hug him but restrained herself. Instead, she smiled and scooted over so he would have a place next to her on the stoop.

Jaime sat down and leaned against her. Martina, afraid to mother him too much, didn't put her arm around him. For a few minutes, they sat in silence. The voices of telenovela characters filtering through the barred windows were the only sounds in the corridor this late in the evening.

When Jaime spoke, in a whisper that made him sound no older than Manolo, it was to tell his mother that he wanted to stop using paint thinner, this time for good. He had a new plan for stopping, he went on to say.

I'm going to go to work with my father, he said, finally looking into her face to gauge her reaction.

It was as if Jaime's and Luis's paths were finally coming together, Martina thought. It gave her pause that they both saw work as the solution. Perhaps she had been wrong to insist he return to the Sierra, she now thought. Here was her son, coming to her with a solution that would give him something to focus on and likely keep him away from paint thinner, just as Luis had said.

Martina reassured Jaime that Luis would be open to this idea and that he would welcome hearing it directly from Jaime. She had understood from their talk that afternoon that Luis wouldn't turn him away again as long as he came back sober and promised to stop using for good. So when she opened the door and saw Luis turn away at the sight of his son, she felt her anger rise. What game was Luis playing? she wondered. Before she could decide how to respond, Jaime spoke.

Papá, he said, quietly.

Luis didn't turn around.

Papá, he tried again. *I'm sorry.*

Still Luis didn't turn.

Jaime couldn't tell what exactly Luis's silence meant. It made him nervous to speak, but he knew he had to keep going. If he let the silence linger, if he didn't break it silence with the right words, Jaime wasn't sure he would ever be welcome in his home.

Papá, after I finish the school year, I want to work with you, he said. He swung his arms slightly as he spoke, and his voice sounded small.

Luis did not turn. But after a few moments, he nodded slightly and pretended to consider Jaime's words. He didn't want to let on too soon how pleased he felt.

If you ever come home high again, you'll have no place here, he finally said in response.

Hot in the sun, cold in the shade
[March 2010]

After Jaime's return, Martina told herself she needed to make a decision about Eugenia's offer to set up shop with her. She had already let Miss Ceci know that Jaime wouldn't be accepting a scholarship for boarding school but Lupita would. With those questions settled, she returned to the urgent matter of earning money on her own. Jaime getting kicked out of the house had unsettled her; she felt powerless to stop terrible things from happening to her son, even at the hands of his father. The idea of having her own income and greater control over her life seemed even more appealing. She hadn't yet discussed Eugenia's proposal with Luis, and after seeing him shut out Jaime, she didn't intend to. He had decided how to handle their son without seeking to reach a consensus with her. She was afraid he would tell her he didn't want her selling her crafts, that she should stick to korimeando, but even more than that, she worried he was now completely disinterested in making decisions collaboratively. At this point, he seemed more likely to forbid Martina from doing something than to take the time to discuss it, as they always had before.

Martina was realizing that korimeando kept her dependent not just on mestizos, but also on Luis. It seemed the only way to gain some control over her family's well-being was to begin earning more money herself. That way she could make sure her children were properly fed, which was the very reason they had left the Sierra in the first place. Keeping them fed and growing was how she showed them that she loved them, and it was one of the best ways to teach them about korima; korima always began with lessons in giving. If she wanted to have any chance of keeping herself and her children tied to the ways of korima, she would have to find ways to teach them herself.

Even so, Martina continued to waver. She feared selling crafts could lead her family away from their Rarámuri identity, a kind of death she wasn't willing to risk. It was a question of deciding where she wanted to fit in, Martina concluded. In El Oasis, women were thought to belong to one of two camps: those who wanted to replicate the lifestyle of the Sierra as closely as possible, and those who believed that retaining Rarámuri identity required giving in to some aspects of modern living. Most women fell squarely into one camp or the other, though each sometimes had to make compromises, often due to scarcity or the desire to keep the system of reciprocity alive. Eugenia, for example, who was in business for herself, often had to give up spending time with other women in order to make enough crafts to sell. Giving her time to her business meant that she participated less in community cooking, races, and rituals. She was so devoted to her business that she wasn't teaching her daughters to sew, though she was proud that they were the best-fed children in El Oasis.

Like many women in El Oasis, Martina believed María Cruz and José's devotion to korima provided an excellent model for Rarámuri children, one reason the community had agreed that José should be made governor. Aligning herself with María Cruz put Martina on a moral high ground in the community. She had always felt some degree of guilt over having abandoned the Sierra, even though she repeatedly told herself and others that the lack of water and food had forced her family out. Being seen as a culture bearer in El Oasis helped her assuage that guilt, distance herself from the Rarámuris who, in her view, had gone too far toward assimilation, and make amends with Onorúame and the Virgen. Yet from the very beginning, she had found María Cruz's way of living too difficult to emulate. She also saw how it burdened other families: María

Cruz's refusal to korimear meant she relied on community members' korima to feed her six children when the mestizos didn't buy enough of her crafts. Martina knew the spirit of generosity was supposed to move her to give, and she often shared what she had with María Cruz, but she found she agreed with others who complained that María Cruz wasn't doing her part.

María Cruz wanted more children and thought family planning was the mestizos' way of controlling the Rarámuri people. Martina completely agreed. The vast majority of Rarámuri women felt certain the mestizos had infused the birth control injections they offered with a poison that would cause them to become very sick and perhaps even die. Hardly any of them used the mestizos' brightly colored cleaning solutions, either, even when they received them for free, believing them to be unnecessary at best, and poisonous at worst. Water alone was enough to keep her family clean, Martina was certain. María Cruz cooked outside more often than anyone else in the community, ignoring the mestizos' warnings that food scraps attracted vermin and campfires could spread to buildings. To them, families like hers were a health concern, their lifestyles likely to correlate with disease. There were two women with tuberculosis in El Oasis that year, and the city government came every week to try to convince them to accept treatment. When the women refused and said that their shaman was caring for them, the mestizos adjusted the focus of their talks on sanitation, explaining that they were trying to help prevent disease and even death. They didn't understand that Rarámuri perceptions of death were not the same as those in the capitalist world, where it was something to avoid at all costs. Rarámuris saw death as a continuation of life. María Cruz didn't want the mestizos to help her avoid dying; she wanted them to let her live as she wished.

Because of their close friendship, Martina was uncritical of the connections Eugenia made with the city and state government, NGOs, and the nonprofits to sell her crafts more widely and for more money. Though Eugenia was respectful of María Cruz's decisions—she, too, had been raised in the Sierra and had lived without the mestizos' soap, birth control, and stoves—she strongly believed that their best chances for cultural survival were tied to making enough money to move beyond always thinking about food, the same line of thinking that had led to the evolution of korimeando. When Rarámuri people were first displaced to the city, they had relied almost exclusively on korima to eat. Families in El Oasis suffered from malnutrition, just as they had in the Sierra. Men were the first to break with korima and obtain jobs as day laborers, in hopes that women and children wouldn't need to do the same, but from the beginning, they suffered wage theft and extortion. Then, in 1992, the state government had established the Coordinación Estatal de la Tarahumara, dedicated solely to the Rarámuri people, and they had gained greater access to shelter and food. Still, they felt trapped by their reliance on mestizos, especially because the state government decided the location and size of the asentamientos, as well as the rules for the community. For the women, it was this feeling of dependence, of impotence, that led to the evolution of korimeando. With their passage from the Sierra to the city, Rarámuri women had expanded the definition of korima to include korimeando as a means of seeking wealth redistribution from mestizos. Then, as Rarámuri people began to realize that they couldn't rely exclusively on gathering coins from mestizos, Rarámuri women began looking to further expand the definition of korimeando in a way that gave them more autonomy over their own lives.

By 2010, hundreds of Rarámuri women were fed up with korimeando, which kept them dependent on mestizos—and on their husbands. They had grown suspicious, too, of the NGOs and nonprofits that bought their crafts, since they were savvy enough to know they were keeping a cut of the profits. Seeking greater control over their labor and time, Rarámuri women began setting up tables to sell their wares throughout downtown Chihuahua City. Like many of the women who set up stalls downtown, Eugenia became convinced that the Rarámuris didn't need to be relegated to asentamientos. There was something more for them, but before they could begin to imagine what it might be, they needed to overcome food insecurity and addiction. The first step toward this goal, according to Eugenia, was to get the mestizos to take them seriously. For years, she had believed the easiest way to do that was to abide by their standards of behavior and cleanliness, even if she didn't share them. Though her Spanish was accented and she often struggled to find words, Eugenia was attentive to the way mestizas talked and tried to increase her vocabulary and emulate their way of speaking. She made sure to keep her house uncluttered, just as the mestizo government required, and she showered each day using soap. She also took care to add details to her crafts—extra embroidery, for example—to make them more appealing to potential mestizo buyers. As a result of her willingness to abide by their standards and speak Spanish, nonprofit workers knocked on Eugenia's door first when they came to El Oasis to buy crafts. She always had plenty of crafts ready to sell, unlike other women, who spent most of their time sewing dresses for themselves and to bet on the races. As a result of Eugenia's crafts-manship and preparedness, mestizos bought the most from her, which made Eugenia the wealthiest woman in El Oasis. She rarely struggled with food insecurity, unlike the vast majority of families in the asentamiento. While some, including María Cruz, criticized her for not sharing her wealth widely, Martina understood when her friend said it wasn't fair for others to take too much from her, espe-cially when they were just as capable as she was of improving their crafts and earning more money.

To further complicate Martina's decision-making, in 2010, the Coordinación Estatal de la Tarahumara and various nonprofits were taking note of the city-dwelling Rarámuri women who wanted to participate in the market economy and building relationships with them to bring greater attention to the Rarámuri peoples' story. State government officials hoped to gain Rarámuri women's trust and to bring them to city and state government events, where the women would share their stories and perspectives, as well as take photos with government officials. These events would possibly be publicized in the national news and gain more attention from the federal government, which did not offer financial support to the

Coordinación Estatal de la Tarahumara. The city and state officials believed publicity would help garner visibility, empathy, and more financial support so that they could continue delivering aid to the Sierra and building asentamientos in Chihuahua City and Ciudad Juárez.

That's what they said, at least, though it's perhaps also true that the city and state government officials saw the publicizing of Rarámuris' stories as a way to attract more national and international tourists. The state had emblazoned their license plates with an image of a Rarámuri woman in traditional dress, and they were now running national and international TV and magazine advertisements for ecotourism in the Sierra. The state government hoped to attract more tourists especially to the Chihuahua al-Pacifico railway, a train that traversed the Sierra Tarahumara from Chihuahua City to Los Mochis, Sinaloa, a coastal city on the Sea of Cortéz. The railway, known colloquially as El Chepe, began in the late 1800s as a way for locals to move between Chihuahua and Sinaloa and to transport their goods, but since the 1950s, the state government had sought to make the passenger train a luxury experience, complete with a restaurant and upscale sleeping cars. The most popular stop on the El Chepe was at Divisadero, close to the town of Creel, where train riders often stayed at the Hotel Mirador, a small luxury hotel perched at the edge of the Copper Canyon. From this hotel, mestizo guides took tourists to see Rarámuri people living in nearby caves, where the families hoped they would receive tips from the tourists. The mestizos also sold tickets to the aerial tram that crossed the canyon, from which tourists could look down and see Rarámuri people struggling to grow their gardens. Aside from the stunning views of the Sierra Tarahumara, a major selling point of the railway was to give tourists access to an Indigenous people who had long resisted contact with the outside world, and whose way of living in the Sierra had remained largely unchanged since they first retreated to the mountains. The romance of this promise appealed widely; in 2010, El Chepe carried passengers from all over Latin America, the US, Canada, Europe, and Australia. The state government's logic to

this plan was that attracting tourists to the region brought in revenue to help the local economy. Job creation in the Sierra was supposed to help Rarámuri people who were no longer able to grow
their own crops. In El Oasis, however, the consensus was that these
developments in the Sierra were set up to benefit mestizos and further harm the land and the Rarámuri people. Rarámuri families in
the asentamiento who had been displaced from the Copper Canyon
region spoke of the sewage water that the Hotel Mirador dumped
into the Copper Canyon, further contaminating the land that should
have grown food for the Rarámuri people.

It was the continued destruction of the Sierra under the guise of
progress that made the Rarámuri people distrust the Coordinación
Estatal de la Tarahumara and other mestizos who claimed to do
good for the Rarámuris, including the half-dozen nonprofits in the
state dedicated to working with the Rarámuri people. Dozens of
families in El Oasis refused to even acknowledge the workers from
the Coordinación Estatal de la Tarahumara who came to El Oasis
to speak with families about the services they offered. Many families interacted with the Coordinación Estatal de la Tarahumara only
when they brought food to the community, and this was only because
they could not make enough to feed their families by korimeando
and day labor alone.

The government's and the nonprofits' message—that a future
was possible for the Rarámuri people if they supported themselves
through the making and selling of crafts—resonated with Eugenia
from the very beginning. By selling the items they made, Rarámuri
women could avoid assimilating into minimum wage jobs that
required them to wear uniforms. They would no longer need to
korimear and could work on their crafts at home while watching
over their children. Despite advantages like these, there were many
women who, like María Cruz, remained suspicious of the mestizo government and refused to interact with them other than to
accept donations. For Eugenia, the question was to what degree she
was willing to cooperate with the nonprofits and the Coordinación
Estatal de la Tarahumara. On a few occasions, each entity had invited

her to city council meetings and had asked her to pose for photographs with government officials. She had agreed to do so, but these interactions made her uncomfortable. She felt out of place among the government officials, the men in suits and ties and the women in pencil skirts and heels. She also wasn't entirely sure to whom her photograph would be shown, and what they would say about her. She would have preferred to simply make her crafts and sell them without having to repay the government by showing up at their meetings and posing for photos.

Eugenia didn't make these feelings known to the government officials, and the Coordinación Estatal de la Tarahumara and nonprofit agencies became only more encouraged by what they perceived to be Eugenia's trust in them. When nonprofit workers visited El Oasis in 2010, they kept an eye out for Rarámuri women who they thought would be receptive to selling their crafts to them and who could be groomed to appear at events, give interviews, and have their photographs taken—though these goals were never shared with the Rarámuri women up front. Seeing Eugenia's financial status improve made a small but growing number of Rarámuri women accept that selling crafts to nonprofits was a safer way to earn more money—though this didn't mean that the women were willing to make every item the nonprofits requested. The nonprofit workers also needed women who would be willing to take some direction from the workers as they came up with new ways to fuse everyday mestizo items with Rarámuri designs, in addition to producing high-quality crafts. It was when they suggested stitching triangles onto T-shirts that some women drew a line—including Eugenia. To women like María Cruz and María José, it was one thing to make a tortillero or set of napkins with the image of a Rarámuri woman; these were household items that Rarámuris didn't use, and were therefore seen as products made specifically for mestizo buyers. Distinguishing between mestizo products and the baskets and pots the Rarámuri women made for their own use was important because it meant that the Rarámuri artisans were not selling the items that had cultural value; they were simply creating products with designs invented to appeal to mestizo buyers. Putting Rarámuri mountains and paths on mestizo clothing, however, came dangerously close to blending the two groups. The mountains and paths sewn onto their own clothing told the Rarámuri peoples' story of continuity. What would it mean for the mestizas to wear clothes with the Rarámuri peoples' story on it? The mestizas couldn't have it all, María José said.

In El Oasis, the nonprofit buyers found two women willing to work with them on a consistent basis: Eugenia and Gloria, both about the same age. Eugenia and Gloria vied with each other to create the most beautiful crafts, and to sell the highest number of them to the nonprofit workers. So far, it was Eugenia's crafts they preferred, which made her feel proud. Eugenia added beaded earrings and necklaces to each of her dolls—an investment in time and effort that Gloria wasn't always willing to make. She gave her dolls smiles instead of straight lines, and often depicted the women carrying babies in rebozos, details the mestizo buyers loved. Eugenia wanted to keep her edge—yet another reason to set up a stall in downtown Chihuahua City. That way, the Coordinación Estatal de la Tarahumara would see her not just as a Rarámuri seamstress who could take direction, but as an entrepreneur capable of surviving on her own. She wanted their respect, if only to prove to herself that she didn't need to depend on government aid or nonprofit buyers to make ends meet. So strong was her ambition to stand alone as a business owner that she dreamt of a day when she could raise her prices and edge out Gloria altogether. Though Eugenia was motivated to invite Martina to go into business with her in part because she wanted to help her friend, she had developed a sense of fierce competition against Gloria, the only woman who could match her in artisanry. Gloria, who was raising three daughters and two sons, resented Eugenia's competitive spirit. Sometimes she walked to Eugenia's house, banged on the door, and yelled at her for hoarding all the money. Eugenia yelled back that it wasn't her fault Gloria's crafts paled in comparison to hers. The mestizos decided which they liked best, and those were the ones they bought.

In fact, one of the nonprofits that bought frequently from Eugenia and Gloria had set its sights on making Eugenia the face of Rarámuri crafts. The organization wanted to increase its visibility throughout the state, in the hopes that the publicity would increase sales. The nonprofit had plans to increase its social media presence and distribute pamphlets and flyers throughout the city advertising the crafts it sold in its store, and featuring Eugenia seemed like a natural choice: she could be taught to pose, the mestizos believed, and would be able to handle the pressure of having her face and story on widely circulated publicity materials. The nonprofit buyers believed that they could garner empathy and sales by telling the stories of the artisans whose work they sold, and they believed that Eugenia was likely to be forthcoming about her story of displacement to the city. Though Eugenia didn't have much of a concept of the reach of this publicity—she had never been on the internet or traveled beyond the Sierra and Chihuahua City—she felt it necessary to trust the mestizos. Without them, she would be back in the situation she had encountered when she first arrived to Chihuahua City: with no choice but to korimear, hoping the mestizos would take pity on her and give her enough coins for some beans.

Martina knew Eugenia and Gloria fought, but she didn't fully grasp why they were so fiercely competitive. To her, the amount of planning and work both women put into craft-making for mestizos seemed absurd, especially when it took them away from community gatherings and dressmaking. The crafts themselves were not items Rarámuri women used in their own households, in the Sierra or in the city. Tortilleros, placemats, tablecloths, aprons, and pillowcases—they were all mestizo objects with the Rarámuri story stitched onto them. Martina didn't particularly enjoy making them either. She loved dressmaking, beadwork, and weaving baskets, all of which resulted in items she personally used.

To Eugenia, stitching the Rarámuris' story onto mestizo crafts was a compromise, similar to korimeando. It required a degree of assimilation into the market economy, but Rarámuri women had some control over the terms. Eugenia thought making crafts was safer and much more enjoyable than korimeando. She enjoyed coming up with scenes to stitch and had even become known for one in particular: a mother carrying a baby in a rebozo, with wild-flowers forming a wreath around them. She distinguished between dressmaking for herself and making crafts for mestizos: while the dresses were made according to her own preferences and inherently told Rarámuri stories, the crafts portrayed an image of the Rarámuri people that was palatable for mestizo audiences. Through trial and error, she had learned that mestizos liked the image of a Rarámuri woman carrying a baby, as opposed to a Rarámuri standing alone. Perhaps this was because the mestizos liked to see the folkloric way the mothers carried their children, in rebozos slung across their backs. The mestizos liked to romanticize Indigenous cultures, so Eugenia and other women included wreaths of flowers and bright suns.

Eugenia and Gloria both envisioned a future in which Rarámuri women could work at home, sewing crafts they could sell to mestizos at a fair price. The future seemed viable, if only more Rarámuri women were willing to cooperate with the nonprofits and the Coordinación Estatal de la Tarahumara, and develop the vision and drive to make better crafts. Eugenia and Gloria were frustrated that the rest of the community didn't see that building a fruitful future required work up front and a small degree of assimilation. They might have to sacrifice time spent sewing or cooking together, but to Eugenia and Gloria, the sacrifice was worth it. With enough effort now, their businesses would one day be established, and they could then dedicate more time to the community events and rituals José and Lucero organized.

Hay que seguir luchando, Martina sometimes told herself in Spanish. It was a phrase she had learned from María José, who had heard it from the mestiza whose house she cleaned. *We have to keep struggling.* The mestiza woman repeated it whenever María José brought up her community's struggles: drug addiction, and earning enough money to pay for food, electricity, and water. She explained that adopting this mindset would give the Rarámuri people a sense of control over their own futures. Instead of giving up, the mestiza said, the Rarámuri women needed to internalize the belief that their destiny was to continue struggling for progress. The mestizos had adopted this mindset throughout the course of Mexico's history, believing that the country's path to an industrialized, light-skinned future was a struggle that they could not give up. That the Rarámuri people didn't want progress—that they saw progress as a goal possible only under linear time—didn't seem to matter to the mestiza who doled out this unsolicited advice.

Martina repeated the phrase in hopes that she would feel the same energy rise in her body and spirit as she did during a race, when women yelled *weriga* and *weh-mah*. Those commands, which Martina shouted even when her heart pumped too hard against her chest and her knees shook, reminded her that her peoples' story didn't have a beginning, middle, and end. It was continuous. To run faster and be stronger, as the words said, made Martina feel that she could run forever, and that her ancestors and family would carry her through anything. *Hay que seguir luchando,* on the other hand, carried a wariness Martina found appropriate for her new life in the city. On the day when she finally started thinking about Eugenia's offer again, her existential questions about how to be a Rarámuri woman in the city no longer seemed to matter. It was like when she sent Lupita out to korimear: she had deliberated for months only to find she had known all along what choice she had to make.

It took just over a week for Martina to make enough crafts to sell at the market alongside Eugenia. She had skipped korimeando on several occasions in order to make tortilleros, dolls, and aprons. In total, she had eleven items to sell. She couldn't tell if selling these crafts would bring her more than korimeando, but she thought it was worth sacrificing korimeando to try. If she made at least as much money as she did korimeando, Martina figured she could at least spend less time on the streets and more time sewing on her front stoop. Finally, on the morning of March 20, the women left the asentamiento carrying plastic shopping bags filled with crafts, two long blankets, and two pails on which to sit. Eugenia had insisted they shouldn't sit on the ground; mestizos would respect them more if they sat on some sort of stool or chair. Martina thought Eugenia had strong instincts, so she did whatever she said without questioning it. She had even worn one of her best dresses rather than one stained with car exhaust from hours spent korimeando, Eugenia's logic being that mestizos would be drawn to Rarámuri sellers who presented themselves as if they knew their value. This logic was lost on Martina, but the instructions were simple enough to follow. Martina had only three dresses she didn't wear korimeando, and she chose a forest-green one with mountains the color of the sunflowers that grow in the arroyo during summer.

Lupita and Manolo accompanied Martina. Normally, Lupita would have been taking advantage of the long breakfast line at the KFC drive-through, but Martina had told her to take the day off, thinking she would probably make enough money to go without Lupita's earnings. Both Eugenia's daughters joined them, since Eugenia didn't want to leave them alone in El Oasis on a Saturday, when she felt adolescents had too much time on their hands. *Go play at the park*, Martina said to Lupita, gesturing to a patch of grass at the center of which stood a monument to a Mexican general. Lupita beamed at her mother—it was the first time in so long that Martina had encouraged her to go off and play—then took Manolo's hand and walked toward the park, followed by Eugenia's daughters.

Standing behind the small folding table lent to her by Eugenia, which she had carried on the bus, her crafts displayed before her in neat rows, Martina found she felt a sense of pride she hadn't expected. Under Eugenia's guidance, she had learned to create scenes of Rarámuris in the Sierra. She'd sat beside Eugenia for hours learning to embroider, a new technique for her. Now, spread before her for the mestizos to see, were the tortilleros, aprons, and table runner she'd made, decorated with Rarámuri mothers and babies encircled by garlands of flowers.

Martina was still soaking in these pleased feelings when an elderly mestiza with red lips and a black handbag approached her table: her first potential customer. Panicking, Martina adjusted one of the tortilleros so the mestiza could get a better look at the woman and child walking through a field of wildflowers. Not knowing what else to do, she put her hands by her sides and returned the woman's smile with her own faint one.

Other Rarámuri vendors had bought fluorescent stickers and written on the prices for each craft. But Eugenia and Martina hadn't yet caught on to this strategy. Soon enough, the woman held up a tortillero and asked Martina the question she had come to loathe when selling monitos on the city streets: *How much?*

Sixty pesos, answered Martina in the clearest voice she could muster. It was the price she and Eugenia had settled on, but saying it out loud filled her with anxiety; she didn't know if she was selling the tortillero for too much or too little. Though she wasn't aware of it, Martina was experiencing the same worries Lupita had felt shopping in the Soriana on her own for the first time. Both had felt uncertain trying to place monetary value on items, not knowing what constituted a fair price or how, exactly, to make sure one wasn't getting stiffed. Eugenia always accepted the prices the NGO workers proposed, so they had agreed to sell their crafts for those same amounts, but neither woman could be sure they were appropriate for a table set up downtown. In any case, Eugenia had coached Martina not to lower any price by more than ten pesos.

I can give you thirty pesos, the woman said without missing a beat.

What came after thirty? Numbers flew out of Martina's head when she was nervous.

Forty pesos, she responded, a note of uncertainty in her voice.

She accepted the bills and coins without counting them, not realizing the mestiza might have shorted her, and offered her a small plastic bag for the tortillero.

Martina rearranged the tortilleros to fill the gap left by the one she had just sold. Her first sale as the owner of a stall downtown—Martina could hardly believe it. It hadn't been much worse than selling a monito; the woman had accepted her counteroffer. It felt good to place the tortillero in a plastic bag, a detail Eugenia had thought of at the last minute, grabbing a handful of old Soriana shopping bags and telling Martina mestizos liked their purchases packaged that way. It seemed like nonsense to Martina, but she was willing to learn. Now, she made a note to start saving plastic bags herself, so she wouldn't have to ask Eugenia to share hers.

A block away, Calle Libertad was bustling with mestizo and Rarámuri sellers and shoppers. While Eugenia enjoyed the lively energy of downtown Chihuahua, especially on weekends, Martina had always avoided the shopping district in the past. She found the crowds overwhelming, the streets dirty, and the rules for buying and selling confusing and frustrating. In the brick-and-mortar stores, Martina had long ago observed that mestizos didn't negotiate; it was only at the stalls set up outside that they bartered to lower the prices. Martina felt this was unjust. Why should the mestizos pay the asking price inside stores, but not the prices set by artisans, many of whom were Rarámuri? After her first customer, Martina realized Eugenia was right; she needed to be more vocal and argumentative with the mestizos, or their business would never be successful.

Martina felt her confidence increasing all morning as she resisted the mestizas who attempted to bargain with her. When a mestiza asked her to lower the price of an item, Martina pointed at it and said, *Mucho trabajo,* which translated to *a lot of work.* To emphasize her point, she lifted the tortillero and pointed to the hand-stitched mountains and doll. *Hecho a mano,* she said in a whisper, breathing in sharply afterward to emphasize her point. She wanted the mestiza to appreciate her embroidery, but defending her work made her nervous, as if she were defying her. In a way, she was: mestizos throughout Mexico were accustomed to driving down prices for artisan products created by Indigenous people.

In the early afternoon, a mestiza with a short column of brown hair set firmly in place by her perm insisted on buying all the tortilleros with purple flowers for half the stated price. She was Martina's hardest test of the day, her tone growing more authoritative and demanding throughout the interaction. She held up one of the tortilleros to Martina's face, leaning halfway across the table and demanding that Martina sell it along with the others for fifty pesos. At that point, Martina became frightened. She took out a plastic bag and handed the tortilleros to the woman, wanting her to leave already. Then she turned around, unable to reach out her hand to accept the payment. The woman threw the money on the table and left.

Martina, worried that Eugenia would start to see her as an unfit business partner, said, *That woman made me nervous with her witch laugh. She would have cursed me if I didn't give her what she wanted.*

At least she only took a few, responded Eugenia, smiling ruefully.

The mestizas she had sold monitos to for ten pesos each had often haggled with her over the price. Martina had found it unjust and infuriating, but now, there was more money at stake, and she couldn't bear the thought of another loss like this one. She'd given up too many hours of korimeando to learn to embroider nearly as beautifully as Eugenia. She'd been more careful about her spending on food, especially since Luis was keeping money for beer. She'd denied herself and her children the raspados and bottles of Coke that broke up the forward motion of the day.

Selling in the marketplace wasn't like korimeando. She couldn't avert her eyes and allow her dress to communicate what she wanted. By acting submissive, she had stoked the mestiza's boldness. What if she returned the next week and demanded the same low price? If she was going to be successful alongside Eugenia, she would need to stand firm and refuse sales to those who asked for unfair prices. She might even need to scream like Eugenia did if a mestiza ever tried to steal one of her crafts. She promised herself she would learn new words in Spanish so she could tell the mestizas what she really thought of their behavior, should it ever be necessary. Martina was done being taken advantage of.

At the end of the day, Martina and Eugenia discreetly counted their earnings behind their tables. At first Martina was sure she'd miscounted, so great was the number. She counted again. Five hundred pesos. It was more than she earned in two weeks korimeando, and it had been just one day. She could buy ground beef and avocado and make tacos for dinner that night, and she would still have enough money left over for the week's groceries.

Eugenia fared a little better than Martina, with six hundred pesos. Elated, the women packed up the crafts they hadn't sold and made plans to return the next day. As they walked down Calle Libertad to catch the bus in front of the cathedral, Martina thought that perhaps with this money she would finally be able to send Jaime to rehab if he relapsed again. She hoped Luis's tactic had been enough and that it would set Jaime on a new path, but she wasn't sure. She wanted to be prepared in case he needed the help.

Thinking of Luis, she realized he would find it odd if she showed up with ground beef and avocados that night. He'd want to know how much money she'd earned at the stall. Perhaps he would want to take some for beer, and not just one can.

The aroma of meat frying on open griddles filled the air. Martina saw some Rarámuri women and their children sitting with steak tacos. She rarely bought meals from restaurants.

Let's eat here, Martina said, her voice light. As she, Eugenia, and their children sat on Calle Libertad with Styrofoam plates of tacos, Martina decided she would put some money in a satchel and keep it in her scrap bag, where Luis never looked. It would be money not for spending, she told herself, but for safekeeping.

Blowing winds

[March and April 2010]

In the spring, the winds blew across the desert floor. They lifted the dust from the ground, swept around buildings, and tore through El Oasis, pulling skirts off the clothing lines and flinging them across the asentamiento. *The wind is playing*, the Rarámuris said, laughing as they retrieved their skirts from corners of the settlement. *The dirty wind*, the mestizos said, taking hoses and soap to their cars to wash off films of dust.

Though each group perceived the wind differently, it lived within both of them. The mestizos contained wind from the demon and Onorúame, and that's why they rejected the Rarámuris and the teachings of korima. Still, the Rarámuris believed they were capable of embodying korima, if only they ignored the demon wind swirling within them. It was the demon that made the Rarámuris view the spring winds blowing across the desert as a nuisance. The Rarámuris believed the winds, like water, fire, and land, expressed themselves with their movements. In March, the winds blew with urgency to remind the Rarámuris and the mestizos that Holy Week, Semana Santa, the most important cleansing ritual of the Catholic calendar, fell on the week of March 28th.

Semana Santa led up to the crucifixion of Jesus Christ on Good Friday, followed by the resurrection on Easter Sunday. In the days leading up to the crucifixion, the Catholic Church asked the devoted to focus on penitence for the sins that had made Christ's sacrifice necessary. In Mexico, the government had declared Semana Santa a national holiday, so businesses closed, traffic decreased, and forward time slowed nearly to a halt. Many mestizos took the week to leave the city and vacation at the beach or one of the thousands of small towns in the country where the sense of time felt gentler.

For the Rarámuris who now lived in the city, Semana Santa was also now the only prolonged period during which they could experience the stillness of circular time. It was another kind of reset for their community, a long pause that allowed them to reflect. The resets they experienced each week through sewing and running were brief interruptions to their workdays, which helped the Rarámuri women resist the rush of urban life. During Semana Santa, however, the deep boom of the drum mixed with the wind embodied the deeper stillness the Rarámuris sought, one that went against the grain of capitalist time, against the destruction of the Sierra and the Rarámuri people. Just as they perceived the wind differently than the mestizos, they saw a different meaning than penitence in Semana Santa.

For the Rarámuris, the ceremonies during Semana Santa were a way of purging themselves of the sins of colonization. Penitence was too passive for them; ridding themselves of the oppressors' sins, rather than repenting, allowed them to move closer to a future that saw their people free.

With her earnings from selling crafts downtown, Martina could afford to buy fabric for a new dress without worrying about taking food away from her children. She had sold her crafts on only three days, but already she had made the eight hundred pesos she needed for the fabric. She had collected, in total, about one thousand eight hundred pesos, almost triple what she collected in one month korimeando. The amount astonished her, and though Eugenia tried to look nonchalant, the sum astonished her as well. Eugenia warned Martina that their sales might be due to the fact that Semana Santa was about to start, and mestizos were feeling more generous. It could also be due to the fact that there were more visitors in town on holiday, since many businesses throughout the country shut down in religious observance. Martina hardly paid attention to Eugenia's attempts to temper her excitement. All she thought about was the fabric she would buy for new dresses for herself and Lupita. Besides, the Coordinación Estatal de la Tarahumara always delivered more meals to the community during Semana Santa, to help sober up the many people who drank heavily during this off week and alleviate the burden of providing extra meals when school was out of session. She figured that with the amount she had made, she would be able to buy the things she needed—new jelly sandals for Lupita, shampoo, soap for the dishes and clothing—and still have money left over.

Luis didn't know about her new business venture; Martina had asked Eugenia and María José not to tell their own husbands about her involvement, and she'd also asked Lupita and Manolo not to mention to their father where they'd gone each Saturday and Sunday morning. So far, Luis had not asked after their whereabouts. Martina supposed he no longer cared, and resented him even more. Still, she felt guilty asking her children to lie. Then she thought about the control her income gave her over her time, and how it enabled her to focus more energy on teaching her children about korima. After just two weekends, Martina's concerns about the ethics of setting up a stall seemed to have gone. Now, she felt the market economy could work in her peoples' favor if they were willing to make some concessions. It seemed to her that Eugenia was right—partial assimilation was not a form of death but a means of survival. Under this logic, the lie of omission seemed like a small price to pay.

Making a habit of setting aside time to produce and sell crafts wasn't as arduous as Martina had expected, at least not so far. She had promised herself not to skip community events, as Eugenia and Gloria often did. So far, she'd been able to make enough items by reducing her hours spent korimeando. She still made sure to go out for a couple hours most days, just in case her sales weren't as strong the following weekend. It helped, too, that the police didn't think to stop her and extort money from her. Luis had no idea that she was earning so much, since she shared only her wages from korimeando and a small portion of what she earned through sales. The solution wasn't perfect; Martina still contended with rude mestizos who pressured her to lower her prices. Yet she'd managed to earn enough to buy fabric for new dresses for her and Lupita and a few necessary household items, and still save some of the money, something she'd never before been able to do. For the first time, she felt some security and a sense of autonomy over her own future.

In previous years, Martina had had to save for months to buy new fabric for her and Lupita's Semana Santa dresses and had sometimes been able to afford only the cheapest cotton, which became discolored after just one wash. Now, with eight hundred pesos in her satchel, Martina knew she would be able to buy the best cotton for not only the dresses but also the loincloths she planned to make for Jaime and Manolo. She wasn't too worried about Luis noticing the new clothing; he didn't seem to pay much attention to what she and the children did these days and now spent most of his afternoons by the arroyo, drinking and talking with his friends. His absence was the only thing that took some of the pleasure out of Martina's increased income, but she tried to block out the sadness it made her feel. It seemed there was nothing she could do about the situation. So instead, she put all her energy into getting ready for Semana Santa, planning to skip korimeando on the last Tuesday of March, to go shopping for fabric with Eugenia. She wanted to make dresses that draped like bells, in thick cotton that swayed only slightly when they walked and the boldest colors she could find.

Telas Parisina was a sea of bolts of fabric grouped by their styles—Egyptian cotton, California cotton, poplin, organza, rayon, and polyester. Martina wandered the aisles, relishing the wide array of prints and colors, trying to picture her new dress in each of them. This time, she didn't pay too much mind to the cartoon images of a Rarámuri woman that marked the laminated cards indicating different cotton and polyester-blend fabrics. They were the mestizos' way of signaling to Rarámuri shoppers where their preferred fabrics were located. Though Martina knew she would end up buying forty meters of the California cotton, a fabric that didn't get washed out and had nice weight to it, she felt luxurious browsing the velvet, silk, and sequined bolts, rubbing the fabric with her forefinger and thumb as she had seen mestizas do.

María José and Eugenia had gone directly to the counter to ask the saleswoman to cut forty meters of floral fabric they had chosen on a previous trip to Telas Parisina. Martina wasn't sure what she wanted, but she didn't feel pressured to make a choice. She knew that whatever fabric she chose, she wanted Manolo to wear a blouse in a matching color, so everyone at the ceremonies would see that one of the youngest dancers belonged to her, a Rarámuri mother raising her children in accordance with korima. For weeks, Martina had been asking Manolo if he wanted to dance matachines with the Rarámuri men in the schoolyard. Yes, he responded eagerly. He and other young children filled plastic bottles with pebbles, then shook them like the men's rattles, stomping hard on the ground. They didn't yet understand that they, too, were keepers of the land, but this play prepared them for the lessons their fathers would teach them.

Twenty minutes later, María José and Eugenia checked in their purchases with the security guard at the front door and joined Martina in wandering the store. Mexican pop ballads played softly from the speakers, a backdrop to the sounds of mestizas giving their sizes to the saleswomen and scissors snipping through fabric. Rarámuris from other asentamientos shopping for fabric greeted Martina, María José, and Eugenia with *cuira*, their peoples' word for *hello*.

Martina had a list of five fabric options in her head, but she didn't want to rush to make a decision. She moved between the five bolts of fabric, trying to decide if she should sacrifice the California cotton for a lower-quality fabric with a print she liked, red hibiscus against a jungle green. That fabric would be beautiful for Good Friday, the day of the cleansing, but Martina was worried it wouldn't look so vibrant after a wash. Finally, having consulted with María José and Eugenia, she chose a deep-purple California cotton with bright-yellow sunflowers. In a section filled with polyester fabrics in solid colors, she chose a phosphorescent green for the road and white for the mountains. The dress would look like late summer in the Sierra, her favorite time of year, a time that meant Onorúame was blessing them with a harvest.

In mid-March, mestizos from local TV stations arrived at El Oasis to request permission to film the Semana Santa festivities. They approached José, who listened patiently as they described the importance of televising the rituals of Chihuahua's first peoples. The journalists told José they wanted mestizos to take pride in the Rarámuri culture that made the state unique, and the best way for them to reach audiences was by broadcasting footage. As good as their intentions may have been, José understood they were building their own careers by filming his people. Besides, many of the articles they published focused on drug problems rather than cultural traditions, even though they promised every year to write respectfully about the community. José found these articles inconsiderate and inaccurate, and so did the rest of the community. He faced pressure from a handful of community members to ban the journalists from the Semana Santa festivities altogether, but it wasn't so simple. Receiving press, even bad press, brought donations in the form of clothing and food. Even José, who believed that the Rarámuri people were capable of making their own solutions, recognized that these donations helped many families.

José allowed the journalists to give their explanations, then pretended to think carefully about his decision. Sometimes he sent them away and asked them to come back the next day for his response, his way of making them feel they did not have the right to his peoples' stories, even if they asked permission before arriving to film. In the end, though, he always said yes, because he believed what the journalists said: putting the Rarámuris' stories out into the world was one of their best strategies for eliciting monetary support and kind words from the mestizos. Thousands of mestizos in Chihuahua didn't even know the asentamientos existed, much less what they were called or where they were located. This was especially true of El Oasis, since Colonia Martín López had a reputation in the city as a neighborhood where people were so desperate for money that they would rob anyone. Television appearances brought an awareness José thought was vital. When the journalists came to record, the Rarámuris of El Oasis held up a white flag with the words "El Oasis: Un Asentamiento Tarahumara" written on it in thick red permanent marker, so people watching them on TV would know the name of their community. Though the Rarámuri people referred to themselves by the name Onorúame had given them, on their flag they used Tarahumara, the name the Spaniards had given them and the one by which they were known to mestizos.

The community was divided over the mestizos' request to film their rituals. Their first year in El Oasis, Martina and Luis had both felt the filming was a form of stealing, even if the mestizos had asked permission. They also hadn't felt moved by the sight of the flag, at first because they hadn't known what it said, since they couldn't read, and then, after María José told them, because they found it superfluous. In the Sierra, no one brought a flag with the name of the municipality to Semana Santa festivities. The names imposed by the chabochis delineated borders the Rarámuris ignored, knowing they were part of the reducción tactic. Martina and Luis had thought the flag was there solely for mestizos watching on their TVs and saw it as one step too far. Martina and Luis believed these cleansing rituals belonged to the Rarámuris. Their Semana Santa festivities were not a spectacle for the outside world, and they were certainly not an advertisement to increase the Rarámuris' likelihood of receiving help from mestizos.

Over the next three years, as Martina began to see korimeando as a form of resistance rather than alms-seeking, she had changed her mind about the flag. Now, she thought it was a way of proclaiming the Rarámuris' presence in the city. Just like the elderly woman she had seen when Martina and her family had first arrived from the Sierra, standing in front of the OXXO entrance and insistently saying *korima*, this flag filled mestizos' TV screens and forced them to accept the city as shared territory. Martina found she looked forward to seeing it at the Semana Santa festivities.

By the end of the third week of March, with only two days before the start of Holy Week, Martina had washed Luis's tagolá, the white linen loincloth that Rarámuri men wore in the Sierra, and sewn him a headband out of the same blue floral fabric she had used for her dress. He had mentioned that he planned to dance matachines along with the other men, and that he planned to play the role of a fariseo, news Martina received with surprise and some warmth. In the narrative that played out during Holy Week, the fariseos defended Jesus Christ from Judas Iscariot's soldados, who sought to kill Jesus Christ. In this ritual dance, which played out over the course of the week, Jesus Christ symbolized the Rarámuris' closeness to Onorúame. The fariseos defended this relationship from the soldados, who represented the chabochis intent on killing the Rarámuris.

To dance as a fariseo, then, was to promise to protect the Rarámuri people and their ways. Martina was delighted because she thought this might have meant that Luis was renewing his vow not only to his community, but to his family. Being a fariseo required discipline the entire week; Luis would not be allowed to drink alcohol, and he would be responsible for setting a strong example to the younger children. Though he had danced in previous years, Martina had thought that this year he might refuse and instead spend the days sitting by the arroyo. He wouldn't work during the week, since the entirety of Mexico shut down for observance. Martina thought that if he was going to dance, he should be dressed like the rest of the family, especially Manolo, whom he was supposed to teach about the cleanse and its importance for their souls.

Martina had made a tagolá for Jaime too. He hadn't danced since before he started using paint thinner, but this year, in an effort to stay in good standing with his father and keep his place at home, he had volunteered to participate as a fariseo. He still cringed at the thought of wearing the tagolá, his bare chest painted with white spots for the reporters and the mestizos watching at home to see.

Proclaiming Rarámuri identity still seemed to him to go hand in hand with a future of extortion and humiliation. But at this point, if it meant pleasing his parents and doing his part to keep the family peace, Jaime was willing.

For the past few weeks, Jaime had stuck to his routine: school, then home. On weekends, he wandered the colonia looking at graffiti art but stayed away from the arcade and the arroyo. It seemed his father's tactic had scared him straight, though it hadn't done much to bring them closer. Instead of feeling eager for his father to come home each day, Jaime felt anxious. Now that he had been kicked out once, he wondered if any future misstep, even if it wasn't using paint thinner, could lead to the same punishment. As a result, he was becoming subdued and distant, two qualities Luis didn't seem to mind seeing in him. Martina, on the other hand, was looking for ways to bring happiness back into Jaime's life. She was pleased that he had agreed to dance matachines as a fariseo, but she feared he was only granting her request rather than feeling the full power of the ritual for himself. She wanted him to feel close to her and his siblings, if not his father.

Semana Santa had always been a time to reset relationships with neighbors and family, though rifts in the Sierra never ran as deep as they did in the city, where so many Rarámuris struggled with addiction. Martina saw moments like birthdays and community celebrations as increasingly important for repairing rifts. José had always treated the week similarly, regardless of whether cameras were present. It was a time when the community, torn apart by drug addiction and economic instability, could come together and reframe their story around survival and resistance.

For the last two years, Martina had tried to convince Luis to carry the flag during matachines and allow himself to be filmed. Luis always refused. As her sense of identity evolved in the city, she became more open to outward expressions of resistance. Luis, on the other hand, continued to feel that the filming was not so different from an extortion: mestizos taking what belonged to Rarámuris and using it for their own gain.

Even knowing Luis's strong feelings, and even with the growing distance between them, Martina decided to bring up holding the flag again that year. Only Luis could teach Jaime and Manolo the meaning of dancing as fariseos during Semana Santa, and it was a lesson Martina didn't want them to miss. Jaime's playing this role alongside his father and the dozen or so other men who volunteered might, Martina thought, help him understand that it took every member to protect their community from outside harm. One part of the beauty of Semana Santa was the passage of knowledge from parents to their children.

Privately, Martina saw Luis's participation as a fariseo as an opportunity for their family to appear as a moral authority in the community once again. She hadn't dared to hope, as she had on Lupita's birthday, that this week would mark a dramatic turning point for her husband or her son; but she did see the fariseo role as an opportunity to convey to the community that her family still lived by korima. The approach of Semana Santa had brought up her desire to once again be a culture bearer, and she imagined the pride she would feel seeing her handsome husband and sons on the evening news, holding the flag, knowing that their image was being transmitted across the entire city, into the homes of mestizos who had no choice but to notice them. Mestizos also danced matachines, but only on Holy Saturday. The Rarámuris, dressed in the clothes that distinguished them, danced the entire week, with little rest.

Wouldn't it feel good to hold up the flag? Martina said to Luis. *Manolo will be proud to see his father dressed as a fariseo, proclaiming his resistance to the white man, his dedication to his community.*

When Luis didn't make any promises, Martina wished she hadn't bothered to sew him a blouse in the same color the rest of the family was wearing.

A deep boom tore through the darkness, traveling up the corridors, entering houses through their barred windows, and jolting sleeping families awake. In the schoolyard on Palm Sunday, the first day of Semana Santa, Venancio, the alapersi—the Rarámuri word for *elder*—who called to the Rarámuris and carried them through the rituals of the week, beat a deerskin drum. There were no police or ambulance sirens that morning, no gunshots, no boom boxes blaring narcocorridos. The birds were not yet awake, and the sun would rest for one final hour before emerging from the desert. Just as he had in the Sierra, Venancio called the Rarámuris to him so they could begin the cleansing that would remind them they were formed from the earth's clay, and that therefore, they would exist forever.

In the glow of a lamp, Martina dabbed her fingers with white paint, the color of the ashen people who sought to kill the Rarámuri. This week, the fariseos would reflect on the sins visited on them by the white chabochis, and struggle against the soldados to purge themselves of these sins. She swirled the paint on Luis's chest, to make a circle as wide as three fingers, then another, and another. She covered his torso, chest, arms, legs, and face as the children watched. When she had finished with Luis, she did the same for Jaime. He stood still and straight, but she noticed there was no tension in his neck and shoulders, as there had been when she cut his hair many months before. His deep, even breaths seemed like a response to her touch, a note of affection in them that Martina hadn't sensed in too long. Her breath catching in her throat, she cupped Jaime's chin in her hand as she had when he was small. He smiled at her a bit nervously, and Martina guessed that he was uncomfortable dressed as a fariseo after all.

Luis, Jaime, and Manolo each wore a white tagolá; Luis wore the sash on which Martina had stitched crosses and the mountains of the Sierra around his waist. Like the women's dresses, the men's ceremonial clothing told a story of displacement just as much as resistance. The main difference was that Luis and the other men could wear this clothing only a few times per year, since they spent the majority of their time trying to fit in with mestizos in order to attain jobs. Martina glanced at Luis, who seemed not to notice his son's discomfort. Martina wished Luis would talk to Jaime about the pride he felt in wearing the tagolá, how this ceremonial clothing was a way to stand apart from mestizos. But since Luis didn't say anything, Martina instead smiled reassuringly at Jaime, hoping that dancing with his father, brothers, and other men would be enough to instill in him the pride she wanted him to feel.

Manolo stood as tall as he could, tapping his feet in anticipation. Each time the drum boomed, his eyes widened with excitement. When Martina had finished staining his skin with white paint, she gave them the koyeras she had made, palm headbands with ribbons that reached to their feet, adorned with fake bird feathers. In the Sierra, Martina had stitched the feathers of birds Luis had hunted to his koyera, as a way to show their connection to the earth. But Luis admired the resourcefulness of the Rarámuri women who found new ways of keeping up traditions. On the day Martina had given him his new koyera, three years before, he had praised how real the fake bird feathers looked: brown and silky, they didn't look any different from the sparrows of the Sierra.

Once dressed, Luis gestured for both boys to follow him. They opened the door to their house and walked toward the drumbeat. Once they turned the corner, Martina joined Eugenia and María José on Eugenia's front stoop, where they sat drinking coffee. She blinked back tears, a bit embarrassed to let on that this was an emotional moment for her. María José, pretending not to notice, went inside to get coffee for her sister. Eugenia sat in silence, staring down the corridor toward the drum beat.

In the Sierra, she had watched Luis dance matachines under a moonlit sky. Here, she watched him and their sons walk through the puddles of yellow light cast by the street lamps. Ceremonies in El Oasis always reminded Martina of what had once been, but this year, the feeling of distance from the Sierra was more pronounced than ever. Luis had always helped her to feel that all was not lost, even if they could never go back. He had always reminded her that their family could live out their days as Rarámuris in El Oasis.

This was the beauty of that week—healing the land was not separate from healing relationships with loved ones. The land and family were one and the same; neither could be healthy without the other.

Standing before Venancio, Manolo felt the drum sound deep in his chest. It was a sound so deep and full that he felt himself grounded, unable to move. Then, as it echoed off the walls, jumping and flowing through the corridors along with the wind, Manolo felt his legs tremble.

It was midmorning, and the men had already been dancing for five hours. The boom of the drum had settled into the chests of every person present in El Oasis that day, including those on the TV crews, who positioned themselves around the perimeter of the schoolyard, blocking some of the women and children who sat to watch the fariseos. Four more mestizos pushed the buttons on their professional cameras, the *click click* of the shutters an unsteady rhythm that threatened to interrupt Venancio's steady beat. Luis, as usual, tried to ignore them. He stood behind his youngest son, shaking a deerskin rattle filled with dried pinto beans. Jaime was behind him, the third in a line of thirty Rarámuri men. Sixty men in two parallel lines all faced Venancio and his drum.

Manolo looked to see what the man in the line beside him was doing. Manolo had played the music for matachines dozens of times before, stomping to the rhythm of his homemade rattles. Now, in the schoolyard filled with Rarámuri women and children, he felt conspicuous and uncertain.

Like this, Luis whispered to his son, taking him by the shoulder and turning him so they were facing each other. Venancio beat his palm against the drum once again, and Luis stomped twice, shaking his rattle. Manolo, encouraged, shook the small rattle Martina had bought for him. He watched his father's feet and tried to imitate the rhythm of his steps. The next beat, he met his father's eyes, grinning with pride.

Luis hadn't beaten a drum since he left the Sierra nearly five years before. Sometimes he wondered what had happened to his deerskin drum, if another family had found it and now used it to call the rain clouds as he once had.

He felt good dressed in the loincloth and blue blouse Martina had made for him. Each year, he found that the clothing returned him to a version of himself he had learned to hide for the sake of obtaining work. When he put on these items, he remembered the forest walks he used to take, the batari he brewed with his family and friends, the many nights they spent beside the campfire.

These memories were from a past Luis had left behind the first time he put on a pair of jeans for work. He had felt, walking out of the Sierra, that he was leaving behind his life for good, but it wasn't until he accepted the shirt and pants Eduardo offered him that he truly stepped into his new reality in the city, as a Rarámuri man caught in a struggle for survival and justice.

Now, in the tagolá, his body covered with white paint, painful memories of the recent past mingling with joyful ones of the distant past, Luis felt ready to join the other men in cleansing their community. No matter what mistakes their people made, no matter how far they strayed from the ways of korima, Onorúame always offered a path back. That's what the mestizos couldn't understand—for them, a path could only be a straight line, filled with struggle and suffering. The Rarámuris' path also contained struggles and pain, but it was within their power to reshape it as a circle, a return to the promise Onorúame made when the chabochis invaded. In returning, Onorúame had assured them, the Rarámuris would always be forgiven.

In the late morning, Luis Fernando hoisted the flag that read "El Oasis: Un Asentamiento Tarahumara" above his head and took his place at the front of the line. The flag waved in the wind, bending and wrinkling, and the cameramen struggled to capture the words. Frustrated, they jostled one another and moved from one location to the next, trying to follow Luis Fernando as he wove between the two long lines of dancing fariseos.

On the other side of the schoolyard, two parallel lines of women dancers had formed. Martina and Lupita, both wearing their light-blue dresses, stepped to the beat of the drum alongside the fariseos. The women accompanied the men in dancing so they wouldn't feel alone. It was not the women's place to hold the flag or to dance through the night. The men bore the full responsibility for cleansing their community of the white man's sins.

Martina tried to keep her rhythm as she looked over at Luis, hoping he would take a turn holding the flag. Jaime danced beside him, and Manolo tried to keep pace just in front of his brother. Luis Fernando was now passing the flag to other men who then wove through the two lines with it. The men danced in perfect rhythm, the flag passing between them, waving in the air so that the name of their community could be captured by the mestizos' cameras. She was proud that their dancing would be transmitted to the televisions of mestizos throughout the city. More than anything, she felt proud to belong to a community that still knew how to live by korima.

She thought perhaps Luis had told the other men not to pass him the flag, because no one offered it to him or to Jaime. They were two of only a handful of men who hadn't carried it. She realized then that Luis had no interest in fulfilling any request she made. She'd sewn his blue shirt, covered his body with paint, and bought food just for him, Jaime, and Manolo, to nourish them throughout the long hours of dancing. Yet he couldn't even hold the flag for a few short seconds to please her.

She was filled with a sense of disappointment that had become too familiar in the past three months. Now, though, she didn't want to waste time feeling anger and regret. Almost immediately, she refocused her attention on her sons, thinking of how she would mold them to be flag carriers in the coming years.

Luis hadn't held the flag because he didn't believe in putting himself on display for the mestizos. He already gave them so much: his money, his labor, his dignity. Though he couldn't force the journalists to leave, nor override the community's decision to hold the flag, he could refuse to participate. He hoped Martina would understand, but lately, it seemed to him that she was focused more than ever on what she wanted. What did a Rarámuri woman understand about extortions and the pressures to provide? He pushed aside his

worries about what she thought and tried to concentrate instead
on what this ceremony was about: cleansing and forgiveness.

With each beat of his drum, Venancio urged them to remember their
origin story. For fifteen hours each day of the six days before Easter
Sunday, the sound of the drum crossed the walls encircling El Oasis
and swirled with the spring winds, reaching as far as the bus stops and
open-air markets in the middle of the colonia. It carried memories
of the Sierra, where the Rarámuris who had remained were planting
their seeds in the dusty earth with great hope. The drumbeat was for
them, those who remained behind to protect the land that Onorúame
had entrusted to them. It was also for the Rarámuris of El Oasis and
all others who now dwelled in asentamientos, so they would remember where they came from: the dark brown earth of the mountains that
had once fed them, from which Onorúame had created them.

On Ash Wednesday, which took place five weeks before Palm Sunday
and marked the start of a six-week penitence to mirror Jesus Christ's
fast in the desert, a Catholic priest dipped his thumb into the ashes of
palms burned the Sunday before, then pressed it onto the foreheads of
mestizos, swiping twice to make a cross. The mestizos wore the ashen
crosses all day, a reminder that they came from the earth and would
one day die. This reminder was meant to inspire Catholics to repent
for their sins and to spend their time living according to Jesus's teachings. Though Catholic mestizos wore the ashes only on this day, they
repented for the six weeks leading up Holy Week, which culminated
in Easter Sunday, the day that Jesus Christ rose from the dead.

For the Rarámuris, ashes were not a symbol of a final death, but
a sign that they were connected to the earth through the fires that
kept them warm. Rarámuris didn't observe Ash Wednesday on the
same day as the mestizos; instead, they observed Ash Wednesday
during Holy Week, the week leading up to Jesus Christ's crucifixion
on Good Friday and his resurrection on Easter Sunday.

On the basketball court on the Rarámuris' Ash Wednesday,
Venancio, who wore his black hair in the chin-length style of the

Sierra, blessed the earth by holding a lit match to four piles of sticks placed on the northern, southern, eastern, and western points of the court. The flames spread to the sticks, creating four small fires that filled the air with the scent of burning wood. For the Rarámuris, this day marked a period in which they would have to make a crucial choice. Venancio took up his drum and beat it faster and louder, to alert the Rarámuris of El Oasis that they were at a crossroads. Would they stand as defenders of Jesus and the land? Or would they go the way of the chabochis and the demon, capturing the good people who protected the earth?

Martina held her breath as she watched the smoke rise. Luis sat beside her, Manolo between them. In previous years, Martina had known Luis felt as nervous as she did, since on this day, Rarámuris had to reaffirm their promise to Onorúame. The year before, she and Luis had sat together in silence until the wood finished burning, and Martina had known that he felt as strongly as she did: they had to continue to live out their story. Now, Martina couldn't tell what Luis was feeling or thinking.

Silently, Venancio asked Onorúame to give the Rarámuris another year of good harvest and good weather, to protect their people against drought, hail, and plague. He prayed that the Rarámuris of the Sierra wouldn't have to leave. He prayed, too, that the people of El Oasis could maintain their connection to the Sierra, and not forget who they were.

On the Rarámuris' Ash Wednesday, Luis danced through the night, his mind empty but for the sound of the drum. He shook his rattle, one made of cowhide that he had bought from another Rarámuri. The rhythm of the rattle was fast and incessant, to signify the growing urgency of choosing a path. The men formed two long lines as they danced, to signify that they would stay on the path of the Rarámuris and never veer off.

The slow and steady beat of the drum had a way of lulling Luis's mind. Though his body stepped to the beat for hours and his feet became sore and blistered, he felt his mind clear of worries.

For Luis, Semana Santa was a kind of rest, one that he got only when he did his prayer dances. It wasn't that his mind was completely empty; instead, he felt settled in each moment, enjoying the time he spent with his sons and friends. He felt a sense of peace in knowing that his sons were with him, dancing matachines to save their souls. There was no future or past; there was only a sense that time had no limitations. Luis could dance without worry about what would come next, or what had come before.

On work days, Luis tried to replicate this feeling by drinking alcohol, but he never felt that his worries were lifted completely; they were simply dulled for a few hours. So far that week, he hadn't experienced a single extortion because he hadn't left El Oasis, not for work and not for errands. He remained at the basketball court, dancing with the other men throughout the day and night. They took short breaks to drink water and eat bean burritos prepared for them by their wives. This week, Luis felt connected to his community by a sense of shared strength rather than shared oppression. *If only every day could be like this,* Luis thought, but almost immediately, he unburdened his mind of wishes or desires. There was nothing more than the drumbeat, nothing more than this single week that carried the Rarámuris' entire past and future.

Jaime noted the way his father tucked his chin into his neck while he danced. This was a way of pointing his energy toward the ground, a giving of a gift to the land in thanks for being given its fruits. With each hour that passed, Luis seemed to gain more strength, as if the dirt under the concrete on which they danced was somehow transmitting energy to Luis. Jaime remembered watching his father dance yumari in front of their house in the Sierra, the way Luis had lifted the dust as he stomped hard on the ground. He had strong recollections of Semana Santa with friends and family too. More than Lupita, he understood the power of dancing matachines in the Sierra because he had felt, as a younger boy, the dirt coating his feet and the wind rushing through the pines. Back then, he had imitated Luis's every step, staying close to him the entire week.

As this Semana Santa progressed, Jaime felt his resentment toward his father lessen. He fell into line with the men, shaking his own deerskin rattle. In those moments, he felt certain that he had a path to follow that would bring him only blessings. Though they didn't exchange many words, Jaime observed the way his father danced and adapted to his style. In imitating Luis's behaviors, Jaime communicated to Luis and Martina that he didn't think his father was weak, at least not all the time. His father had qualities that Jaime gravitated toward—resilience, strength, and hope—so much so that he chose to imitate his father in the hope that he might one day embody these qualities as well.

When the sun reached the top of the sky on Good Friday, Luis, Martina, and the rest of the community descended the rocky slope of the arroyo to bury Jesus Christ. According to the Bible, Jesus Christ had been crucified that morning. In the churches, mestizos cried and repented. The Rarámuris, too, felt sorrow for Jesus and for the earth, which seemed destined to turn into brittle soil.

Then a troupe of six Rarámuris dressed in white loincloths came out from behind the mesquite trees carrying a large white rag doll. The Rarámuris called the doll Judas, the Roman apostle who, according to the Bible, ordered Jesus to be crucified. In their view, Judas represented the colonizer, the bringer of death. He was not the Biblical Judas, but a relative of Hernán Cortés and the many chabochis and mestizos who followed, and also of the demon who created the chabochis. In the decades after the Spaniards introduced Jesus to the Rarámuri people, and as they mixed elements of Christianity into their religious practices, they came to identify with him because of his moral superiority and the persecution he suffered for his way of living.

Luis, a fariseo, ran toward a soldier and took him by the shoulders. The soldado, a teenager named Lorenzo, did the same to Luis. Now was the time to make the decision: would they give in or would they fight for the Rarámuri people? Around them, other fariseos and soldados were locked in a five-hundred-year-old battle for the Rarámuri soul. Jaime, following his father's example, locked arms with a soldado twice his age. The soldado was taller and thicker; it seemed that Jaime wouldn't stand a chance. Yet Jaime bore his feet into the ground and pushed as hard as he could against the soldado. Perhaps it was seeing his father struggle against his own anger and addiction that week that made Jaime believe that he, too, could be strong enough to resist. Semana Santa revealed aspects of character that stayed hidden during the daily hustle of work. There were no mestizos exerting pressure on their community. It was only the Rarámuri people, narrating their story to themselves so they could continue to hold on to korima. Now, as they danced and ate together, Luis and Jaime both found strength in that narration, and Jaime recognized the strength in his father too.

The night of Good Friday, when the fariseos had triumphed over the soldiers, the fariseos and soldados again danced matachines in straight lines. Like the paths the women stitched onto their dresses, these lines symbolized paths. Onorúame had created them to keep the Rarámuris safe; all they had to do was follow.

In the morning, a young man named Samuel laid Judas at the center of the basketball court.

Venancio swung his arms back, then forward, beating the drum with his palms. He seemed to never tire or grow too old to make the drum sound through El Oasis.

Samuel, a young man who worked in construction and had once been jailed for refusing to empty his pockets for police officers, threw a lit match onto the doll.

The small flame spread, and smoke began to rise. Men, women, and children now crowded around the doll, calling for Judas to burn so Jesus and the Rarámuri people could be cleansed. To kill Judas, as Jesus had been killed, was the only way to restore balance. Jesus had given his life so the Rarámuris could live. Now, the Rarámuris took Judas's life. As long as Judas remained, as long as the chabochis remained, the Rarámuri people needed to resist.

The Rarámuris took turns kicking and stomping on Judas. In doing so, they reenacted the fight between good and evil, brown and white, Indigenous knowledge and the white man's oppression. Martina, Lupita, and Manolo stayed at the edge of the circle, preferring to let the others complete the purge. Martina thought that the purge itself was violent; participants sometimes bumped into each other, causing bruises. She preferred to watch instead of participate, and Lupita followed her cue.

Luis trampled Judas, the pain of the past year and his hope for the future in every stomp. Around him, other men who worked day jobs, who had been kidnapped, who regularly gave up their wages to police officers, kicked Judas too, calling for him to die.

How could they return to the ways of korima when work and wages dominated life and police officers trapped them in a cycle of abuse they alone could not break? Perhaps only the strength of their community could defeat the white man's sin. Jaime, stomping on Judas for the first time, began to feel that he had inherited his father's resilience and not simply his struggle. Perhaps, he thought, he could persist as a Rarámuri man too, just as his father was doing.

A cleansing smoke rose from the doll. Luis inhaled deeply.

Hard, silent desert

[April 2010]

One month earlier, as they prepared for Semana Santa, Luis had told Martina that he expected Jaime to quit school at the end of the school year and start working with him. This was what Jaime had proposed to Luis when he returned home after getting kicked out of the house. Martina had hoped that they would revisit the agreement that Luis and Jaime had arrived at; she didn't want her son to leave school and start working in the city. She had hoped that she could convince Luis and Jaime that going back to the Sierra would be best for him. But Luis had left no room for discussion when he told Martina what he wanted. Martina had spent the night worrying that he would also demand Lupita stay in El Oasis. She had been searching for the courage to send Lupita off, even if Luis disagreed. But the next morning, he'd surprised her by telling her he thought Lupita would be safest in the Sierra. Martina had noticed he'd said "Sierra" and not "boarding school"; she took this to mean that he thought the mountains themselves would protect Lupita. Whatever his meaning, though, she was relieved. Lupita, at least, would be safe. Martina had delivered the news to Miss Ceci a few days later. She had waited in the hopes that Luis would change his mind about sending Jaime, but he hadn't.

In the period between Luis's decision to send Lupita to boarding school and the start of Semana Santa, Martina, for the second time that year, told Lupita of her decision, though this time she sat her down and asked her how she felt about it.

I'm scared, Lupita said, after a few moments' consideration. She remembered living in the Sierra, but since they left, she had come to think of it as a place filled with bad mestizos and starving Rarámuris. She worried, too, about dangerous wild animals in the Sierra, like bears and wolves.

Martina smiled at the mention of bears and wolves. *You'll live in a school with a tall gate around it,* she told Lupita. She had been worried Lupita would take the news badly, and though she had never imagined her daughter would rely on gates for protection, she understood. It was another irony, the first being that Martina and the other mothers now found themselves having to send their children back to the Sierra to protect them from the dangers of the city.

Though there wasn't enough room to play in the asentamiento, and it was often dirty, Lupita had no desire to return to the Sierra. She didn't miss the pine trees or the mountains. Here, she sat on front stoops and whispered secrets to her friends. She skipped rope in the schoolyard and carried stray puppies in one of Martina's old rebozos, pretending they were her babies. There were restaurants she thought she might one day have enough money to try; McDonald's and Domino's Pizza were two of them.

Lupita thought about asking her mother to let her stay in El Oasis. She had hoped all the hours she spent korimeando would make her mother pay more attention to her in the present, but now, even as she encouraged her to share her feelings, Lupita understood that her mother's focus had been on deciding her future. It was yet another disappointment, but one she thought she might get over if she put it behind her quickly enough.

The Monday after Semana Santa, Lupita and the rest of the third graders sat at their desks, struggling to keep their eyes open as they tried to complete worksheets. Eventually, their teacher, Miss Lucia, handed out paper and crayons instead. There was no point in teaching anything that day, not when the children had gotten so little sleep over the weekend, busy as they were celebrating their peoples' triumph over evil. The night before, Lupita had stayed up with Martina, drinking Coke and running back and forth across El Oasis to watch Rarámuri women, tipsy on batari and beer, twirl until their skirts fanned around their ankles. Lucero had brought out her boom box and turned the dial to a station that played reggaeton, and teenagers danced to the Caribbean rhythms and sang along to Daddy Yankee and Don Omar.

When the paper and crayons didn't wake up the children, Miss Lucia decided to share some news she'd received that morning, which she was sure would energize and motivate them for their lessons. She told the class she had a special announcement.

Lupita perked up.

What is it? asked Camila.

Miss Lucia held them in suspense a moment longer, then said, *To celebrate Día del Niño, you'll be going to a water park.* Her words had just the effect she had wanted: the children erupted in murmurs of excitement.

Your mothers are invited to attend too, Miss Lucia went on. *So make sure to tell them after school.*

The thought of a day at the water park with her mother didn't thrill Lupita as it would have a few months before. Though she had enjoyed the community festivities, she'd been plagued by the thought that this would be her last Semana Santa in El Oasis, at least for many years. She hadn't seen much of a point in doing more than her mother expected her to—sitting and watching the matachines and the burning of Judas—now that she knew she would be leaving for boarding school in the fall. In boarding school, she wouldn't be allowed to attend Rarámuri Semana Santa activities; she would instead go to Mass and do the rituals that the mestizos deemed appropriate. Her only comfort was that Camila would be going too. Violeta would stay behind; her parents had refused to let her go, for reasons that weren't clear to the girls. Lupita was trying to detach from her family and community to avoid the feelings of rejection she had been struggling with since her mother informed her of the decision to send her off. So while the day at the water park still felt like a special treat, it didn't excite her the way it would have previously.

She told Martina about it that evening, not expecting that she would care about her mother's reaction. She was surprised at the pleasure she felt when Martina told her that she had already learned of the excursion and made plans to skip korimeando that day. Instantly, though, she felt afraid of her happiness. Her mother spending a whole day with her seemed too good to be true.

Eight million years earlier, the gray mountains the Rarámuris left behind had lain submerged. Five years before, the Gutiérrez family had traveled across land strewn with thousands of brachiopod and crustacean fossils, the curved ridges on the sea creatures indicating that they were from the Cambrian period. Most Mexicans think of the Chihuahuan Desert as devoid of water, but forceful currents once molded and shaped the tops of its mountains, which had risen even earlier, when tectonic plates trembled and crashed. Water has always been part of this land.

Though the Gutiérrez family had never visited the Chihuahuan Desert before leaving the Sierra, and it had been centuries since their people relied on the rivers running through it to nourish their crops, Martina and Luis could recognize signs of water there. The arroyos sprinkled throughout the desert held creeks the family drank from during their journey. Dark gray clouds glided across the sky, and though they didn't release their water while the Gutiérrez family walked, Martina and Luis knew the rain had to fall sometime, for the cacti and rabbits they saw.

When they entered the city for the first time, the presence of water no longer felt obvious to Martina and Luis. As they walked down the busy road called Avenida Zarco, the family heard cars rumbling, sirens wailing, music blaring, and vendors hawking their wares through megaphones. They passed storefronts displaying items they'd never seen, whose uses they couldn't imagine. This concrete city contained every sound and object, but there was no sign of water. That afternoon, once they reached María José and Eduardo's home, they drank water from plastic cups, but they didn't know where it came from.

It wasn't until the next morning, when Martina stepped out of their house, that she heard water gushing. At first, she couldn't identify the source of the sound and thought there might be a small waterfall nearby, perhaps in the arroyo. She descended the two steps from the door and glanced up and down the corridor, but all she saw were colorful skirts stretched across clotheslines from one house to the next.

Not wanting to go farther, Martina sat on the bottom step. That was when she noticed a trickle of water approaching her. Baffled, she watched it spread across the cement. A few moments later, when María José emerged from the house and pushed aside one of the skirts hanging on the clothesline, Martina saw that the water was flowing from a faucet into the large basin of a utility sink. The sight of this small waterfall located right outside the houses filled her with a sense of relief so immense, she wanted to cry.

Martina knew now that in the city, her children didn't often feel the presence of water, wild and free, either. They had become accustomed to turning the faucets of the utility sinks and seeing perfect cylinders flow until they closed the levers, once again trapping the water. Having endured thirst, then experienced the ease of drawing water from a pipe, it was easy for Martina to forget that water became angry when trapped. She had learned that lesson from the elders in the Sierra, who had seen how the cutting of forests made the rain stay away. Water was sensitive, wanting to feel welcomed and loved, just like the wind, land, plants, and animals. The pine trees were the only ones who knew how to invite the rain in just the right way. Without the pines, the rain didn't feel welcome in the Sierra. It was important to care for the land and the water in particular ways, just as it was important to care for one's family and friends. Martina wanted her children to know that water was generous and life giving, and not because the mestizos had learned to confine it. The water loved the Rarámuri people, and she made it her goal to teach her children how to love the water in return.

Sometimes Martina described korima to them as a fast-flowing river that winds through the canyons of the Sierra. She reminded them that they had once drunk from a river and carried water in clay jugs for the plants that fed them. She didn't want her children to see water as devoid of feeling, or as a nuisance, the way the mestizos sometimes did. Water, like wind, loved to play, bubbling over rocks in the creeks, splashing against boulders, and pinging lightly against the roofs of buildings in the city. Sometimes the wind blew as water fell from the sky, creating a sheet that caught the Rarámuris and mestizos in its folds, soaking them until, gasping in disbelief, they arrived to their shelters. Martina wanted her children to laugh at the pranks the wind and the water played. They enlivened the world, bringing humor to the Rarámuris' lives.

Water, she often said to them, was not an individual entity; it belonged to korima, like all living beings, and that's why it had such a giving nature. She made sure to tell them that they could learn to be giving by following water's example. Many mothers in El Oasis told similar stories about water, careful to teach their children about Onorúame's abundance and not simply the scarcity they knew. At school, the teachers reinforced these lessons by asking the children to draw parcels of corn and Rarámuri families with rain falling on them. Children growing up in the city couldn't experience korima each day as they helped their parents in the garden or walked barefoot on the land Onorúame had created for them. Stories and drawings were the closest they could get.

Sometimes Martina took Lupita and Manolo to the man-made lake at the top of a hill filled with mestizo houses. El Oasis sat at the bottom of the hill, and up above, a dam built in 1968 held back the water for Colonia Martín López and five other neighborhoods. The lake was one mile around, and its water was diverted from the Río Chuvíscar. Many Rarámuris went there for leisure. Though the water was controlled by the mestizos, a fact Martina found disturbing, she wanted her children to experience how soothing a lake could be. She had loved sitting beside the lakes of the Sierra as a child, dipping her feet in their coolness and caressing the smooth pebbles that washed ashore. She and María José sometimes swam as their parents fished, giving over their entire afternoons to the water.

It was the lake up above El Oasis that Lupita daydreamed about as she sat at her desk in the classroom. She used to go and lounge on its grassy shore with her mother and Manolo. Once, Camila and Violeta came along and brought a fishing rod. Martina and the three girls sat for hours looking out over the vast blue until something tugged hard on the line and Camila jumped to her feet and reeled it in. From the water, she pulled a long wriggling fish with a metal hook snagged in its mouth. Later, the girls skipped through the dusty streets of the colonia, taking turns holding the fish, singing the entire way. They saw mestizos outside their homes, watching the sun set behind the eastern mountains, drinking a beer at the end of a work day, or watering their flowers with green hoses, and some even smiled at the girls. At home, Martina fried the whole fish.

Like the ones I used to catch in the streams of the Sierra, she said to her daughter and Lupita's friends. Martina left the second part unsaid—*before the water dried up*—but the young girls understood their mothers were always thinking of a time when the water filled lakes and rivers and provided enough fish for everyone. Though she tried to speak of the water's abundance, she couldn't forget that the lack of it in the Sierra was the source of their displacement. Lupita understood that about water better than her mother's teachings about a living water. For her, the story of water was one of theft and scarcity, no matter how hard her mother tried to paint it otherwise.

Martina and the other women had never been to the water parks that were cropping up on the outskirts of the city almost as quickly as the housing developments. She had seen the vast pools and waterslides advertised on TV but assumed the parks were far from the city and the desert. She couldn't imagine that much water in one place; the pools in the commercials seemed larger than the lake at the top of the hill. She decided to skip korimeando that day out of curiosity as much as a desire to put Lupita and Manolo in touch with water. In the sewing circle, other women said they would skip korimeando too: this outing was too interesting to pass up. The official from the Coordinación Estatal de la Tarahumara who had told the teachers about it had even said the state government would provide a meal and transportation. All they had to do was be ready by nine in the morning, and the rest would be taken care of.

On the morning of Friday, April 9, Martina, Lupita, and Manolo rode a bus along the two-lane highway, headed toward Ciudad Juárez and the US-Mexico border. Martina had never been so far north and expected they would soon reach a new kind of landscape filled with lakes. Instead, the desert extended to the horizon, slate-gray mountains rising from the land as the bus traveled forward. There were few homes beyond the outskirts of the city, only the land, vast like the ocean it had once been.

Then the bus reached a series of water parks, their white and sea-green waterslides rising toward the bright sky. Lupita turned and pressed her face against the window, and Manolo squirmed to get a better view, tucking his head under his sister's arm. Through the tall white gates that enclosed the parks, Martina could see the pools, aquamarine circles that held water still. She could almost feel their coolness against her skin.

Martina and the other Rarámuri women didn't know that the water parks throughout the Chihuahuan Desert, all the way to Ciudad Juárez, had been built by private companies. The temperatures in the region were rising, just as they were throughout the world. Water parks near cities in the desert—cities where governments set watering restrictions and asked residents to be mindful of their water usage— were a lucrative venture. Working- and middle-class mestizo families who couldn't afford to build swimming pools in their backyards made day trips to these water parks, especially during the summer months, when the temperatures regularly rose to 110 degrees. Then there were the neighborhoods in Chihuahua City that relied on the city government to deliver water, because water lines hadn't yet reached them. These citizens, some of whom were Rarámuris who didn't qualify for government housing due to a shortage, didn't have water to drink or bathe in, much less water for recreation.

Vast amounts of land in Chihuahua were privately owned, since the government preferred to give control to the cattle ranchers who brought millions of pesos in revenue to the state. Privatization meant that the poorest citizens—the Rarámuris—couldn't access most of the state's land and water. The majority of the state of Chihuahua was made up of desert, with the Sierra Madre mountains spanning the western part of the state, Sinaloa, and Sonora. Here, in the water parks carelessly strewn throughout the desert, the mestizos were once again hoarding water, giving access to Rarámuris only when they chose to do so.

To Martina, the difference between a public space and a private one was in whether or not she felt welcome. Even at public parks, like the reservoir, Martina and other Rarámuris were aware that they were in mestizo territory and could be sent back to El Oasis at the mestizos' slightest whim. At the water park, a group of government officials, each wearing jeans and polo shirts with the insignia of the Coordinadora Estatal de la Tarahumara, welcomed the families and offered them seats at picnic tables. Still, the Rarámuri mothers moved uneasily, lingering at the edges of the tables, the water slides twisting around each other behind them. The children stared at the water, some of them open mouthed. There was no one in the entire park that day but their group of seventy, the six officials from the Coordinadora Estatal de la Tarahumara assigned to them, and a couple of park employees. It was an event so out of the ordinary that none of the Rarámuris knew where to look or stand, so they remained still. The mestizos, unsure how to help them feel at ease, hovered nearby awkwardly.

Does anyone want some soda? one of them, a young woman, asked.

There was a murmur within the group, but not about the soda. Cuquita, one of Martina's good friends, had nodded at a patch of wide-stemmed grass growing by the fence.

Guasoliki, she had said, trying to keep her voice low despite her excitement.

Martina turned to look. It was indeed the herb she loved searching for inside the city's arroyos, one she liked to use for broth. The mestizos sold three hundred native plants in their markets, for food and medicine, but Rarámuri women, including Martina, were accustomed to using more than five hundred. Guasoliki was one of the herbs the mestizos had forgotten about, and the Rarámuri women foraged for it.

Now, instead of sitting at the picnic tables neatly set with bottles of soda and small Styrofoam cups, the Rarámuri women knelt beside the fence, picking guasoliki.

Do you have some plastic bags? María José asked one of the officials. Amused and slightly frustrated, he rummaged in a large duffel bag. He gave María José a handful of bags, which she then distributed to the women.

With the mothers occupied, one of the officials, another young woman who seemed eager to please the Rarámuri visitors, beckoned the children over to the pool. She coaxed them to dip their toes in the water, then to jump into the shallows. First, a few of the more daring children jumped in. Then the others jumped, and laughter filled the park.

The sun moved across the sky, the heat deepened, and the children splashed in the water. In its coolness, the heat felt like a warm caress instead of a punishing hand. In the same desert where the Rarámuri people once swam in the waters of the Río Conchos, the same river that had nourished their gardens, the Rarámuri women and children of El Oasis refreshed themselves in the mestizos' chlorinated pools.

Two hours passed before any child was brave enough to scale the metal steps and descend from the enclosed tubes. A fifth grader named Miguel went first, the rest of the children, the mothers, and the mestizo workers watching from below.

The water rushed down the tubes with the force of a river. The mestizo in charge of the slide gave Miguel an inner tube and helped him settle into it, holding it by a cord so it wouldn't be taken by the water before Miguel was ready.

Children gathered at the bottom of the slide to await Miguel's descent. The mothers watched from the picnic tables, where they drank cups of Coke and sewed. Their frequent glances toward the water slide were the only indication that they, too, were waiting for Miguel to emerge.

The mestizo sent Miguel down. Inside the enclosed green waterway, the inner tube sped along, rocking from side to side. A grin spread across Miguel's face. He let out a yell the children and mothers could hear one hundred feet below. They could see the outline of the inner tube as it made its way down the slide.

Keep the opening clear, one of the government workers yelled as children began crowding it. Within seconds, Miguel's inner tube flew out and landed with a splash.

Martina didn't get into the pool, preferring to sit in the grass and watch the children play. She'd filled a plastic bag with guasoliki, and by midday, she was eating ground-beef tacos the officials had prepared on a comal. Lupita and Manolo splashed with the other children, not tiring of the water.

Martina couldn't stop thinking about the strangeness of the aquamarine pools in the middle of the desert. Where did the water come from? Had the mestizos diverted it from the Río Chuvíscar too? She'd heard stories from other women about mestizos releasing chemicals into the air to make the clouds rain only where they wanted them to. Martina had thought those claims were exaggerations—not even the mestizos could control the clouds. But now, seeing the water they maintained only for their own pleasure, water that didn't even nourish the desert plants on the other side of the fence, it seemed to her that the stories could be true. The possibility horrified her.

When the day was over and the fun the children had had was becoming a memory, several mothers stepped off the bus and walked straight to the Soriana to buy bags of beans and packets of tortillas for dinner. Others went to street corners to earn the coins they needed for that day. Martina joined a small group of women who walked back to their houses to rest.

The image of the vast pools in the middle of the desert stayed with Martina, giving her pleasant, cool sensations but also a feeling of discomfort. She had always known the mestizos hoarded water; she had simply never seen evidence of it in Chihuahua City. The trip to the water park gave her an impression of a world beyond the places she knew. In her nearly five years in El Oasis, she had learned about this world by watching the local news: she heard reports about a water crisis in southern Mexico, which was pushing Indigenous peoples from their land to the north, where many hoped to cross into the US. Martina imagined that country—which was four hours away by car, but might as well have been at an impossible distance—as a land filled with water. She now wondered if it was possible that the US was as filled with water as she had thought.

This hard desert was teeming with life—life that was made possible by water. Seeing those pools locked behind gates, Martina began to sense that the water crisis extended beyond Mexico; how far, she wasn't sure. From local news stations, telenovelas, and other programming, she had learned that there were immense bodies of water called oceans, and beyond those, even more land. That the world was far larger than the Sierra and Chihuahua City both terrified and fascinated Martina. At Telas Parisina, a mestiza worker once told her the floral fabrics she loved were made in China. *Across the ocean,* the worker had said as she cut a length of it for Martina. Even since, Martina had imagined that China must be filled with the many flowers that appeared on the prints of her fabric. She had imagined rain fell every day, enough to keep the flowers full all spring and summer. Now, she began to question her assumptions about water in the US and China. No Rarámuri person in El Oasis could be sure, so she asked the few trusted social workers and anthropologists who visited the community. They confirmed what the news reported—the water crisis touched all people, everywhere in this vast world.

For days after returning from the water parks, Martina discussed the excursion and the feelings that had been brought up in her by the knowledge that these water parks existed. Through conversations, she and the other women came to the collective conclusion that the private pools were manifestations of the mestizos' selfishness. That they had been invited was not an act of generosity, much as they and their children had enjoyed their day; it was merely a crumb tossed to them. The water parks were evidence that water was more plentiful in the desert than they had previously thought. The water parks were also proof that the mestizos hoarded water. Martina and the other women had been raised with the knowledge that mestizos were corrupt, so much so that they allowed Rarámuris to die before they shared their wealth. Yet there was always the hope that life would be different in the city than it had been in the Sierra. Sometimes this hope was poignant, and other times it felt like it had disappeared and would never come back. Every Rarámuri person who came to El Oasis felt this sense of hope at some point.

By mid-April, Martina was pleased with the success of her stall downtown. She was earning enough money to buy beans, tortillas, and vegetables for her children, and sometimes even meat and fruit. She could even spare a few pesos for Lupita and Manolo to have ice cream on Saturday afternoons. Martina didn't worry much about extortions, since police always assumed Rarámuri women didn't make much money. From Luis she asked only for enough money to pay the utility bills, and she let him keep the rest to spend as he pleased. While she thought that Luis must have noticed that food was more plentiful in the house, he didn't ask where the money to pay for the food came from. Martina assumed he either didn't care or was satisfied with the fact that he didn't need to provide for the family any longer. They had reached a new stability, one that Martina controlled. This sense of control gave her confidence to manage the family's money and make decisions about what her children would have.

The day at the water park shifted this perception. One afternoon, Martina told María José that she was worried that the mestizos might one day stop buying her crafts. It was her first time thinking directly about the instability of the market, and though she didn't make the connection to the water park excursion herself, the worry about the market entered her mind when she and other women were having conversations about the future of water in the desert. In a way, the visit to the water park was a wake-up call. Martina had been lulled into a sense that she could carve a future for herself out of a sliver of the market economy. She thought she had figured out a long-term solution to her problems. It was at the water park that she realized the way this economy worked—through the hoarding of wealth—wouldn't let her rest easy. She would always have to be on guard, because the mestizos could change the course of her future on a whim, and she would perhaps not see it coming. The sense of control she felt she had gained was more precarious than she thought.

If only all people, including the mestizos, danced yumari together on the streets, just as the Rarámuris danced on the sidewalk outside El Oasis. They would call the water forth with yumari; together, their feet and the drumbeat would bring the clouds. If only people danced yumari in every place the rain clouds didn't visit, Martina thought.

In two months, the rains would return to the Chihuahuan Desert, if they were lucky. But in the days that followed the visit to the water park, Martina realized she hadn't danced yumari in a year. In fact, neither had anyone else in the community. At the beginning of the summer before the men's kidnapping, women and men had often danced yumari inside El Oasis. Dancing was as spontaneous as running: the Rarámuri people danced because they felt moved to do so. But the practice had fallen away in the months that followed, due to the stress of the missing men and the increased need to korimear. Realizing this, Martina worried that she and others had let go of the belief that yumari was a way for the Rarámuri people to communicate with the land and the water.

But no, Martina thought—it wasn't a lack of faith. It was that their time had been filled with worries about the present. Yumari was ancient, and it was new. Like korima, it belonged in every space, in every time. She supposed she and her community had forgotten about it because it didn't fit within the rigid constraints of forward-moving time.

Martina wondered if it would ever become easy to look ahead, to plan for the future. Most days, a quiet, constant dread now sat in the pit of her stomach. In a few weeks' time, Jaime would graduate from elementary school, and Lupita would finish third grade. Summer would arrive with its unrelenting heat. She would take Lupita to the Media Luna park as often as she could, then prepare to send her off to the Sierra.

Martina tried constantly to remind herself that in a sense, Lupita was returning. The mountains needed her—even Luis thought so. Though she doubted the nuns would teach Lupita yumari, Lupita's teachers had told Martina the children at the school would meet with Rarámuri teachers, men and women who would pass down their traditions, once a week. *She won't forget what it means to be Rarámuri, then,* Martina thought, and that was the most important thing. What would the Sierra be without the Rarámuri people? What would the desert, their first home, and most likely their permanent future home, become?

Return of rain

[April, May, June, July, and August 2010]

The beginning of April brought another extortion, one that stripped Luis of the money meant for that week's utility bill. Martina and Luis were faced with a choice: pay to have light, or pay to have food. They chose food. Or at least, Martina thought they had; Luis had been calm, clearheaded, and responsive when she said they could do without TV and light for a few weeks. She hadn't counted beer as part of their nourishment, though. Luis now bought three or four cans two or three times per week, spending what a packet of tortillas and a bag of beans would have cost on alcohol that served only him. Martina felt her resentment growing. She didn't want to touch the money she'd started saving, knowing Luis would spend it. Luis sensed her judgment and stopped speaking to her again. They carried on, the children noticing yet another shift in the mood between them, the penitence and hope of Holy Week now preserved only by the past.

One April afternoon, Lupita, Camila, and Violeta sat together on the curb outside El Oasis, sucking on lollipops that stained their lips and tongues blue. It was one of the rare afternoons when all three were in El Oasis instead of out korimeando. As they talked, the girls watched toddlers wander up and down the sidewalk, their mothers sewing in a circle beside the entrance gate. Even without being asked, the girls kept an eye on the children who wandered toward them, eager for a taste of their lollipops. To distract them,

Camila offered each of them one potato chip from the bag the girls had bought.

Lupita and Camila were discussing their future at the boarding school while Violeta listened. Both girls had agreed to return to the Sierra, but they hadn't yet had time to delve into the matter together. Now, Camila relayed to her friends that her mother was sending her back because she couldn't afford to take care of her, especially not since her father had left them to be with another woman. She didn't want to go back to the Sierra, she admitted. She had only agreed because she didn't want to burden her mother. Lupita told her she'd made her decision for the same reason.

You really don't want to go back? asked Violeta wistfully. All three girls had born in the Sierra and brought to El Oasis when they were not yet five years old, but it wasn't so much nostalgia as the prospect of a warm bed and three meals a day that made Violeta wish she could join her friends. She wasn't worried about wolves or bears or running into bad mestizos. She wanted her friends to say they were excited so she could imagine a path out of her home in El Oasis. Perhaps in a year or two, if she collected enough coins, her parents would see how responsible she was and allow her to go too. But she hadn't told them yet that the idea appealed to her. She didn't think they would listen, even if they were sober.

Lupita and Camila considered the question. Neither had been back to the Sierra since they were displaced. They knew it only through vague early-childhood memories. Lupita remembered playing in the clearing in front of the small wooden house. But she couldn't remember the scent of the pines, which her mother sometimes recalled. Camila and Violeta, too, remembered the homes where they were born, but not much else.

I don't want to be so far away from my mother, Lupita admitted. It felt arbitrary to her that the school was in the Sierra; it could have been in the desert nearby, and she still wouldn't have wanted to go. She knew her mother felt like she was sending Lupita to live with family, but Lupita didn't think of the mountains and the pine trees that way. They were part of a landscape, the one her parents had been forced to leave. Her life was in the desert, in the city, where her mother was.

I wish I could, Violeta said. Lupita and Camila let the words stand, aware that their friend would not have this or any other desire fulfilled. Her parents continued to leave El Oasis for days at a time, to drink in other asentamientos. Both Lupita and Camila were learning what it meant to have fathers who drank, but their mothers drank batari only on special occasions.

I don't remember the Sierra, so I don't care about going back, said Camila, a note of defiance in her voice. *When we leave, our families will forget about us. But they won't care, because they'll have more money.*

Camila spoke confidently, as if she believed her prediction was bound to come true. She was only eight, but life had taught her that money created rifts even between parents and children. Ever since Lucero decided to send her back to the Sierra, the distance between them had felt wide. Lucero, like Martina, said being in the Sierra would help her connect with Onorúame and learn what it meant to be Rarámuri, but Camila knew money was the real root of her mother's choice, just as it was the root of so many choices Rarámuris in El Oasis made. At least, that's how Camila saw things. She didn't yet understand that her mother was backed into a corner, overwhelmed by the task of caring for three children on her own. No decision she could have made would have given her what every woman in El Oasis wanted: autonomy from mestizos, and the ability to raise children by the values of korima and still have financial security.

It was the first time Lupita had heard her worst fear vocalized. All along, she had trained her mind on the benefits her leaving would have for her family, especially Martina and Manolo. She hadn't stopped to fully process what leaving would feel like for her. Without seeing Lupita every day, maybe Martina would think of her less often, just as she now thought of the Sierra less often. She wouldn't stop loving her all at once, but she would begin to forget her. Distance had that effect, which was why Rarámuri people in the

Sierra ran to each other's homes as frequently as they could. If her family were still there, Lupita might have left her mother's house in six years to start her own family, but they would have visited each other often, exchanging gifts from their gardens. Now, Lupita and Martina would be too far apart to run to each other, and Lupita would be locked in a schoolroom or a dormitory. She'd return home only on holidays.

Lupita began to cry. Camila, surprised, looked at her friend and then began to cry too. Violeta nudged her friends to stand and led them to the edge of the arroyo. The men hadn't arrived home from work yet, so the area was free of people drinking, though they knew that in the depths of the arroyo, there were boys sniffing solvents, hidden beneath a canopy of mesquite trees. There the girls sat, at the arroyo's edge, looking out at the gully and the mestizo houses dotting the hills of Colonia Martín López.

They were still there when purple and pink splashed across the sky, when strings of orange and yellow unwound, then became tangled. The sky was a palette of colors that bled into one another, creating new shades. Every minute, it offered a new scene to witness. Finally, when night covered the city, Lupita returned home.

How are you? Martina asked, smiling. She was sitting on the mattress, stitching a Rarámuri mother and daughter onto a tortillero.

Hearing her mother's question, Lupita felt the hurt well up inside her. She bent her head and sobbed silently into her hands. Her shoulders shook, and she fell to her knees. She held her breath to try to keep in her sobs, but they broke through with torrents of tears.

Speak, little mouse, Martina said. She began to feel alarmed. Lupita never cried like this, not even when mestizos hurled insults at her or she quarreled with Camila. Martina worried something terrible had happened.

Did someone hurt you? she asked, trying to keep her voice steady.

Lupita shook her head no. She looked away, distraught that she couldn't keep from crying. Manolo wrapped his arms around her shoulders. *Don't cry, sister,* he said.

A key turned in the lock. Luis had returned from the arroyo. Martina hurried back to the stove to resume chopping a stalk of celery. Lupita hastily wiped her tears and shifted so she was facing the back room. Even Manolo knew to sit on the floor and busy himself with a toy car.

Luis walked in, his eyes bloodshot. They had learned not to speak to him when he was drunk, since he took words as provocations. He went to the back room to lie down.

Martina decided not to finish the tortillero or the vegetable broth. Instead, she lay down beside Lupita, who had buried herself under her blanket. Manolo sat beside her, running a car over her legs. They listened to one another's breathing, not saying a word.

In late April, the seamstresses often followed the sun out of the asentamiento gates to the edge of the arroyo. They settled in one long row, more than twenty of them against a backdrop of dense brush and desert hills dotted with houses. After a long winter, the spring sun, which was not yet searing, felt like a gift.

With the end of the school year approaching, Martina felt time with Lupita slipping away. Soon the sun would burn the desert floor. The weeks would pass in a flurry of craft-making, selling, cooking, and cleaning. Then Lupita would board a bus and leave for the Sierra. She wouldn't be back until Christmas.

When she wanted to escape the forward motion of time and there was no race or community gathering to help her, Martina left El Oasis for the police stables at the edge of the colonia, where there was a grassy area and a creek. One afternoon, she decided to skip korimeando and to take Lupita and Manolo there. That afternoon, some mestizo boys were coming as part of a school program to play basketball with Rarámuri boys in El Oasis; Jaime decided to stay behind and join in the game. Martina's desire to spend more time with her daughter wasn't her only motive. All year long, she had intended to teach her how to sew, but beyond threading a needle and making a few practice stitches on a piece of scrap, Lupita showed little interest in learning. Martina's day-to-day worries had kept her from insisting. This afternoon, though, she wanted to spend time teaching and encouraging Lupita, as her own mother had taught her.

Martina, Lupita, and Manolo walked past cinder-block casitas, and Martina admired the sunflowers and geraniums mestizos had planted in their front lawns. They passed a mestiza woman watering her garden. Lupita and Manolo darted over to ask if they could have a drink of water. The mestiza, used to these requests from the Rarámuri children, held out the hose and let the siblings drink. Soon they continued on, past neon poster boards advertising homemade tamales and raspados. Even the mestizos were trying to collect enough coins to pay for what they needed and wanted, Martina thought, though she felt the mestizos' shared knowledge of Spanish made it easier for them.

When they rounded a corner, they came upon a forested path. The sounds of cars quickly faded away, and the chirping of birds filled the air. They followed the path along a creek that bubbled and gurgled, and soon, they came upon the fenced enclosure for the horses. Lupita and Manolo ran to greet the horses, who recognized them immediately. They wandered over, flicking flies away with their tails, and nuzzled Lupita's hands to check for food. As she and Manolo spoke softly to them, Martina found a patch of soft grass in the shade of a mesquite tree. This was the place Martina came to feel close to the Sierra. Opposite the stables, the old aqueduct stood against a cityscape of freeways and newly constructed houses. Sometimes brides and grooms came to pose for photos in front of the aqueduct, but mostly the park was empty except for the horses' caretaker, an elderly man who didn't mind when Martina came by. She sat down facing the stables and sewed.

Perhaps because she sensed Martina's sadness, Lupita quickly joined her for her sewing lesson. Manolo was too afraid of the horses to be left by himself, so he ran after Lupita and looked for insects in the grass by his mother and sister. The first step was learning how to thread a needle, which Lupita had done a few times. She sat dutifully beside her mother, holding the needle a short distance from her face and trying to guide the thread through its eye. Martina showed her how to wet the tip of the thread with her tongue so it would stiffen. But Lupita struggled with this crucial and seemingly simple step. She brought the thread to the eye of the needle, and each time she thought she had it, she missed it entirely. She thought her eyes were playing tricks on her.

Martina laughed. In the Sierra, she and María José had sat with her own mother in the shade of the pine trees, straining in just the same way. Her mother had told them to sit and practice until they got it right, and Martina said the same thing to her own daughter.

But Lupita found the task tedious. To sit trying to thread a needle when there were horses and an expanse of green meadow felt impossible. Camila had recently learned to sew, though she didn't like it either. Violeta's mother wasn't even willing to teach her. Perhaps because many of her peers weren't learning or because other things seemed more important, Lupita didn't care much for these lessons. She tried to hide her disinterest well, choosing, as usual, to please her mother. Yet Martina sensed her daughter's frustration and offered encouragement.

You're going to learn to sew beautifully, she said, smiling.

When Lupita finally threaded the needle, she felt triumphant. Martina handed her a small rectangle of fabric.

Now make the stitches. Make sure they're small and even, she said, indicating with her forefinger and thumb how tiny they should be.

Do you remember the mountains and the forest? Martina asked suddenly, her tone wistful. She thought about how Jaime usually answered that question. *No,* he would say defiantly, though as the oldest, he was the most likely to have retained memories.

Yes, Lupita answered honestly. *A little.*

We'll go back and visit someday, Martina said, even though she knew she couldn't save enough money for the bus fare.

May afternoons, dark clouds swept across the sky. They emerged together from a distant point on the horizon, which appeared to be the edge of the world. Dimming the desert sun, they released a rain that lifted the sand. There was no wind, only a curtain of water that sometimes turned to small pebbles of ice. Lupita thought the hail was miraculous: ice that fell to the desert floor and didn't instantly melt. It was only after the clouds had moved across the sky and returned the sun to the land that the hail disappeared. The clouds, moving fast then slow, carrying water, had more strength than the ever-present sun. It was like they were running, Lupita thought; they could choose, like the Rarámuris, when to move and when to be still. Lupita had made a choice too: she was returning to the Sierra, carving a future for herself, making life a little easier for her family. She was relieved that she would no longer have to korimear, and it pleased her to imagine her parents, especially her mother, not having to worry about her. They would know she was responsible enough to make smart choices not only for herself but for her entire family. Not like Jaime.

One early May morning, Rarámuri men built a makeshift stage where the sixth-grade graduating class would receive their diplomas. They carried dozens of folding chairs loaned by the Coordinadora Estatal de la Tarahumara from a delivery van and filled half the basketball court with them. They strung a large handwritten banner that read "Felicidades, Graduados" from poles on either side of the stage. Jaime would graduate that day and walk across the stage to receive his diploma. Lupita would sit in the third row until her third-grade class was called up to receive certificates of their own.

That morning, Martina separated Lupita's hair into three thick sections. Dipping her fingers into a cup of water, she moistened the strands to help them stick together. Then she braided a single plait that reached Lupita's waist.

Lupita wore a new dress Martina had made for her. It was midnight blue, the color the girls in her class had chosen for their graduation dresses, with white piping. There was a path of triangular peaks and valleys on each layer of the skirt. Martina had cut the small, even triangles from the same color fabric as the piping. She loved the way the mountains were all the same size, a pattern that repeated just as the actual mountains extended toward a horizon that seemed to have no end.

Jaime dressed in jeans and a button-down shirt his teacher had given him. He allowed Martina to comb his hair for the last time. Jaime had been waiting for this day all year. The end of school. The beginning of something better. Not adulthood, and not quite adolescence, either, but something like independence.

Lupita took her place on a folding chair beside Camila and Violeta, who greeted her with smiles. Violeta had a large bruise on her forehead. Though she wouldn't say how she had gotten it, Lupita knew that her parents, who were not at the ceremony, had most likely hit her the night before. Violeta was in the same blue dress she had worn every day since school started. A neighbor had realized her mother no longer sewed or knew her daughter's needs and made it for her. That morning, she had showered at the neighbor's house, since her parents no longer paid the utility bills.

Lucero had asked for the day off so she could watch Camila walk across the stage. She was thankful that her manager had said yes—she had heard of employees who were fired when they asked for a sick day or time off. But the manager of the hotel was pleased with Lucero's work ethic and wanted to keep her. She told her she cleaned better than most of the other women. Now, she sat at the basketball court next to Martina, her hands folded tightly in her lap as she waited in anticipation to see her daughter graduate.

Mothers, fathers, and their youngest children sat on the ground around the perimeter of the basketball court, as they did for government-sponsored events, observers on the other side of the line between them and their city-raised children. And yet no adult felt the same mixture of solemnity and joy that the Virgin's feast day or Holy Week brought. Though the fathers and the mothers, in hand-sewn dresses that carried a continuum, knew completing a grade was a worthy accomplishment, they saw the graduation ceremony, the procession of children across the stage, as another occasion that marked the passage of time. It was both a starting point and an ending, which made time's fleetingness especially palpable.

This was why most Rarámuris didn't celebrate birthdays. But the graduation ceremony was different, because the Rarámuris themselves had advocated for the school to be built, back in the 1980s. Young parents at the time, among them José, had argued to the state government that their children would continue to live in poverty unless they had a chance to gain an education. Getting this education was impossible in the mestizo schools, they said; there was too much harassment. The solution lay in building a school just for Rarámuri children within the walls of El Oasis. It was the only asentamiento school for over a decade, until newer asentamientos began to replicate the model. Having the school inside the walls meant that children could walk to school without fear of harassment, and that they could get to school without having to rely on their parents. Every elementary-age child in El Oasis attended the school, which meant that the city-born generations all learned to read, write, and do math, including counting money. There was never a guarantee that children would continue their schooling beyond the sixth grade, and for more than half of that sixth-grade class, this would be their final ceremony. For many, it marked the passage between childhood and adulthood in a way that their parents didn't understand, but that they felt keenly. Some of the boys, like Jaime, would go straight to work; most of the boys and girls would attend a mestizo middle school and drop out within the year, usually because they needed to work or because they were expecting a child.

Then there were the children who would be sent to boarding school, in an attempt to save them from the fate that awaited those who completed the sixth grade in El Oasis. In Lupita's third-grade class, a handful of the children would not gather in these folding-chair seats next year to celebrate their fourth-grade graduation. Some, like Lupita and Camila, would be in the Sierra, studying at the boarding schools through high school, trying to make a path to college. The forward motion of time continued to pull apart families and friends.

One of the teachers opened the ceremony by speaking about the children's accomplishments and the importance of education for a better future. In the mestizo schools throughout the city, teachers delivered similar lectures. The mestizo children understood that they carried the promise of a future where economic stability was the central focus, an achievable goal. For most of the children in El Oasis, the end of the school year marked the beginning of a summer of food insecurity, since they would no longer receive lunch in the school cafeteria and would have to rely on korimeando and their parents' wages to have enough to eat. Though it was hard for the children to conceptualize the teacher's words—for many, a better future meant having enough to eat that evening—the children heard the solemnity in her voice. The power of the ceremony lay not in the words the teacher spoke, but in the fact that the teachers had taken the trouble to set up a stage and a balloon arch, and to deliver remarks in a serious tone. This alone made the children feel important, and planted the seed that there was a place for them in the wider mestizo world.

Martina and Luis gleaned this feeling too, though they had a more vague sense of it than the children. Moving forward, progressing—these ideas didn't resonate with Martina, Luis, or the dozens of other parents who listened to the teacher speak that day. They couldn't imagine their children in a profession, no matter how hard the teachers tried to present this possibility to them and their children. This was a main reason the teachers encouraged parents to send their children back to the Sierra. There, the teachers would instill in the children the idea that higher education would bring them economic stability, and allow them to contribute to the world in a meaningful way. For the parents, the importance of the ceremony lay in the fact that trusted mestizos were paying attention to their children. As they had each learned since coming to the city and beginning to korimear, the kind of attention mestizos gave them could mean the difference between life and death.

Butterflies fluttered in Lupita's stomach as the principal began to speak. The smaller children, in kindergarten and first and second grade, were called to the stage, and then it was time for the third graders to go up. The students sat in rows behind the sixth graders, who would be the final ones to go up. Lupita squeezed Camila's and Violeta's hands. A row of girls in navy-blue dresses and boys in jeans and long-sleeved button-downs filed past their teacher and received their diplomas. Lupita thought about how she was one step closer to the end of her time korimeando. Hundreds of children throughout Chihuahua City would continue, enduring heat, pollution, and threats from mestizos. Soon, Lupita would be spending her days in an orderly classroom. When classes let out, she would play and run in the fenced-in yard and take field trips into town to buy candy. She would sleep in a dormitory filled with identical twin beds with pink coverlets. During holidays, she would ride back to El Oasis in a van, where she would hug her mother and tell her she had seen her grandparents once that semester.

Lupita returned to her seat and grasped Camila's and Violeta's hands once again. They had completed third grade, together. There were moments when Lupita felt a deep sense of gratitude for her two best friends, and this was one of them. Without them, Lupita wasn't sure she could have focused on school; she would have been too worried about learning to korimear. But Camila and Violeta had helped her, and this had allowed her to pay attention in class. She was proud not just because she had graduated third grade; she had also learned more math and gained proficiency in reading. It felt good to be smarter; it felt wonderful to have friends who could help her.

The sixth graders, who were marking the end of their elementary years, were called up one by one. When his name was called, Jaime rose from his seat and walked across the stage for the final time. He walked with his head slightly lowered, and extended his arm hesitantly to receive the diploma. Though his teachers had never spoken harshly to him about his paint-thinner addiction, he suspected that they saw him as a delinquent. Perhaps they thought he wouldn't be anything more than a drug user, and they gave him his diploma only because they felt sorry for him. He didn't look out at the younger children, a little afraid they would be mocking him instead of watching him in admiration, as he had observed they did the other sixth graders. In past years, he had stored his diploma in a folder he kept in a plastic bag that held his clothes. That paper had marked his passage into the next year, and like Lupita, he had looked back on his accomplishments of the year with satisfaction. Now, Jaime dreaded receiving the diploma. It was a reminder of everything bad that had happened this past year, and nothing more.

Then, as Jaime shook his teacher's hand and received the scroll tied with a blue ribbon, he realized that the piece of paper marked his transition from schoolboy to worker. Until then, Jaime had felt that school was endlessly long, and that he was forever trapped in the role of paint-thinner-sniffing schoolboy. Now, with this final act as a student, Jaime was free from this role, at least the schoolboy part. There was possibility in his future, he thought, though as he walked back to his seat, he began to feel fear about what would come next. He would go to work, but to what end? Would he become a victim of weekly extortions, like his father? Or would he be smart enough to evade the extortions, and keep all the money he earned?

Jaime watched as the final six students in his class were called up. Once the last student had received her diploma, the principal congratulated the sixth-grade class and asked them to rise. The teachers, standing in a line behind the principal, applauded the sixth graders. The children joined in next, and then a few of the parents. Most of the sixth graders around him grinned with pride; Jaime smiled a little, the sound of applause lifting his insecurities. The teacher beckoned for the sixth-grade class to file up to the stage once again, where the class stood together under the balloon archway, looking out at the younger students and their parents, and smiled for the camera.

The summer months arrived, and heat bore down on the desert once again. Children with holes in the soles of their shoes stuffed cardboard and tissue inside to shield their feet from the burning sidewalks. Someone had donated a box of Barbies in princess gowns, doctors' coats, and business suits, and girls played with them, setting them on the sidewalks to watch boys play at matachines, shaking water bottles filled with pebbles as they stepped to the slow rhythm.

Some girls let their Barbies nap in rebozos made of fabric scraps they tied across their backs. One afternoon, María José collected the dolls and put them in tiny Rarámuri dresses the mothers had made in their sewing circle. Then she lined them up like women dancing matachines. The mothers smiled at the blond and brunette dolls, whose skin color carried the colonizers' stories, now wearing colorful, ankle-length dresses patterned with tiny mountains on luminous paths.

Lupita spent her summer korimeando, trying to provide her parents with as much money as she could before she left for boarding school. Martina had said she could join her at the market stall downtown, which she and Eugenia were now setting up every day. But soon after graduation, Lupita noticed weekday sales were slower and convinced her mother to let her korimeando until the day she left. The money would come in handy, she told her mother. Manolo was growing and needed more food. Jaime had started working but was spending a portion of his money on the jerseys he had long wanted.

When they weren't at their posts at the KFC and the intersections near the roundabout, Lupita, Camila, and Violeta got together to jump rope or run alongside women in the footraces that were now taking place nearly every evening. The summer months always saw more races, since the late afternoons were cool. Runners could breathe without their throats burning, and the sun warmed without scorching. Camila and Lupita felt worried thinking that they would soon be separated from their friend. They weren't sure if anyone would notice if her parents hit her or forgot to give her food. Their own parents, María José, Eugenia, and other kindly neighbors might not notice if they were busy korimeando or selling crafts. Violeta would likely be too ashamed to ask for help. There wouldn't be anyone to make her laugh or play with her; Violeta didn't have friends besides Lupita and Camila. Violeta, not wanting them to feel guilty for leaving her behind, told them she was glad to be staying in El Oasis; she liked her teachers and recess on the basketball court. In truth, Violeta wanted badly to go to the Sierra, but knew her parents would never grant her permission because they needed her to korimear. She never mentioned her parents, and Lupita and Camila had stopped asking about them, sensing that talking about a problem that seemed to have no solution only brought her more pain.

It was a summer of goodbyes for the girls, whose bond, formed before they ever wore matching graduation dresses, was about to be weakened by distance. Violeta's life would change when her two best friends were no longer there to bring lightness to it. Martina, Lucero, and other women would continue to look after her, offering her meals and a place to sleep, but the patchwork of support never dulled the pain and isolation of being a child with parents who felt the cut of history too deeply to look after their daughter. Violeta would become pregnant five summers later, when she was fourteen. The father would be a man thirty years her senior, a man most Rarámuri parents wouldn't have approved of for their young daughters because of the age difference. Violeta would not go on to attend middle school; instead she spent her afternoons korimeando, her infant son wrapped snugly in a rebozo across her chest. Though she loved her son and being a mother, Violeta would often wonder what it would have been like to attend boarding school with her friends, whether in the Sierra she would have finally felt the sense of security she never experienced with her parents.

Martina stands in front of the stove, stirring onions and jalapeños in oil. She sprinkles in a pinch of salt and listens as the oil crackles. She wants the onions to soften and brown a little; she likes to scrape out the burnt pieces and eat them straight from the pan.

It's August 15, and it's hotter than it's been all summer. The pavement burns to the touch by mid-morning, and women have retreated to their homes to cook and sew. Outside, in the shaded corridors, children are slapping pogs on the pavement and talking excitedly in a mix of Rarámuri and Spanish. Their voices become louder as María Cruz walks down the corridor with a chicken, still alive. She carries it by its legs, and its beady eyes dart around, taking in the children and their game. Soon, the smell of meat frying in oil will waft through the barred windows María Cruz keeps open and mingle with the scent of onion and jalapeño from Martina's kitchen.

On the other side of the room, Lupita is folding her dresses and tucking them neatly into a duffel bag. Tonight will be the family's last meal together until Lupita returns for Christmas break in December. She is leaving at six the next morning, in a van driven by one of the girls' fathers. He is taking the children to the boarding school in Carichí, a municipality close to where the Gutiérrez family once lived. It seems like another lifetime, especially after this year, the year Chihuahua City brought new dangers into their lives. Martina and Luis don't know if their old wooden house is still in the clearing, if drug traffickers have taken it or burned it down. Martina likes to imagine a family has arrived and planted seeds in the garden. She hopes a woman is using the loom she left behind to make blankets and rebozos. She hopes children collect pinecones to play with, and that a family dances yumari together in the evenings.

Martina has sent word to her parents, through a friend, that Lupita will be at the boarding school in Carichí. She hopes they will visit her, and that the nuns will allow her to travel to their home on weekends. Though Martina isn't sure what to expect from the nuns, she believes being back in the Sierra will not only keep Lupita safe but guide her. She will be breathing the very air Onorúame made for their people.

At school, you'll have time to practice sewing, Martina says. She spoons the onions and jalapeños out of the pan and onto a small dish. *You'll be able to sew your own dresses.*

I think I'll have to. I heard the nuns hit the girls' hands when they don't make perfect stitches.

It'll be better than watching mestizos pass chicken and coins back and forth.

Lupita laughs. *Yes, it'll be better than that.*

Manolo reaches into Lupita's duffel bag, trying to pull out one of her folded skirts. To stop him, Lupita squeezes him to her and tickles him. Manolo, a boy who runs and kicks balls with other children in the corridor, is old enough to understand that Lupita is leaving and to tell her, *Don't go, sister.* In response, Lupita tickles him until he howls.

Will you come visit me? Lupita asks her mother. It is the closest she has come to saying she will miss her mother terribly, that she already misses their afternoons sewing at the police stables, their walks to the reservoir.

It is a blessing to have a daughter. A blessing not only for Martina, but for the Rarámuri people, who will continue to be Rarámuri because their daughters take care to live by korima. Even if Martina spends the rest of her days missing Lupita, she knows the mountains will be thankful to have her back. Of that, Martina is certain.

She breathes in, trying to remember the scent of the pine trees and the rosemary Luis used to bring her.

I'll be waiting here for you, Martina says, her voice catching in her throat. *You'll tell me what the Sierra is like.*

Epilogue

In July 2021, Martina and Eugenia sat on the floor of Eugenia's kitchen counting the money they had begun saving twelve months before, soon after Chihuahua City shut down to slow the spread of COVID-19. Martina counted the bills, and Eugenia, the coins. They had to work quickly or risk being caught; their husbands, who were drinking at the arroyo, didn't know they were part of a group of women putting aside money for a parcel of land in the desert. They were planning to build a new settlement.

This new path would finally lead Martina and her family to greater security. Her friends had begun discussing the idea as early as 2016, when a handful of Rarámuri women went to work at a mestiza-owned clothing shop that claimed to be a socially conscious business because the owner hired only Rarámuri seamstresses to create and sell Western garments decorated with Rarámuri designs. Martina and Eugenia took the job, the promise of a regular paycheck too good to pass up. Then the owner cut their wages with no explanation, and a couple of women quit. The owner later showed up at El Oasis and threatened to sue the women for selling sweatshirts and T-shirts with mountains embroidered on, claiming they had stolen her designs. At that point, every seamstress quit. Some of them attended a sewing workshop founded in El Oasis in 2017 by Gloria, the woman who had once vied with Eugenia to sell the most crafts to the nonprofits. For years, Gloria had been envisioning a workshop where Rarámuri women could make garments and crafts in the comfort of their community, with their children playing nearby, and sell these garments to clients. She saw it as the best way to ensure a steady income and give them more control over their time and interactions with mestizos. Even Eugenia, who continued to feel a sense of rivalry with Gloria, joined the workshop. But the women struggled to gain clients, even as the mestiza's clothing brand garnered national attention—a fact that frustrated the women to no end. They recognized that the mestiza had sales and marketing savvy, which she had put to use to build a trendy website filled with slender, light-skinned models in adaptations of Rarámuri clothing. Most Rarámuris and many mestizos saw her business as exploitive: yet another way the mestizos stole Rarámuri knowledge for their own profit.

In the sewing circle, the idea of building a new community, complete with another sewing workshop where Rarámuri women could sell directly to their own clients, began to gain momentum. Owning land was the first step toward the autonomy they recognized as imperative to their survival. They could then decide who came onto their property, and turn away government officials, police, drug traffickers, child traffickers, journalists, and anthropologists as they saw fit. The women would design the community to fit their needs. The corridors would be wide enough to let in sunlight, and there would be plenty of space for children to play. There would be an elementary school, and the basketball courts would always be open, so the older children could play sports. There would also be a carpentry workshop, which the Rarámuris would maintain without having to ask the government for help. It was a future Martina wanted so completely that she no longer wondered whether it was possible to be Rarámuri in the city. By that point, El Oasis had grown from a community of five hundred people to approximately eight hundred, nearly all of whom sought refuge from the drought and the drug growers in the Sierra. It was more apparent than ever to Martina that their people would have to find ways to enact korima in the city—even if it meant evolving the definition of korima.

Each day, women brought whatever money they could spare to Eugenia or Martina, who kept it in a cloth pouch they took turns hiding in their scrap bags. The women couldn't let their husbands find out what they were doing, for fear that one of them would demand the money for alcohol or drugs. It was safest to keep the money a secret, as Martina and dozens of other women already did if their husbands had a habit of hoarding their wages or stealing the coins their wives earned korimeando. The women's goal was to reach twenty thousand pesos, or about two thousand dollars, the cost of a parcel of desert thirty minutes outside the city. The landowner, a rancher they met while searching the city outskirts for For Sale signs on empty parcels of land, had warned the women that there was no running water that far outside the city, but it didn't deter them; they would pay a mestizo with a car to drive into the city, buy the water, and deliver it to the settlement.

Martina and the Rarámuri women of El Oasis became more adamant about forming a new community on the outskirts of the city after meth overwhelmed the asentamiento in the summer of 2019, taking dozens of children and teenagers. At first, the mothers didn't realize what their children were taking. It was only by surreptitiously following them through El Oasis and the wider colonia that they learned mestizos were selling them small snow-white pills, assuring them the drug would give them a high far better and more joyful than the brief euphoria they felt after sniffing paint thinner.

It was no longer just the local shop owners selling paint thinner who were victimizing Rarámuri youth. As the federal army burned hidden fields of marijuana and poppies, the Juárez and Sinaloa Cartels switched to making meth in laboratories hidden throughout the Sierra and the cities. In Colonia Martín López, it sold for little more than a can of beer, and the high did, indeed, last far longer. News began to spread, and more youth began taking the pills; some would crush and inhale them. The Rarámuri mothers found meth far more terrifying than paint thinner. While paint thinner made their children dull and listless, meth caused hallucinations and paranoia. Boys and girls on the cusp of adolescence began threatening their families and fighting among each other.

Jaime's addiction to meth came fast and furious. By August 2019, he was scouring the house for extra coins, shaking and nervous between pills. When he didn't find coins, he took bags of his family's beans and sold them to mestizo neighbors for less than they cost at the store, then spent the money on meth. Martina, distraught, tried to enlist Luis to help her talk Jaime into finally going to rehab, though Luis had never agreed with the idea, feeling the daily treatment program was too expensive and probably wouldn't work anyway.

The siríame, a middle-aged woman named Jimena who sewed dresses every day despite quietly suffering from liver disease, asked the mestizo police to make daily rounds through the El Oasis community. Taking a different approach than José or Lucero, who had gone on to serve as siríame from 2014 to 2018, she urged the police to arrest youth who were using drugs in an effort to scare them. The police filled their patrol cars with teenage boys and girls and jailed them for twenty-four hours. Mothers borrowed bus fare from one another to travel downtown to the offices of the Coordinación Estatal de la Tarahumara and plead for rehab scholarships, which were given only to families who couldn't afford the facility's daily fee of fourteen dollars, in cases that couldn't be helped by other means. Some of the adolescents lived in the rehab home for a full three months, completing a detox program, psychological evaluations, and talk therapy sessions. Jimena thought the detox program seemed to work, though she recognized that the adolescents returning to an environment where drugs were sold caused many of them to fall back into addiction almost immediately. The new settlement in the desert would be a way of removing children and adolescents from the source of the drugs, but while the mothers saved enough money to buy the land, they agreed that using the police to scare the adolescents was the only option. When Jimena returned to the Sierra to die, in December of that year, the police continued making their rounds, arresting a handful of youth each week.

Martina had never stopped wanting Jaime to go through the detox program, even in the years just after he began working, when he became known as a quick learner among mestizos and Rarámuris, and young women admired the muscles he'd developed doing hard labor. He sniffed paint thinner intermittently during this time but avoided alcohol altogether, fearing he would become potbellied like his father. When he began a relationship with an old schoolmate and welcomed a daughter just after his fifteenth birthday, Martina hoped he would finally stop for good. But abuse from mestizo managers and frequent extortions wore him down until he saw no point in quitting. When a drug peddler came to El Oasis selling pills, Jaime decided to try them.

Luis's alcohol dependency had grown stronger over the years for the same reasons, but he still wasn't able to address Jaime's addiction in a productive way. When Jaime became belligerent that fall, Luis kicked him out of the house again, telling him not to return until he was sober. Jaime's partner, a young woman who wore hoop earrings and black eyeliner with her hand-sewn dresses, stayed with him in the back room, which Luis and Martina had given to the young family. Luis watched his son leave: Jaime's head was bent low toward the ground, and his arms hung stiffly by his sides. Then Luis walked to the edge of the arroyo, where he drank with Eduardo and other men until they fell asleep on the sidewalk.

Lupita and Manolo both witnessed their brother's decline. Lupita now had a husband, and a one-year-old son she sought to protect from Jaime's violent outbursts. Manolo, a teenager himself, worked in construction and rarely visited. He lived with his girlfriend and her family in another asentamiento.

In fall 2018, one semester before she graduated, Lupita was kicked out of boarding school for becoming pregnant. Her boyfriend, a young man named Javier, was allowed to remain. At Martina's urging, Lupita returned to her parents' house in El Oasis to wait to give birth. She cleaned a mestiza's home in the colonia, and in her free time, she sat on the front stoop with Violeta, who had a newborn son and a husband who spent most of his time on ranches outside the city. They lived in the same house where Violeta was raised, which she kept after her parents' deaths three years before. Lupita practiced holding the infant, trying to imagine what it would feel like to look into her own child's eyes. She had mixed feelings about the baby. She'd wanted to graduate high school and go on to nursing school, where she had hoped to wear a white Rarámuri dress. She had seen Rarámuri nurses wearing such dresses and thought they signified what she had become: a Rarámuri woman capable of reading and writing, able to maintain her cultural identity even as she made a path for herself in the city. But with the baby growing in her belly, she wondered if this aspiration would ever become a reality. Diapers and formula were expensive; she often walked by the locked case where the formula was kept at the Soriana. How would she pay tuition at the Instituto de Estudios en el Área de la Salud Florencia Nightingale when there was barely enough money to buy groceries, much less the formula the baby would soon demand?

Now, in 2021, Lupita and Violeta still met on the front stoop to talk. They rarely spoke of Camila, who had died by suicide one year before. Soon after she had returned to El Oasis, after graduating from boarding school, she had moved in with a Rarámuri man her age. She became pregnant and told no one that her husband had started to hit her. No one knew him well, not even Lucero, who hadn't wanted her daughter to marry so young. Six months into her pregnancy, Camila took her own life, alone in the apartment her husband had insisted they rent on the other side of town. She became one of the many Indigenous women across the Americas to die young, another casualty of a system that made men violent and trapped women in endless cycles of abuse.

Lupita was in the Sierra visiting her grandparents when Lucero created an altar for her daughter a few weeks after her death. Martina told her the news over the phone. She also shared that the police report Lucero tried to file had been ignored. Though an anthropologist who had gained the Rarámuris' trust over the years tried to insist to the police that a proper investigation was warranted, his urging came to nothing. The mestizos thought the Rarámuris were too broken to warrant an adequate investigation into Camila's death. *These things happen,* they said to Lucero, shrugging. *She probably didn't do what her husband wanted, and that's why he hit her. No one killed her, she did it to herself, there's no one to blame but her.* Lucero's house was filled with food and flowers, the Rarámuris of El Oasis coming together once again to help one another. Martina, María José, and Eugenia sat with Lucero for many nights, telling stories about Camila and joking with her spirit. The Rarámuri soul never wants to depart from Onorúame's beautiful world. Only when other Rarámuris gather to keep it company does the soul, feeling loved and supported, decide to join Onorúame in the sky.

Even after the death of her dear friend, and even as she watched her brother succumb to a more potent drug, Lupita kept her mind trained on the future. She supported the women's goal of buying land, agreeing it was the best way to finally gain control of their lives. Some evenings, she kept watch outside while her mother and Eugenia counted coins, ready to alert them if one of their husbands was returning early.

When Martina first heard about the virus on the nightly news, she shrugged it off, thinking it seemed far less threatening than the meth still tearing through the community. It wasn't until mestizos stopped showing up at El Oasis to hire men, buy crafts, and deliver donations that Martina and the other women became fearful of its effects. At first, becoming ill seemed a small concern; so many members of the community, particularly the youth using meth, were already gravely ill. Even when Calle Libertad emptied of pedestrians and potential customers, the virus and its potential to cause death continued to feel abstract. Martina, María José, Eugenia, and the other women weren't entirely sure that the COVID-19 virus could even infect them. They regarded the virus as a chabochi illness, one that touched only people who exploited the land. They regarded most of the diseases the medical doctors warned them about in this manner. Sometimes, Martina even joked about it with María José and Eugenia. *At least the government has a good plan for dealing with this,* she'd say, referring to the trucks that drove up and down streets, spraying sidewalks and people with disinfectant.

By the end of March, food insecurity had reached a level no Rarámuri had ever before experienced in the city. In those first days after the shutdown, when Martina tried to go out to korimear, she found the streets eerily empty save for a few houseless people. Staying home wasn't an option for the Rarámuris in the city, who to eat needed to collect coins every day. With no jobs for the men and no mestizos to give korima or buy crafts, the community depended entirely on the sacks of beans and rice from the Coordinadora Estatal de la Tarahumara and the food box donations from NGOs, churches, and private citizens, all of which were weeks late in arriving. The Rarámuris' network of help kept the children from starving, as those in the Sierra were, but the instability led to other problems. Without work, Luis was drinking even more often. Jaime, desperate to find money for pills, became increasingly violent. But still Martina would not abandon her family.

Each time they sat down to anxiously count their savings, which they did once or twice a week, Martina and Eugenia hoped they had made a great leap toward reaching their goal, but earnings had been even more sparse than before. Martina sat inside the house, listening to news reports on TV, her purse empty. She had no beans or tortillas, no squash, no potato chips or lollipops. She had only the water streaming fast and cold from the faucets of the utility sinks.

One evening that June, the clouds released a rain that did not stop for an entire day. Water dripped through the laminated roofs of the houses, and Rarámuri families shivered. Hail covered the ground in white. The torrent fell like a curtain and turned the streets of Chihuahua City to fast-flowing rivers. Into the arroyos it ran, dragging along trash and stray dogs and cats.

In the hours before the water turned dangerous, Lupita's fifteen-year-old cousin Lorena, María José's daughter-in-law, decided to take a shortcut through the arroyo to her mother's house, where she planned to wait out the storm. She descended into the arroyo, just as she had hundreds of times. At the bottom, she waded through ankle-deep water, her skirt hems instantly drenched. When a flood of water poured into the arroyo, it knocked her off her feet and pulled her across the arroyo's floor, then into a canal the mestizos had built to carry floodwaters. The waters grew faster and deeper, and no one knew she had been crossing through the arroyo on her way to her mother's house. It would be hours before anyone suspected she had drowned, and ten days before a search and rescue team composed of Rarámuris from El Oasis, the police, and workers at the Coordinadora Estatal de la Tarahumara located a body that appeared to be hers.

After the flash floods, the dark clouds continued gathering, but no more rain fell. Soon, the water in the arroyo dried up, and the desert once again thirsted for more. The nopales and lechuguilla kept a store of water in their bodies, and the Rarámuris of El Oasis collected it in buckets. The community mourned Lorena, who had died in the water that should have given her life. Her mother created an altar in her home and talked with her daughter's spirit, urging her to travel to the sky, to be with Onorúame.

The Rarámuris had noticed that these flash floods were happening more frequently. First long periods of droughts, then violent rains that swept people away. Some of the older Rarámuris attributed this to the mestizos' cars and factories filling the air with smoke, which frightened the clouds and caused them to release angry torrents of rain. *If the foolish mestizos would only stop harming the land and the sky, the clouds would feel peaceful and provide us with the right amount of water,* they said among themselves. Others said the heavy rains were their peoples' fault for failing to dance enough yumari.

Younger Rarámuris, Lupita among them, relied on news reports of the climate crisis to broaden their understanding the struggles they were facing. They understood that the clouds' strange and threatening behavior was not unique to Chihuahua City and the Sierra. These kinds of weather events were happening everywhere, even in faraway countries, where people spoke different languages. Though they now shared Western-based ways of thinking about the climate crisis, the youth agreed with their elders on two important things: that the Rarámuri people deserved land justice, and that they had the power, supported by Onorúame's blessings, to determine and carry out their own solutions. Rarámuri people have always done this, even in the face of colonization and forced assimilation. Their story is not one of the present or the past. It lies outside linear time and comprises adaptations only they are brave enough to imagine.

The effects of meth and the virus ravaged El Oasis well into 2021. Despite these challenges, the community continued engaging in the same rituals that had always held them together. They sacrificed a cow, dancing matachines on the school basketball court and praying to Onorúame to protect even the chabochis from the virus. During Semana Santa, they burned Judas for the sake of the entire world. Youth like Lupita saw climate change as a sin of colonization and believed the cleansing ritual would give them the strength to organize and protect the land and the water. The women continued to save up money for their own land, but the new settlement was still a far-off possibility. It helped that the city had reopened. Martina agreed to let a nurse give her the first dose of the COVID-19 vaccine, even though she was certain that no Rarámuri had ever caught the disease. She believed that the people in her community who had gotten ill the past year had been afflicted with another illness. Usually, Rarámuri people became sick because they were not living by korima. Still, she thought, it couldn't hurt. But the fever and chills she suffered after the first dose were so bad that she told the mestiza nurse she would never accept another vaccine again. Martina and Eugenia resumed selling crafts downtown, and María José continued to clean houses for mestizas. Slowly, their savings grew, their dream becoming more viable with each coin added to the purse.

Then, in March of 2022, Lupita caught wind of some plots of land that had just gone up for sale near the Cerro de la Cruz, in the eastern part of the city. They were small parcels, just enough for one house. Eugenia, Martina, and María José, realizing they had enough money, decided to buy parcels next to one another. They didn't tell their husbands, fearing that the men would force them to hand over the money. The land was on the outer edges of a mestizo neighborhood, a fact that none of them liked. But the land was affordable to them, and the three of them were eager to get out of El Oasis. Martina's house was too crowded now that Lupita lived there with Javier and their toddler, a little boy with Martina's smile, and she was tired of the constant presence of mestizos and drugs. On this parcel of land, she could build a two- or three-story house, and still be neighbors with María José and Eugenia. They could live a little separate from mestizos, and have easier access to the desert, where they could go for runs and look for herbs. The three of them tried to convince other community members to buy up parcels of the land, but most stuck with the original plan of buying the land out in the desert, farther from the city. Their refusal didn't disappoint Martina and María José enough to keep them from going forward with their plan, and it didn't bother Eugenia at all. Eugenia carried resentment toward Gloria for gaining so much success with her sewing workshop, and she didn't mind that she would be living far away from her.

With the parcel of land purchased, Martina then scrambled to gather enough money to lay down the first bricks. She feared that someone else would lay down bricks first, stealing the land for themselves, and that no authority would help her get back what she had rightfully purchased. She heard that this sometimes happened, and so she urged Lupita and Javier to add to her purse. By October of 2022, she had saved enough to buy just the cement and cinder blocks needed to lay the foundation of the house. On a Saturday afternoon, Javier took the bus to Martina's land and mixed the cement. He laid it on the dirt, then carefully placed the cinder blocks around the perimeter. It would take years, perhaps, to save enough money to build their new home, but that didn't bother Martina. This land, a small reclaiming of what had been taken from her ancestors, was now hers.

In late afternoons, the sound of thunder rumbling in the near distance drew Rarámuris to the sidewalk outside El Oasis, where they watched dark clouds converging over the city. A few dozen Rarámuris danced yumari on the sidewalks, coaxing a gentle rain. Dancing was as spontaneous as running—they danced when they felt moved to. Yumari was ancient, and it was of the moment. Like korima, it belonged in every space, and every time. Rarámuri men made their way up the street around the dancers, dishrags and squeegees in hand, on their way to wash car windows at intersections throughout the city. Others wandered the streets, high on paint thinner and meth. A group of children pushed an electric toy car with a dead battery to the top of the hill. Five of them piled into the two seats, two pushed the car down the hill, and others cheered. Mothers laughed and scolded. They left their sewing on the ground and rose to join in dancing yumari, their desire for peaceful rain too great for them to keep sitting.

Martina still believed the Rarámuri people of El Oasis didn't dance enough yumari, and that was one reason the clouds didn't share their water the way they used to. But now she also believed the mestizo people, and the people of the wider world, should join the Rarámuris in dancing. *The rain should reach everyone,* she said, *and we must all take care of the water.*

Author's Note

I met Lupita one September evening in 2009, when the late-afternoon heat had eased enough for the women to race in daylight. I was sitting on the curb, listening to them debate the quality of their dresses, when a little girl with long dark hair and a chubby face sat down next to me. *What's your name?* she asked me in Spanish, with the same candor so many of the children had when they spoke to me. I told her, and she asked me a few more questions: Why was I there? Where did I come from? What was my family like? When she learned that I was a researcher with an agenda, most interested in grasping the steps to the dress-betting process, she began to explain what was happening and even to translate bits of conversation she thought I should note. That evening, eight-year-old Lupita became the first Rarámuri person to guide me through El Oasis, explaining aspects of her community and sharing insights I once thought well beyond the scope of a child her age. Lupita was a special young girl— and is today a special woman—but I realized after a few months of field research that children are among the most astute observers of their own communities and families. Her perceptions helped color my understanding of El Oasis that year, and in the following thirteen years. Her influence is all over this book.

I was twenty-five years old that September and had recently started a year-long Fulbright fellowship in Chihuahua City, four hours south of my hometown, El Paso, Texas. From September 2009 through August 2010, I spent my days and many nights in El Oasis. According to my grant proposal, I was there to collect oral histories

from the Rarámuri people, whom I had grown up seeing on weekend trips to Ciudad Juárez, across the border from El Paso, so I could
understand what it meant for them to be displaced from their homeland. I had written the proposal during my senior year of college at
Northwestern University, where I had seized opportunities to take
classes in Latin American history. It was in the old classrooms of the
history building, the heaters chugging as the snow fell quietly, that
I began to expand my family's story of five generations in the border cities of Ciudad Juárez and El Paso, and Chihuahua City four
hours south. It was there, too, that I first noticed my Mexican family stories were only one version of events; there were Rarámuri
and Nde (Apache) people who had stories older than mine, stories
that deserved to be widely heard. I told the grant committee how
my mother had taught me to give my spare change to the Rarámuri
women who approached my family outside restaurants and shopping centers in Ciudad Juárez, distinctive in their colorful ankle-
length dresses. She repeated what she had been told by her parents:
that the word Rarámuri people said when they approached us—
korima—meant *limosna,* or alms. Their people had come from the
Sierra Madre mountains seven hours southwest of our home because
they were poor, she would tell me. But as I listened to professors lec-
turing on historical inquiry and the dangers of repressive histories, I
began to sense that there was something missing in my mother's telling of the Rarámuri story. While I gathered the facts and context that
surrounded their displacement—not their migration, as everyone I
knew had always called it—I understood that mining and logging in
their homeland, coupled with seasons of drought, had forced their
people out of the Sierra and to the cities. But no historical or ethno-
graphic account I read—all of them written by Mexican mestizos or
European men—explained what I wanted most to know: how it *felt*
for the Rarámuris to leave the mountains and maintain their identity
in a Spanish-speaking city.

Though I couldn't articulate it at the time, I now understand
that in pursuing knowledge of something so intimate as a person's
lived experience, I was searching for deeper knowledge of myself

and my family's story in the Chihuahuan Desert. Although I am a mestiza—a woman of mixed Indigenous and European ancestry—I know very little about my Indigenous heritage. Family members say we had a Rarámuri ancestor generations ago but the stories have since been lost. This is a common occurrence among mestizos, who form the majority population of Latin American countries and have most fully assimilated into the Spanish colonizers' culture, taking on the Spanish language and currency. The only tangible way in which my Indigenous heritage lived on is through the corn tortillas my abuelita used to make, the pinto beans she boiled each morning. I had grown up thinking my Mexican culture was beautiful because it combined elements of Indigenous cultures and Spanish culture. I had always been proud to be Mexican, proud of my family's role in the Mexican Revolution and our remaking of the country in the decades after. I had never seen the silence around my Indigenous ancestry as a loss to be mourned. It was simply the course of history, I had thought—the result of a Spanish conquest that created a new people. But the year I spent collecting oral histories from Rarámuri people, most of them women, I began to question the narratives I had grown up hearing, not only about Rarámuri people but about Mexico and the mestizo peoples' relationship to our Indigenous heritage. I didn't yet understand that *korima,* an ancient word spoken every day on the streets of Ciudad Juárez and Chihuahua City, holds rivers running unbridled, rain that falls from the clouds with abandon, and handwoven baskets filled with the same corn tortillas my abuelita made. It took years of oral history collection, living among Rarámuri people, and writing for me to begin to comprehend that. In listening to Rarámuri people tell their family stories, I realized I was gathering an entirely different and rarely heard history of the country.

Lupita introduced me to Martina that same evening. I'd already seen her around the community, in the sewing circles I watched from a distance, and the communal kitchen, where I sat on a stool in the corner, an eager field researcher dying to stand beside the women to shape balls of sticky flour into tortillas. We hadn't yet spoken, though. In those first weeks, I spent entire days in the community, introducing myself and asking permission to sit and watch the women as they engaged in their activities. Though I was eager to learn their names, get to know them, and join in whatever occupied them, I understood they were suspicious of me, a white mestiza who carried the legacy of pillaging and erasure that their people had to resist. I had already learned about the missing men through Lucero, and I understood I had come into the community during a particularly distressing time. That's why I was so moved when Martina sat on the curb next to Lupita and me that evening and offered me sips from her bottle of Coke as we watched two young runners race up the hill.

Over the following year, our friendship grew deeper, in large part thanks to Lupita, who spoke kindly and enthusiastically of me to Martina and Luis. Without her, I'm not sure the Gutiérrez family would have opened up to me as they did. By October 2009, my second full month of field research, I was in the habit of walking straight to Martina's house every morning and joining her in whatever household task she was working on. I got to know her sister, María José, and her best friend, Eugenia, by maintaining a near-constant presence in the community and being honest about my intentions. Maintaining a constant presence and being transparent and sincere about my intentions formed the foundations of the trust I wanted to build, and I tried hard to let them guide my actions. It helped that whenever I felt greed take over, a Rarámuri woman—though never Martina—put me in my place. A few times, I let my desire to cook alongside the women get the better of me and insisted they include me when they simply didn't want to. That they told me no gave me an opportunity to show them my character: other journalists who came through El Oasis gave up and abandoned their projects when the Rarámuri women hid for hours in their homes or maintained stony silences in their presence.

By the end of that October, I was joining the Rarámuri women in most activities and was fully engaged in the participatory research methods I had hoped to use. I wasn't simply observing the races: I was running in them. I was sewing my own dress and searching for guasoliki in arroyos. The only activity I didn't participate in was korimeando; this I observed from a close distance. I didn't take breaks during the day. This meant that I ate when they ate, which meant that I often didn't eat at all. Though I realized that I could never embody Rarámuri peoples' lived experiences, I wanted to come as close as I could. So I gave every waking hour to my participatory field research that year. This method of field research, developed by anthropologists and sociologists, seemed to me the only way to deepen trust and engage the community in storytelling.

I think of participatory research as an attempt to level the power imbalances inherent in the researcher–research subject relationship. Too often, social scientists and journalists don't do enough to dismantle the structures that give them greater power than their subjects, instead allowing themselves to be guided by the ultimate goal of extracting the material they need to write their articles or books. The goal of participatory research, on the other hand, is to build relationships, and the writing is a byproduct of those relationships. Though it might seem counterintuitive to those of us who think of writing as a career—and how can we not, when we, like everyone else, live under the constraints of a capitalist economy that rewards monetizing your personal interests, no matter the personal cost—I believe writing can be deeper and more insightful when it is the result of a trusting collaboration with the subjects it depicts. This process takes more time than scheduled interviews, but I long ago came to terms with that. The book I wanted to write would be done when it was done.

But I was still new to field research, twenty-five years old and one year out of college, with a double major in history and creative writing. I didn't understand, beyond what I had learned through reading, how much endurance it had taken for the Rarámuri people to keep alive Indigenous knowledge, and I made many mistakes during my year with them. Perhaps my biggest logistical error was that I never hired a translator. I took Rarámuri language classes and kept Enrique Servín Herrera's incredible Rarámuri dictionary close. But beyond those resources, I relied on children, especially Lupita, and the women to translate conversations in real time. I kept a recorder on me, but sometimes the women didn't give me permission to turn it on, I suspect because they saw their refusal as one of the ways to level the power imbalance. The depiction of the Gutiérrez family's story of leaving the Sierra is based entirely on oral history collection, secondary sources, and my own visits to the portion of the Sierra Madre mountains inhabited by the Rarámuri people. Martina and Luis recounted their journey to me over the course of the year I spent with them. We spoke in Spanish, which is my first language and their second language. When they struggled to find the words they wanted in Spanish, or when I struggled to understand their descriptions, Lupita, who is fluent in both Rarámuri and Spanish, helped translate for us. These factors impacted the dialogue in the book, which I approached in three ways: In the first four chapters, when the family leaves the Sierra and arrives at El Oasis, I created dialogue based on Martina's and Luis's descriptions of events. In the rest of the chapters, as well as the epilogue, I relied on Lupita to translate words I had captured on my recorder, or I drew from Lupita's and Martina's memories of what was said. In some instances, I edited the translations because I wanted to heighten tension; in others, I wanted to convey Martina's dry sense of humor, which simply couldn't be left out.

I believe firsthand experience is the best way to understand the rhythms of a person's life, and the emotional significances behind the activities that make up their days. That's why I cooked, sewed, washed clothes, collected edible herbs, danced, and ran alongside Rarámuri women. The only two activities I observed from a close distance were korimeando, as I've already noted, and the sacrifice of the cow, because in those instances, my participation would have impeded the community's goals. While I'm not a Rarámuri, and can't become one, I was able to gain insight into the

Rarámuris' lives by spending my days alongside them. I've relied on close observations, conversations, and my own experiences to color my descriptions of day-to-day life in El Oasis.

I was lucky to have the guidance of anthropologists from the Escuela Nacional de Antropología e Historia in Chihuahua. The most important piece of advice I received from them, which I followed from day one, was to show up every day, even when I was tired, even when the weight of what I was witnessing felt like too much. I wanted the community to see, through my presence and the active interest I took in their lives, that I was there not merely to extract stories, but to build relationships.

I can't call this project truly collaborative, at least not in the sense of calling the Gutiérrez family my cowriters. Martina and Luis don't know how to read and write, and they see books as belonging to mestizo culture. While they've always been supportive of this book, they've also been baffled by my insistence on writing it. To them, stories are meant to be shared in community, not bought and consumed individually, as is done with books. It was through them, and others in the community, that I realized writing for the sake of sharing stories and knowledge is not enough, not when Indigenous cultures and their lands are in peril.

Lupita, Violeta, and other women their age have read my reportage and are increasingly seeing the value of taking control of their own narratives through Facebook posts, TikTok, and Instagram and sharing them with the world. This is one rift in perspective between generations raised in the city and those raised in the Sierra, though Martina sees Lupita's interest in writing and journalism more as a point of disconnect than a problem. In the last five years, Lupita and her peers have become active on social media, developing and sharing images, memes, and posts that speak to their desire to keep alive Rarámuri identity; they understand that this form of storytelling is one way to counter the mestizos' narratives about Indigenous people. They have also begun to share their ideas about

Rarámuri futures, and have played a big role in shaping Martina, María José, Eugenia, and other women's tactics of resistance. For example, one thirty-three-year-old Rarámuri nurse named Liliana encourages community members to get the COVID-19 vaccines as well as to engage in traditional herbal medicine. She believes that traditional medicine helps the community maintain physical health, and that it's also a way for the Rarámuri spirit to resist assimilation. Yet she maintains that Western vaccines protect Rarámuri women, just as they protect the rest of the world. To help spread the idea of resistance to and acceptance of new ideas, she has taught women to sew facemasks with Rarámuri designs on them—and she displays them on social media. This helps the women take ownership of their own health and gain even greater pride in their sense of identity. Posting on social media has helped spread word throughout the city, and women in other Rarámuri asentamientos now make these facemasks. Martina, who still refuses to get her second vaccine dose, wears the facemasks of her own design each time she enters a store.

To recreate the scenes that took place in 2005—the drought the Gutiérrez family experienced in the Sierra that culminated in their leaving—I relied on my field notes, recordings, and photos. When I arrived in 2009, I was in the habit of taking notes as I conducted my research, but I ultimately felt that writing in a notebook while living alongside Rarámuri women was antithetical to my goal of showing up. My workaround was to type up everything that had happened each evening when I got home. Where there were discrepancies in my notes, I relied on the memories of Martina, Lupita, María José, Eugenia, Lucero, Camila, and other women to fact-check and shape my interpretations of events.

At their request, I changed the first and last names of every character in this book. In the story of the men going missing, I've altered a few details to avoid making the rancher identifiable. I made these changes because retribution for reporting is a real threat in Mexico, where journalists and the people who aid them put their lives at risk. Keeping the Rarámuri community of El Oasis safe was my highest priority.

These years later, I still feel the power imbalance between me and the Rarámuris when I visit El Oasis, but a little less each time. Though I am still a researcher, my relationships there grow deeper each year. I'm not sure if the power imbalance will go away as I continue to work to build trust; I suspect that it won't, not really. But to help mitigate this power imbalance, I remind myself when I arrive that I know nothing. I frame it that way—sternly—because I know it's important to set my ego aside, especially among people who always prioritize the community over the individual. The Rarámuris are the experts on their own community, their history, and what they need for the future they envision. I've kept that in mind while writing this book in my home in Minneapolis, just as I have and do at El Oasis. For example, I've taken care to prioritize Rarámuri versions of history over the Western textbooks. I've presented the origin story as a history that is more important than the history of the conquest. I focused all my oral history collection on Rarámuris, intentionally avoiding speaking too much to workers at the Coordinación Estatal de la Tarahumara or other mestizos. I didn't want mestizo perspectives to color my perceptions more than they already were. These decisions helped frame the way I wrote the chapter of the feast day of the Virgen de Guadalupe and Semana Santa, as well as how I discussed the sanitation problems in the asentamiento. While I recognize that the Coordinación Estatal de la Tarahumara (today known as the Comisión Estatal para los Pueblos Indígenas to accommodate the growing number of Indigenous refugees from other parts of the country) offers crucial services, I wanted to convey Rarámuri perceptions of the Coordinación as I have observed over the years.

I chose to widen the scope of the book to include historical and political context not known by many Rarámuris, who, for the sake of their peoples' survival, have tried to prioritize their ancestral knowledge by reducing engagement with the outside world. I've never imagined that Rarámuri readers would find anything in my writing enlightening—they have their own storytellers, people in every stage of life who share knowledge and lessons, weaving past, present, and future into the fabric of their everyday lives. This book, then, is for non-Rarámuri audiences, so they may know the lives and histories of a people and actively support them.

I suspect readers may wonder why it took me so long to write and publish this book, when I have known this community, and have had these stories, since 2010. My best answer is that I took the time I needed to think through everything I saw and experienced, to consider what my position is relative to the community of El Oasis, and to realize what I hope my writing will accomplish. I've returned to El Oasis eight times since my initial yearlong stay, and each time I have deepened my understanding of Rarámuri culture, history, and current challenges, including the ways the Rarámuris see their people evolving in our era of global capitalism and climate change. Along the way, I had one miscarriage and three children of my own—blessings that deepened my understanding of Martina's love for her children and inspired me to be patient with my writing process.

In 1943, the prominent American anthropologist Robert Zingg published his personal travel narrative, *Behind the Mexican Mountains.* After riding the Chihuahua al-Pacifico train into the Sierra Madre, Zingg, echoing the Spaniards who followed the Rarámuris into the Sierra with the aim of exploiting them and their land, proudly proclaims, "At last we had the elusive Tarahumara right under our noses for observation." The title itself suggests a quest, as if Zingg had discovered a people who, instead of strategically dispersing throughout the Sierra and developing skill for long-distance running to deliver aid to one another, had wandered there without aim or purpose. In the chapter titled "Personalities Emerge from Wooden Indians," Zingg weaves together his initial impressions of Rarámuri people with details of their daily life and the intersections and tensions between them and the mestizos, peppering the narrative with judgments that academic institutions considered too subjective to include in ethnography but found entertaining and acceptable in this personal journalism. "Such is the blind, unreasoning conservatism of primitive culture, they will even make tremendous sacrifices to raise corn," Zingg wrote, observing that the Rarámuri people remained staunchly committed to cultivating labor-intensive corn instead of potatoes, which were brought by the Spaniards and which Zingg considered easier to raise. "This unquestioning adherence to traditional patterns is the essence of the primitive," he concluded, before offering a list of ways—starting with the potatoes—that Rarámuri people might utilize the Sierra's resources to improve their livelihoods. That the Rarámuri people viewed cooperative labor and connection to the land as equally essential to their survival as food was lost on Zingg, who embodied capitalism's values of efficiency and high yields. His narrative has been applied not only to the Rarámuri people but to Indigenous people across the world. This was the first book I read when I started my field research. I returned often to the passages I underlined for historical contexts, and to others where I wrote notes arguing with Zingg's depictions. My book was born out of these arguments I started with Zingg on the margins of his book. I offer it as a counternarrative, one that seeks to elevate the Rarámuri peoples' stories and offer truth about their lives.

I owe much to two anthropologists and their research with the Rarámuri people. First, *Género y Etnicidad Rarámuri en la Ciudad de Chihuahua: Organización y participación de las mujeres en los asentamientos congregados* by the anthropologist Marco Vinicio Morales Muñoz gave me additional history on the origins of El Oasis, and offered analysis and insights on El Oasis that helped inform my own thinking. Marco is beloved by the Rarámuri people of El Oasis, and the depth of research that went into the writing of this ethnography clearly shows that the work of anthropology is the work of building relationships. The anthropologist Jerome Levi, whose work was introduced to me by a history professor in college, shaped the way I think about passive resistance and its many fascinating manifestations. I've read and re-read *Hidden Transcripts among the Rarámuri: Culture, Resistance, and Interethnic Relations in Northern Mexico* throughout the years. I'm grateful to these works in particular for showing me how to "do" anthropology, and how to write with respect and care.

When my mother was a little girl, Rarámuris would come to the farm my grandparents had built near the town of Delicias, located forty minutes south of Chihuahua City. When my abuelita answered the door, a Rarámuri woman, usually accompanied by children, would say *korima*. My abuelita would respond, *I have a day's work for you, and I'll pay you*. When the Rarámuri women were silent, my abuelita would shut the door.

While I can't confirm what the Rarámuri families thought or felt when my abuelita abruptly shut the door on them, I've spent enough time with Rarámuri people to know that they most likely went on to knock on other doors, asking mestizos to share their wealth. They likely found gifts on their walks from farm to farm—an apple tree, or a walnut tree—and asked each plant's permission before taking. In the evening, when they arrived home, perhaps they placed these gifts, and anything the mestizos had given them, into hand-woven baskets. When another family arrived at their doors, they would have shared the baskets and water from jugs. They would have invited their neighbors to drink.

Acknowledgments

I'm filled with thanks for Monica Odom, my incredible literary agent, whose belief in this book from the beginning helped see it to fruition. I'm grateful for your care and for our collaboration on this book—and the books yet to come.

Thank you to Mary Wang, my developmental editor, who helped me shape *Out of the Sierra*. We worked together through the hardest months of the pandemic, sometimes with infants in our laps. I'll always be grateful for your thoughtful and insightful notes and conversations, and your unwavering advocacy for me and my work. I truly couldn't have done this without you.

Thank you to Lizzie Davis, who also edited my book, bringing her keen editorial eye to every word.

Thank you to Chris Fischbach for acquiring *Out of the Sierra*.

Catapult, *Guernica*, and the *New York Times* published early essays that helped shape my thinking for this book. I'm thankful to these publications, especially two editors: Megha Majumdar, my editor at *Catapult*; and Mary Wang, my editor at *Guernica*, who helped me expand my essay into the book.

My gratitude to *Water-Stone Review* for publishing an excerpt of *Out of the Sierra*.

Bridget Mendel, Florencia Lauria, and Scott Parker: for all the late-night discussions about literature, for reading and conversations over very early drafts of this work, for the many cups of coffee and glasses of Malbec enjoyed on the back deck. For watching

Andre while I went to campus to teach, attend class, and draft chapters of *Out of the Sierra*. Your friendship means everything.

Thank you to the Loft Mentor Series 2017–18 cohort. I'm grateful for your generous readings of my work, and your friendship.

Thank you, Kathryn Savage, for your friendship, for your notes on *Out of the Sierra*, and for navigating motherhood and the writing life alongside me.

Claire Boyles, for encouragement and care, and for understanding how hard it is to write a book.

Beth Cleary, Mackenzie Epping, Dana Brummit, and Sarah Quimby, my writing group and dear friends these last eight years: for rigorous discussions about our work, for delicious snacks, for friendship. Thank you.

Kendra Atleework, your friendship pulled me back into writing at a time when early motherhood felt like it might consume me. I'm always energized and inspired by you; you help me remember that writing is fun and worth giving yourself to.

To Tania Anchondo, who took the beautiful photograph for this book cover. Conversations with you about art, feminism, Rarámuri culture, life in El Oasis and Chihuahua, the borderlands, the desert, and so much more have deepened my understanding of home and my place in it. Thank you for answering my questions and helping me think through the hardest parts of writing this book. Thank you, also, for always indulging my appetite for enchiladas when I'm in Chihuahua.

Many organizations supported my field research and writing: Fulbright funded my first year of field research; Global Spotlight Research Grant, Community of Scholars Program Travel Grant, and the Judd Fellowship, all from the University of Minnesota, funded further field research; Community Development Action Fund from the US Department of State allowed me to work hand in hand with Amalia Holguin in El Oasis to develop culturally relevant programming for Rarámuri youth; Coffee House Press In the Stacks gave me the time and space to write at the beautiful East Side Freedom Library; the Roxane Gay Fellowship in Nonfiction funded writing time and mentorship during the Jack Jones Literary Arts retreat for women of color; the Culture, Too conference by Jack Jones Literary Arts gave me the opportunity to deepen my professional connections; and the Artist Initiative Grant from the Minnesota State Arts Board allowed me time to write this book. I am thankful to each and every one.

Matetera-ba to the Gutiérrez family—especially Martina and Lupita. Living alongside you and growing our friendship over these last thirteen years has been a tremendous gift. Thank you for opening yourselves to me; for teaching me to sew and cook and run; for patiently answering my many, many questions; and for allowing me to write about your beautiful lives.

To my mom: if there was any concern when I professed that I wanted to be a writer and not a doctor, you didn't show it. All you've ever shown is love and support. I am so grateful to be your daughter.

Andre, Sebastian, and Oliver, you were so patient while I wrote this book. Thank you, my loves.

Enrique, mi amor. For the life we've built together, our beautiful children. For the conversations about our home that helped shape my feeling and thinking, and therefore, this book. For taking care of our children and home while I spent many hours putting words on paper. For your countless acts of love, big and small, that bring light into my days. My heart is yours.

Coffee House Press began as a small letterpress operation in 1972 and has grown into an internationally renowned nonprofit publisher of literary fiction, essay, poetry, and other work that doesn't fit neatly into genre categories.

Coffee House is both a publisher and an arts organization. Through our *Books in Action* program and publications, we've become interdisciplinary collaborators and incubators for new work and audience experiences. Our vision for the future is one where a publisher is a catalyst and connector.

LITERATURE
is not the same thing as
PUBLISHING

Funder Acknowledgments

Coffee House Press is an internationally renowned independent book publisher and arts nonprofit based in Minneapolis, MN; through its literary publications and *Books in Action* program, Coffee House acts as a catalyst and connector—between authors and readers, ideas and resources, creativity and community, inspiration and action.

Coffee House Press books are made possible through the generous support of grants and donations from corporations, state and federal grant programs, family foundations, and the many individuals who believe in the transformational power of literature. This activity is made possible by the voters of Minnesota through a Minnesota State Arts Board Operating Support grant, thanks to the legislative appropriation from the Arts and Cultural Heritage Fund. Coffee House also receives major operating support from the Amazon Literary Partnership, Jerome Foundation, Literary Arts Emergency Fund, McKnight Foundation, and the National Endowment for the Arts (NEA). To find out more about how NEA grants impact individuals and communities, visit www.arts.gov.

Coffee House Press receives additional support from Bookmobile; the Buckley Charitable Fund; Dorsey & Whitney LLP; the Gaea Foundation; the Schwab Charitable Fund; and the U.S. Bank Foundation.

The Publisher's Circle of Coffee House Press

Publisher's Circle members make significant contributions to Coffee House Press's annual giving campaign. Understanding that a strong financial base is necessary for the press to meet the challenges and opportunities that arise each year, this group plays a crucial part in the success of Coffee House's mission.

Recent Publisher's Circle members include many anonymous donors, Kathy Arnold, Patricia A. Beithon, Andrew Brantingham & Rita Farmer, Kelli & Dave Cloutier, Theodore Cornwell, Jane Dalrymple-Hollo, Mary Ebert & Paul Stembler, Jennifer Egan, Kamilah Foreman, Eva Galiber, Jocelyn Hale & Glenn Miller Charitable Fund of the Minneapolis Foundation, Roger Hale & Nor Hall, William Hardacker, Randy Hartten & Ron Lotz, Carl & Heidi Horsch, Amy L. Hubbard & Geoffrey J. Kehoe Fund of the St. Paul & Minnesota Foundation, Hyde Family Charitable Fund, Kenneth & Susan Kahn, the Kenneth Koch Literary Estate, Cinda Kornblum, the Lenfestey Family Foundation, Sarah Lutman & Rob Rudolph, Carol & Aaron Mack, Gillian McCain, Mary & Malcolm McDermid, Daniel N. Smith III & Maureen Millea Smith, Vance Opperman, Mr. Pancks' Fund in memory of Graham Kimpton, Alan Polsky, Robin Preble, Ronald Restrepo & Candace S. Baggett, Steve Smith, Lynne Stanley, Jeffrey Sugerman & Sarah Schultz, Paul Thissen, Grant Wood, and Margaret Wurtele.

For more information about the Publisher's Circle and other ways to support Coffee House Press books, authors, and activities, please visit www.coffeehousepress.org/pages/donate or contact us at info@coffeehousepress.org.

COFFEE HOUSE PRESS began as a small letterpress operation in 1972. In the years since, it has grown into an internationally renowned nonprofit publisher of literary fiction, nonfiction, poetry, and other writing that doesn't fit neatly into genre categories. Our mission is to expand definitions of what literature can be, what it can do, and to whom it belongs.

FURTHER NONFICTION TITLES FROM COFFEE HOUSE PRESS

American Precariat:
Parables of Exclusion $19.95
EDITED BY ZEKE CALIGIURI ET AL.

With Bloom Upon Them
and Also with Blood:
A Horror Miscellany $17.95
JUSTIN PHILLIP REED

In Vitro: On Longing
and Transformation $16.95
ISABEL ZAPATA (TRANS. ROBIN MYERS)

This Wide Terraqueous World:
Essays in Fiction $16.95
LAIRD HUNT

Bard, Kinetic $19.95
ANNE WALDMAN

Groundglass: An Essay $16.95
KATHRYN SAVAGE

When Woman Kill:
Four Crimes Retold $16.95
ALIA TRABUCCO ZERÁN
(TRANS. SOPHIE HUGHES)

Brown Neon: Essays $16.95
RAQUEL GUTIÉRREZ

the déjà vu: black dreams
and black time $17.95
GABRIELLE CIVIL

Borealis: An Essay $14.95
AISHA SABATINI SLOAN

The Breaks: An Essay $16.95
JULIETTA SINGH

Madder: A Memoir $16.95
MARCO WILKINSON

Time Is the Thing a Body Moves Through:
An Essay $16.95
T FLEISCHMANN

Socialist Realism $16.95
TRISHA LOW

Mean $16.95
MYRIAM GURBA

The Latehomecomer:
A Hmong Family Memoir . . $17.95
KAO KALIA YANG

Tell Me How It Ends:
An Essay in Forty Questions . . $16
VALERIA LUISELLI

Civil Disobediences:
Poetics and Politics in Action . . $18
EDITED BY ANNE WALDMAN
AND LISA BIRMAN

Screaming Monkeys: Critiques of Asian
American Images $22
EDITED BY M. EVELINA GALANG

For more information about Coffee House Press and how you can support our mission, please visit coffeehousepress.org/pages/donate

Professors may request desk copies by visiting coffeehousepress.org/pages/educators

Photo © Jessica Strobel

VICTORIA BLANCO's essays have been published in the *New York Times*, *Guernica*, *Literary Hub*, and *Catapult*. Her field research has been supported by awards from Fulbright and the University of Minnesota. She received her MFA from the University of Minnesota. Born and raised in the sister cities of El Paso, Texas, and Ciudad Juárez, Chihuahua, Victoria now lives in Minneapolis with her husband and three sons.

Out of the Sierra was designed by
Bookmobile Design & Digital Publisher Services.
Text is set in Ten Oldstyle.